TWO
VIEWS
ON

HOMOSEXUALITY,
THE BIBLE, AND THE CHURCH

Books in the Counterpoints Series

Church Life

Evaluating the Church Growth Movement
Exploring the Worship Spectrum
Remarriage after Divorce in Today's Church
Understanding Four Views on Baptism
Understanding Four Views on the Lord's Supper
Who Runs the Church?

Bible and Theology

Are Miraculous Gifts for Today?
Five Views on Apologetics
Five Views on Biblical Inerrancy
Five Views on Law and Gospel
Five Views on Sanctification
Five Views on the Church and Politics
Four Views on Christianity and Philosophy
Four Views on Christian Spirituality
Four Views on Divine Providence
Four Views on Eternal Security
Four Views on Hell
Four Views on Moving Beyond the Bible to Theology
Four Views on Salvation in a Pluralistic World
Four Views on the Apostle Paul
Four Views on the Book of Revelation
Four Views on the Historical Adam
Four Views on the Role of Works at the Final Judgment
*Four Views on the Spectrum of Evangelicalism Genesis:
History, Fiction, or Neither?*
How Jewish Is Christianity?
Show Them No Mercy
Three Views on Creation and Evolution
Three Views on Eastern Orthodoxy and Evangelicalism
Three Views on the Millennium and Beyond
Three Views on the New Testament Use of the Old Testament
Three Views on the Rapture
Three Views on the Doctrine of the Trinity
Two Views on Women in Ministry

TWO VIEWS ON HOMOSEXUALITY, THE BIBLE, AND THE CHURCH

Megan K. DeFranza

Wesley Hill

Stephen R. Holmes

William Loader

Preston Sprinkle, general editor
Stanley H. Gundry, series editor

ZONDERVAN

Two Views on Homosexuality, the Bible, and the Church
Copyright © 2016 by Preston Sprinkle, William Loader, Megan K. DeFranza, Wesley Hill, Stephen R. Holmes

This title is also available as a Zondervan ebook.

Requests for information should be addressed to:
Zondervan, *3900 Sparks Dr. SE, Grand Rapids, Michigan 49546*

ISBN 978-0-310-52863-0

Cover design: Tammy Johnson
Cover image: Ben Greenhoe

Printed in the United States of America

HB 01.12.2024

CONTENTS

LIST OF ABBREVIATIONS

Ancient Texts
Miscellaneous

Pss. Sol.—Psalms of Solomon
T. Benj.—Testament of Benjamin
T. Levi—Testament of Levi
T. Naph.—Testament of Naphtali
4Q177 4QCatena[a]—(MidrEschat[b]) Catena[a], also *Midrash on Eschatology*[b]
4Q270 4QD[e]—Damascus Document[e]
4Q270 4QD[f]—Damascus Document[f]

Philo

Abr.—De Abrahamo, On the Life of Abraham
Contempl.—De vita contemplative, On the Contemplative Life
Deus—Quod Deus sit immutabilis, That God Is Unchangeable
Ebr.—De ebrietate, On Drunkenness
Her.—Quis rerum divinarum heres sit, Who Is the Heir?
Hypoth.—Hypothetica
Ios.—De Iosepho, On the Life of Joseph
Mut.—De mutatione nominum, On the Change of Names
Prob.—Quod omnis probus liber sit, That Every Good Person Is Free
QG—Quaestiones et solutiones in Genesin, Questions and Answers on Genesis
Somn.—De somniis, On Dreams
Spec.—De specialibus legibus, On the Special Laws
Virt.—De virtutibus, On the Virtues

Josephus

Vita—Vita, Life
Ap.—Contra Apionem, Against Apion
A.J.—Antiquitates judaicae, Jewish Antiquities
B.J.—Bellum judaicum, Jewish War

Plato

Leg—*Leges, Laws*

Ovid

Metam.—*Metamorphoses*

General Abbreviations

AB—*Anchor Bible Commentary*
BETL—Bibliotheca ephemeridum theologicarum lovaniensium
Ms—manuscript
NovT—Novum Testamentum, New Testament
SemeiaSt—*Semeia Studies*
WBC—*Word Biblical Commentary*

William Loader

ELJ—William Loader, *Enoch, Levi, and Jubilees on Sexuality*
(2007)
DSS—William Loader, *The Dead Sea Scrolls on Sexuality* (2009)
PS—William Loader, *The Pseudepigrapha on Sexuality* (2011)
PJT—William Loader, *Philo, Josephus, and the Testaments on*
Sexuality (2011)
NTS—William Loader, *The New Testament on Sexuality* (2012)

INTRODUCTION ████████████████

PRESTON M. SPRINKLE

Few topics have become as volatile, confusing, and debated in contemporary religious and political discourse as homosexuality. The sanctity of same-sex relations is one of the most pressing ethical questions facing the church today. Unlike other topics that Christians debate—the rapture, the millennium, speaking in tongues, etc.—homosexuality affects the very core of human persons. It is, as I have stated elsewhere, not just an issue to be debated, but touches the heart and humanity of real people.[1]

Homosexuality is not *just* an issue, because people are not mere issues. But it does include issues—several issues in fact. Issues informed by Bible passages and doctrines and biblical-theological themes related to human nature, marriage, gender, and sexuality. A full-bodied understanding of homosexuality demands that we dig into the ancient Near Eastern and Greco-Roman context of the Bible, study the perspective on same-sex relations in Judaism and early Christianity, and consult recent works in psychology, sociology, and biology. Homosexuality also involves listening. Listening to and entering into the lives of real gay, lesbian, and bisexual people.[2]

When I began my own study of the topic, I cracked open dozens of books and hundreds of articles and began inching my way through what seemed like an insurmountable pile of research. I learned a lot about Hebrew and Greek words, a biblical view of sexuality, complications about a biblical view of sexuality, church history, sexuality in ancient Mesopotamia, and that body of ancient pornography otherwise known as Roman poetry. But it wasn't until I got to know and love gay and lesbian people that I started to understand the "topic" of homosexuality.

---

1. See my book *People to Be Loved: Why Homosexuality Is Not Just an Issue* (Grand Rapids: Zondervan, 2015).

2. Ethical questions related to other sexual minorities, such as transgender persons, are just as pressing as ones related specifically to sexuality, but are beyond the scope of this volume. Therefore, I will avoid using the acronym LGBTQ+ unless appropriate.

This is what excites me about this book. In the following pages, academic erudition will be put on display. The contributors we've enlisted are accomplished scholars in the fields of biblical studies, theology, and topics related to sexuality and gender. But none of these authors have studied this topic in the lofty cell of an ivory tower that soars high above the lives of real people, gay and lesbian people—humans, who are not mere issues.

A Flurry of Books on Homosexuality

The topic of homosexuality was largely untouched by biblical scholars and theologians until 1980, when John Boswell published his provocative book *Christianity, Social Tolerance, and Homosexuality*.[3] Boswell argued that early Christian tradition has always had a place for same-sex couples, and that the Bible forbids only certain forms of exploitative homosexual behavior. Boswell's book was roundly criticized by biblical scholars,[4] but it opened the door to a different way to read the Christian Scriptures that would allow for the full inclusion of gay and lesbian couples in the church.

Several studies followed in the wake of Boswell. Interestingly, the majority of books written by historians and biblical scholars, while disagreeing with several of Boswell's arguments, also concluded that the Bible's prohibition of same-sex relations does not address or condemn consensual, monogamous, same-sex marriages.[5]

Non-affirming scholars have responded with counterarguments, which have sought to lend biblical and historical credibility to Christianity's traditional sexual ethic. Among the most significant work has been Robert Gagnon's massive book *The Bible and Homosexual Practice* published in 2001,[6] which continues to be the largest and most in-depth biblical study of the topic from a conservative position.

---

3. John Boswell, *Christianity, Social Tolerance, and Homosexuality: Gay People in Western Europe from the Beginning of the Christian Era to the Fourteenth Century* (Chicago: University of Chicago Press, 1980).

4. See especially Richard Hays, "Relations Natural and Unnatural: A Response to J. Boswell's Exegesis of Rom. 1," *Journal of Religious Ethics* 14 (1986): 184–215.

5. Among the most significant are Robin Scroggs, *The New Testament and Homosexuality: Contextual Background for Contemporary Debate* (Philadelphia: Fortress, 1983); William Countryman, *Dirt, Greed, and Sex: Sexual Ethics in the New Testament and Their Implications for Today* (rev. ed.; Minneapolis: Fortress, 2007); Daniel A. Helminiak, *What the Bible Really Says about Homosexuality* (Estancia, NM: Alamo Square, 2000); Dale Martin, *Sex and the Single Savior: Gender and Sexuality in Biblical Interpretation* (Louisville: Westminster John Knox, 2006); Martti Nissinen, *Homoeroticism in the Biblical World: A Historical Perspective*, trans. Kirsi Stjerna (Minneapolis: Fortress, 1998).

6. Robert Gagnon, *The Bible and Homosexual Practice: Texts and Hermeneutics* (Nashville: Abingdon, 2001).

The last few years have witnessed a new wave of studies that have come to different conclusions on what the Bible says about same-sex relations.[7] Despite the growing number of books and articles devoted to the topic, there remains a great need for fresh work and refreshing dialogue across disciplines and viewpoints.

A Fresh Contribution

There are several aspects of this Counterpoints volume that add a fresh perspective on this well-worn debate.

First, this book is the first of its kind to be published by an evangelical Christian publisher. I don't think a book like this would have been possible ten or even five years ago. Until recently, there was only one view of homosexuality within evangelicalism: the so-called non-affirming view. Conservatives may protest or simply disagree, but the fact is that there are a growing number of Bible-believing, gospel-preaching, card-carrying evangelicals who are either exploring the affirming view or who have embraced it and aren't looking back. I'll never forget talking to an affirming gay Christian friend of mine, who referred to me as being "more liberal" than he was. When I asked him who his favorite preachers were, he said John Piper and David Platt. Another friend of mind recently met a Bible thumper on an airplane. She was extremely vocal about her faith. With an open Bible on her lap, she was sharing Jesus with everyone around her and telling them they would go to hell if they didn't believe in Jesus. He later found out she was a lesbian pastor.

No longer is this a Christian versus non-Christian debate. The debate about homosexuality, the Bible, and the church is currently an inner-Christian discussion, even if some may think there is only one true Christian view. Christians can no longer hide behind what the Bible *says*; we now must do the hard work of figuring out what the Bible *means*—in conversation, of course, with our rich history of received tradition.

Second, discussions about Christianity and homosexuality have been dominated by biblical exegesis. And, as a biblical scholar, I believe this is where the discussion needs to start. Indeed, any discussion about

---

7. On the affirming side, see, e.g., James Brownson, *Bible, Gender, Sexuality: Reframing the Church's Debate on Same-Sex Relationships* (Grand Rapids: Eerdmans, 2013); Robert Song, *Covenant and Calling: Toward a Theology of Same-Sex Relations* (London: SCM, 2014). On the non-affirming side, see, e.g., Kevin DeYoung, *What Does the Bible Really Teach about Homosexuality?* (Wheaton, IL: Crossway, 2015); Sprinkle, *People to Be Loved.*

Christians and homosexuality must keep the Bible open from the time you begin the discussion to the time you close in prayer. Every author in this volume maintains a high view of Scripture. However, what's been lacking in the conversation is more attention to historical and systematic theology. Biblical scholars keep talking about Greek and Hebrew terms, while theologians keep talking about Augustine, Barth, and how—not whether—the Bible applies to contemporary ethics.

In the following pages, you're going to see both. Even though this is a "two views" book, we've intentionally enlisted one theologian and one biblical scholar to articulate and defend each of the two views. This way, you'll see how Leviticus 18:22 and Romans 1:26–27 relate to Augustine's *On the Good of Marriage*. We will set theology and the Bible down at the table for a good, honest conversation about their perspective on same-sex sexuality.

Third, unlike most heated—and quite obnoxious—debates about homosexuality, you are going to experience a very different tone in this volume. You're about to enter into, perhaps for the first time, a dialogue between people who disagree on significant ethical and theological matters, yet still maintain a respectful and humanizing posture. In my experience, loud and angry debates don't foster understanding. It's when people sit down and truly listen to each other that constructive dialogue can happen.

This doesn't mean that we need to agree with each other. None of our contributors changed their view by the end of this project. (That certainly would have been awkward for the publisher—contract in hand—no doubt!) What you'll find in this book are robust and pointed arguments for each of the two views; the responses in particular are exceptionally insightful and worth the price of the book. Our authors are able to be direct without being demeaning, forthright without being fearful or feisty.

Introduction to the Authors

Finding the best contributors for a volume like this is no easy task. The criteria are manifold. Every author needs to be an accomplished scholar in their field of theology or biblical studies, demonstrated through published books and peer-reviewed articles. They must be able to communicate to a fairly broad audience (not just pastors or scholars) and model constructive and humble dialogue with their fellow contributors. Moreover, for this present volume, we made sure we found contributors who don't see homosexuality as a scholarly battle to be fought and won, but understand the personal impact their views have on real people.

In light of these criteria, I could not be more thrilled with our lineup. Each of our contributors excels in all the areas mentioned above.

Dr. William ("Bill") Loader (Dr theol, Mainz, Germany) is widely regarded as the foremost scholar on sexuality in ancient Judaism and Christianity, having written five scholarly volumes on the topic, which he recently summed up in a popular-level volume *Making Sense of Sex*.[8] Bill argues for an affirming view of same-sex relations; however, he fervently believes that we must take the Bible seriously and that the Bible prohibits all forms of same-sex relations. What the Bible says and what the Bible means are very clear—same-sex relations are wrong. But every faithful application of the Bible to contemporary ethics must consider advancements in biology, anthropology, sociology, and other fields related to sexuality and gender. For hermeneutical and ethical reasons, Loader affirms the sanctity of faithful, monogamous, same-sex relations.

Dr. Megan DeFranza (PhD, Marquette University) is an emerging leader in the theological study of sex, gender, and sexuality. Her pioneering book *Sex Difference in Christian Theology* explores how intersex persons challenge the assumption that all people are born clearly or exclusively male or female. Studying the complexity of biological sex development and the challenges of interpreting the Bible for contemporary theology and ethics opened the door for her to reconsider the non-affirming view of homosexuality that she grew up with. Megan argues that the prohibition passages are better understood when read in

---

8. William Loader, *Making Sense of Sex: Attitudes towards Sexuality in Early Jewish and Christian Literature* (Grand Rapids: Eerdmans, 2013). Loader's other volumes include *The New Testament on Sexuality* (Grand Rapids: Eerdmans, 2012); *Philo, Josephus, and the Testaments on Sexuality: Attitudes towards Sexuality in the Writings of Philo, Josephus, and the Testaments of the Twelve Patriarchs* (Grand Rapids: Eerdmans, 2011); *The Pseudepigrapha on Sexuality: Attitudes towards Sexuality in Apocalypses, Testaments, Legends, Wisdom, and Related Literature* (Grand Rapids: Eerdmans, 2011); *Sexuality in the New Testament* (London: SPCK, 2010); *The Dead Sea Scrolls on Sexuality: Attitudes towards Sexuality in Sectarian and Related Literature at Qumran* (Grand Rapids: Eerdmans, 2009); *Enoch, Levi, and Jubilees on Sexuality: Attitudes towards Sexuality in the Early Enoch Literature, the Aramaic Levi Document, and the Book of Jubilees* (Grand Rapids: Eerdmans, 2007); *Sexuality and the Jesus Tradition* (Grand Rapids: Eerdmans, 2005); *The Septuagint, Sexuality, and the New Testament: Case Studies on the Impact of the LXX in Philo and the New Testament* (Grand Rapids: Eerdmans, 2004).

the light of ancient sexual landscapes, dominated as they were by human trafficking, economic exploitation, and differences of power related to assumptions about gender and social class. Biblical passages are not focused on consensual, monogamous, same-sex unions.

Dr. Wesley Hill (PhD, Durham University) is an accomplished biblical scholar and theologian who has written several books and essays related to our topic. Moreover, Wesley is a self-identified gay Christian who has a lot of skin in the game, as it were—as you will see from his opening paragraphs of his essay. Wesley argues for a non-affirming view of same-sex relations by revisiting the prohibition passages (Lev 18:22; 20:13; Rom 1:26–27; 1 Cor 6:9; 1 Tim 1:9–10) and setting them in conversation with an overarching theology of marriage, sex, and procreation, and enlists Augustine as his primary dialogue partner.

Dr. Stephen Holmes (PhD, King's College, London) is a prolific theologian with a long list of highly acclaimed published works. Stephen's essay focuses on a theology of sex and marriage and argues that the so-called prohibition passages (Lev 18:22; Rom 1:26–27; et al.) are important, yet secondary to the debate. A Christian theology of sex and marriage alone rules out the sanctity of same-sex relations on the grounds that sex and marriage are oriented toward procreation, and same-sex couples cannot procreate. Stephen looks to Augustine's influential treatment of marriage as the foundation for subsequent Christian theological reflection on homosexuality. Even though Stephen argues for a non-affirming position, he explores the possibility of some sort of pastoral accommodation for gay and lesbian couples in the church, similar to the way Christian leaders have accommodated heterosexual couples who have been remarried after divorce.

Each of our contributors exhibits a high view of Scripture, a commitment to the gospel and the church, and a love for people—especially the people who are most affected by this topic. You will not find arguments based on emotional sentimentality or postmodern views of love—"If you love me, you must affirm everything I desire to do." If you follow along with a studious mind and compassionate heart, you will see that all of our essayists wrestle deeply with the Bible and theology because they believe that God is the author of Scripture and has mediated his truth to humanity through human writers, a truth that has been refracted and reflected upon through centuries of Christian thinkers.

A Word on Terminology

One of the most difficult things about discussing homosexuality is language. (The very word "homosexuality" is offensive to some.) People who explore these issues for the first time are confronted with a whole new set of terms and face the threat of being cited by the self-appointed language-police, who liberally dish out moniker violations. This is why the authors of this volume and I spent a good deal of time figuring out what terms we should use to describe each of the two views. We considered every term that's often used in the discussion—conservative, liberal, historical, progressive, revisionist, orthodox, and many more—and found most of them to be invested with problematic implications. The terms "affirming" and "non-affirming" are growing in popularity and almost made the cut, but the word "non-affirming" could be understood as unnecessarily negative, and there are many things that "non-affirming" people *affirm* about gay people. As it stands, there is no perfect pair of terms to describe the two views represented in this book.

After much discussion, we decided to use the terms "affirming" and "traditional" in this book. They aren't perfect, but they seem to be better than the other options—especially when the reader understands exactly what is (and isn't!) meant by each term. The term "affirming" is used to describe Bill Loader's and Megan DeFranza's view that consensual, monogamous, same-sex relations can be blessed by God and fully included in the life of the church. These relations, in other words, are not inherently sinful. We've labeled the other view held by Wesley Hill and Stephen Holmes as "traditional," with the understanding that this label describes only the position that all forms of same-sex sexual behavior are prohibited by Scripture and Christian theology. This does not mean that Holmes and Hill simply adopt a "traditional" view of marriage, or of same-sex orientation, across the board. As you'll see, some of their thoughts on marriage and sexuality may be deemed *untraditional*. Likewise, Loader and DeFranza don't necessarily affirm everything about gay and lesbian relations or the concerns of activists in the political arena. The term "affirming" refers specifically to their view that gay and lesbian marital relations are sanctifiable before God.

Challenge to the Reader

I recently served as the general editor for the Counterpoints book *Four Views on Hell*—another highly contested topic! My challenge to the reader in the introduction to that volume rings all the more true for this current subject:

> It's common, perhaps likely, that unexamined beliefs become detached from their scriptural roots over time and through repetition. We become convinced of certain truths, but don't know why. We believe particular doctrines, but can't always defend them biblically. Yet this is unacceptable for anyone who claims to believe in God's inspired Word as the ultimate and final authority of truth. We should be reformed and always reforming.[9]

Scholars in the Protestant tradition coined the phrase *ecclesia semper reformanda*, or "the church is (reformed and) always reforming." This has been my heart in studying and rethinking the topic of homosexuality. When I began my (ongoing) study of the Bible and homosexuality, I made a personal and public commitment to go where the text leads. And I challenge you, the reader, to do the same. Bible-believing Christians should never be satisfied knowing *what* they believe, but must explore *why* they believe it. Unfortunately, conservative Christians often approach the topic of homosexuality with a preconceived commitment to a particular view—regardless of whether they know *why* they believe this. Progressive Christians are guilty of the same. If something even smells remotely conservative, they pivot around and run the other way.

I encourage you to avoid both of these approaches. Instead, put your high view of Scripture to the test. Read all the essays with an open mind and an open Bible. Have the courage to go where the text leads and explore how it applies to the twenty-first-century church.

---

9. Preston M. Sprinkle, ed., *Four Views on Hell* (Grand Rapids: Zondervan, 2016), 15.

HOMOSEXUALITY AND THE BIBLE

WILLIAM LOADER

Human Experience in Our World

In recent times, more and more people have come to acknowledge openly that they are gay. Among them are highly respected leaders, committed Christians, and much-loved ordinary citizens. Not many decades ago, such people would not have spoken openly. Indeed, under the legislation of many countries, the suspicion that they might have expressed their homosexuality actively would have brought prosecution. What began perhaps at first as a fringe protest of the young, daring to "come out" and at times flaunting their freedom before a suspicious society, has come to be a relatively normal occurrence. People acknowledge in the media that they are "gay" without fanfare and with much less fear. There remains, however, a level of fear in contexts where being gay is still seen as something shameful (for the gay person and often also for their parents). We still hear stories of children thrown out of their homes and stories of suicides.

Sometimes these tragedies occur in contexts where religion and faith play no role. This is not always the case. Therefore it makes sense to approach the issue from within a context where religion and faith do play a role, in particular within the Christian tradition. There are now many personal stories of families, often in traditional Bible-believing contexts, where parents, instead of responding with shock, disapproval, and rejection, have acknowledged something they had always seen in their child. I have heard it so often: "He was always like that from when he was a little boy," or "She was always like that. We noticed it in her when she was little." It seems that increasingly people are recognising that there are some—a minority, but a significant one—for whom the natural sexual orientation is toward people of their same sex. The more people share such experiences, the more it has become widely accepted as something that just happens and that this is the way some people are. This is why increasingly governments are legalising gay marriage, seeing it as doing what is just and right for citizens who are gay.

People are now also more likely to know of other variations, such as when a child is born with genitalia that are incomplete or ambiguous. It does in fact happen also that a person can feel male inside but look female outside and vice versa. There are many variations, both physiological and psychological, when it comes to sexuality. Many of these are observable also in the wider mammal world. Not all people are simply either male or female. The matter is even more complicated because one's orientation can change over a lifetime, and for some their orientation is in both directions, homosexual and heterosexual. Most have long since abandoned the belief that any such variations are to be accounted for by deliberate perversion on the part of the individual.

Relating Experience to Faith: Changing People?

For people in a faith tradition, to come to such a realisation is only one step along the way. What is the individual to do? And, in the case of families, what is a family to do? Why do they need to do anything? The answer to this question lies in the fact that traditionally Christian faith has indeed seen such orientation as perversion, or at least as a pathology, and its expression as a serious sin. In some contexts, especially Bible-believing contexts, the scriptural prohibition collides with what people are experiencing, creating a crisis of faith. For some, then, there are two alternatives: abandon my faith or abandon my child. For others, the consternation and pain which this crisis evokes have led to what seemed to be more caring and compassionate alternatives. People have given themselves or their children treatment to undo the homosexual orientation and install a heterosexual one. Such therapies have, however, had minimal success. There are many stories of people who believed they must either have this done or tried to do it themselves and who in the process have put themselves through terrible stress and great suffering. There are too many of them to be ignored.[1]

---

1. See the sensitive assessment in Wesley Hill, *Spiritual Friendship* (Grand Rapids: Brazos, 2015), 73.

Relating Experience to Faith: Changing Scripture?

Some choose a different path. Instead of changing themselves, they ask: Does our understanding of Scripture need to change? What if we can show that the Bible does not condemn homosexuality or homosexual acts after all? The former might be easier to show than the latter, although some did begin to mount arguments that really the kinds of acts which were condemned were limited to certain contexts or only certain people. They were when heterosexual people engaged in homosexual acts, not when homosexual people did so. Or they were about homosexual acts only when they occurred in cult centres associated with idolatry. Or they were only about the relatively widespread pederasty which exploited minors in the ancient world, not about homosexual expressions of mutual love between adults. Or, in the case of women, there have been attempts to show that this was never condemned, and that assumptions that it was are based on misreading the texts.

In relation to homosexual passions, the argument has been mounted that Scripture does not judge a person because of their orientation, including their feelings, but condemns only the act and the intent to act. For many this has been a huge relief. It is okay for them to be gay and have homosexual feelings as long as they do not act on them. As we shall see, this softening of the biblical position does not do justice to the text, which sees the orientation itself as a symptom of sin. It has, however, enabled many to accept their homosexuality without feeling guilty about it, and to hold together their understanding of themselves and their understanding of Scripture by binding themselves never to express their sexuality, at least not in the form of those acts which are condemned. Thus some make the choice of lifelong celibacy, and there are many stories, some of them very moving, of people who have chosen this path and hold to it heroically, which some, however, might deem as tragic. For others, this is not a realistic or, at least, a healthy option. Choosing celibacy is one thing. Obliging it by implication on all who are gay, so that they must never give natural expression to their sexuality, is another.

Relating Experience to Faith: Upholding Both?

A further path, which some are more willing to tread than others, is to ask whether what the biblical writers believed and said about homosexual orientation and activity should itself be questioned as to its accuracy and sufficiency. Such an approach is not new and has needed to be taken in relation to many issues on which biblical writers held beliefs and attitudes which for good reason we no longer share. Indeed, the list is long: the age of creation (it must be more than 6,000 years old!); the sequence of creation; the origin of women; the origin of labour in giving birth, in working poor soils, in controlling weeds; the origin of languages; the world as flat or as a sphere which the sun goes around. These reflect ancient views of the universe and how it came into being. Some ancient views have moral and ethical implications, including views about the status of women as in some sense inferior (which can play a role in the ordination debate); marriage and divorce (always to be forbidden? always to be required after adultery?); slavery (ever acceptable?); and much else.

In all of these we have needed to update biblical writers' understanding and assumptions and respectfully acknowledge that their witness, which we treasure and in which we hear the word of God, was expressed in the language and thought-world of its time. Is homosexuality another one of those areas where we need to update our understanding from their beliefs? If they, as it seems, saw homosexual desire and action as deliberate perversion and sin, is it legitimate for us to add: but in many cases which we observe this is not the case. Where it is, the condemnation remains; but where it is not, we must find a new way of responding. It would be irresponsible simply to sustain the condemnation without reassessing the situation.

Scripture and Its World
Approaching Scripture

Such solutions all depend on how we understand Scripture on the one hand and contemporary experience on the other. In what follows, I will focus on Scripture. In doing so, I take the position that I need as accurately as possible to describe what is said. I firmly believe that I should listen to what was said in its own language and context, including its religious and cultural context. It is important that I do not read into the text what I might like to hear, but bring what it was saying to expression, whether I might like it or not. To guard against the inevitable blind spots which I might have—everyone has them—I need to do my investigation in company with others who can keep me focused and help me to not miss what I might otherwise overlook, and I have done so.[2]

My approach to interpretation of Scripture is informed by respect and reverence. I indeed apply these principles to all relationships. We all know people who listen selectively, hear only what they want to hear, or read into what we are saying what we never intended. Respect for others means acknowledging also that we can never fully know another, that our knowing will always have limitations. It means humility. This approach also informs my relationship with God. I need to listen to what God is saying—whether I like it or not. I need to acknowledge that I can never fully know God. That does not prevent a relationship. In some ways it makes it possible. As I hallow God, so I need to hallow others, and in the same sense I also hallow the text.

I come to the biblical texts primarily as a New Testament scholar with a specialist interest in attitudes towards sexuality in early Jewish literature up to the end of the first century CE. My approach to the Old Testament texts will be informed not just by what they say but also by how they were used and understood within early Judaism and the New Testament.

Old Testament
Leviticus

The primary Old Testament references are the two prohibitions in Leviticus:

> "Do not have sexual relations with a man as one does with a woman; that is detestable." (Lev 18:22)
>
> "If a man has sexual relations with a man as one does with a woman, both of them have done what is detestable. They are to be put to death; their blood will be on their own heads." (Lev 20:13)

---

2. My book *Making Sense of Sex: Attitudes towards Sexuality in Early Jewish and Christian Literature* (Grand Rapids: Eerdmans, 2013) is a summary and contains a subject index for my five research volumes published by Eerdmans: *Enoch, Levi, and Jubilees on Sexuality* (2007) (=*ELJ*); *The Dead Sea Scrolls on Sexuality* (2009) (=*DSS*); *The Pseudepigrapha on Sexuality* (2011) (=*PS*); *Philo, Josephus, and the Testaments on Sexuality* (2011) (=*PJT*); and *The New Testament on Sexuality* (2012) (=*NTS*).

It is possible to read the Hebrew in both instances as saying, "Do not lie with a man as a woman does," which would then be focusing on the shame of a man acting as a woman. However, primarily anal intercourse is in view, and Leviticus 20:13 condemns both parties to death.

These prohibitions come alongside a number of others, including in Leviticus 18: various forms of incest (18:6–18); intercourse during menstruation (18:19); adultery (18:20); offering children to be sacrificed to Molek (18:21); and sex with animals (18:23). These, it claims, characterise the evils in both Egypt and in Canaan (18:1–3, 24). The same concern underlies the prohibitions in Leviticus 20, which also lists sacrificing offspring to Molek (20:4), witchcraft (20:6); adultery (20:10); incest (20:11–12, 14, 17, 19–21); sex with animals (20:15–16); and intercourse during menstruation (20:18). Cultic concerns are part of the mix, and the word "detestable" (NRSV: "abomination") puts the offence in more than just a moral category, but one can hardly on that basis conclude that the prohibition of same-sex intercourse pertains only to cultic contexts, such as in cultic prostitution, since the other prohibitions clearly show more than a cultic concern. The text gives no rationale for the prohibition beyond its offence against divine will.[3]

The concern might have been that such activity failed the purpose of sexual intercourse, to beget children, which would apply also to sex with animals and during menstruation, and cohere with the prohibition of sacrificing children, but adultery and incest scarcely fit here. The concern might have been mixing substances: semen and blood. More broadly, the concern of inappropriate mixing, blurring of categories, may have played a role. Inappropriate mixing applied in many areas (e.g., "Do not mate different kinds of animals. Do not plant your field with two kinds of seed. Do not wear clothing woven of two kinds of material" (Lev 19:19). It also pertained to cross-dressing: "A woman must not wear men's clothing, nor a man wear women's clothing, for the LORD your God detests anyone who does this" (Deut 22:5), which may well serve as evidence that there were indeed people who engaged in such practices in the community.

Once the prohibitions of Leviticus 18:22 and 20:13 were read within the Pentateuch (the first five books) as a whole, hearers might well have

---

3. On the Old Testament references, see *NTS* 22–31.

made a connection with the creation story, understood as limiting sexual union to heterosexual intercourse. Whatever rationale people might have brought to the prohibitions, these prohibitions were certainly understood subsequently as absolute and, as we shall see, extended also to same-sex relations between women.

Beyond Leviticus

The creation stories in Genesis 1 and 2 make no reference to a homosexual possibility, but present humankind as created male and female in the first account of creation (1:27) and, in the second, explain how woman was created from the first man's rib (2:15–23) and how then in sexual union (and more than that) the man and woman join, by implication to create kin (2:24). Read as explanations of divinely intended order, the creation stories leave no room for notions of people being anything other than heterosexual and so imply that to depart from that order is sin. The issue of same-sex orientation, let alone action, goes unmentioned, including when the outcomes of the first couple's sin are elaborated in 3:16–20.

The use of the word "sodomy" to describe engaging in same-sex relations derives from a story in Genesis 19 in which the men of Sodom wanted to rape Lot's male guests (who were in fact angels). Lot offers his daughters instead, an appalling proposal reflecting the traditionally low view of women, but the men refuse. The angels then step in, rescuing Lot and his family. A similar act of male aggression occurs in Gibeah, according to Judges 19, resulting in the horrific abuse and eventual death of the Levite's concubine. The focus of the Sodom and Gomorrah story is crass inhospitality and male rape. One can speculate that perhaps they also engaged in consensual same-sex relations among themselves, but that is not said. Later allusions in biblical writings to the story mostly stress the inhospitality (Isa 1:10; 3:9; Jer 23:14; Ezek 16:48–50). The story makes its return in Jewish and early Christian literature, as we shall see.

There is little else pertaining to same-sex relations in the Old Testament. One might speculate that Ham not only saw his father Noah naked but also raped him (Gen 9:20–27). Some see allusions to male cult prostitution in Deuteronomy 23:17–18,[4] but this is far from certain. Others cite the friendship between David and Jonathan as an example

---

4. 1 Kgs 14:21–24; 15:12–14; 22:46; 2 Kgs 23:7; Job 36:13–14. Robert A. J. Gagnon, *The Bible and Homosexual Practice: Texts and Hermeneutics* (Nashville: Abingdon, 2001), 100–103.

of a homoerotic relationship, not least because of the allusion to their love as surpassing the love of women (especially 1 Sam 20:41–42 and 2 Sam 1:17–26), but this is doubtful. Nowhere in early Jewish literature is there any indication that it was read in this way, which would have almost certainly have occasioned efforts to explain it differently. Close friendship between men need not have been homoerotic.

Early Jewish Writings

Early Jewish Writings in a Mainly Jewish Context

When we consider the wide and diverse body of Jewish literature produced in the four centuries up until the end of the first Christian century, we find that the issue of same-sex relations mostly arises when authors are warning about the evils of the non-Jewish world.[5] We find nothing in the collation of writings in 1 Enoch and in Jubilees, written in the early second century BCE.[6] It regularly warns against the sexual immorality of the non-Jewish world (e.g., *EJL* 7:20–21; 9:15; 30:3), but nowhere mentions same-sex relations. Its generalising depiction of the people of Gomorrah as sexually immoral (*EJL* 16:5–6; 20:5–6) probably assumes it, but this is not said. Similarly, among the writings collected in the Qumran caves by the Dead Sea, including sectarian documents, we find at most that the prohibitions of Leviticus are repeated alongside others in their context,[7] including prohibition of cross-dressing,[8] but otherwise it is never a theme.[9] One document may be referring to it in its mention of disgusting acts and people wallowing together in Sodom and Gomorrah,[10] and sexual immorality is assumed to characterise those cities, as in Jubilees.

Early Jewish Writings in a Non-Jewish Context

One finds more specific references in texts which directly address the evils of the outside world, especially where people were writing in predominantly Gentile contexts.[11] The earliest stratum of book 3 of

---

5. On references in Jewish literature, see *NTS* 32–33.
6. On 1 Enoch and Jubilees, see *EJL*.
7. 4QD^e/4Q270 2 ii.16–18/6QD/6Q15 5 3–4.
8. 4QD^f/4Q271 3 3–4; 4QOrd^a/4Q159.
9. On the Dead Sea Scrolls, see *DSS*.
10. *4QCatena*a/4Q177 iv.10.
11. For the following writings, see *PS*.

the *Sibylline Oracles*, a book of poetic oracles, accuses the Romans of male-to-male intercourse, pederasty, and male prostitution of boys.[12] Elsewhere the book broadens its scope to similarly attack a large number of nations because of their "impious intercourse with male children."[13] It became common to supplement the prohibition of adultery in the Ten Commandments with the prohibition of same-sex relations. Indeed, in most manuscripts of the Greek translation of the two Old Testament accounts of the Ten Commandments, the order puts the prohibition of adultery as number six; in other words, as the first in the second table of commandments. We see the two linked in *Sibylline Oracles* 3:764 and also in books 4 and 5 of the *Sibylline Oracles*, written slightly later within our period. Thus *Sibylline Oracles* 4:33–34 associates adultery with "hateful and repulsive abuse of a male" and 5:166–68 attacks Rome for its "adulteries and illicit intercourse with boys," declaring it an "effeminate and unjust, evil city" and "unclean" (similarly 5:387, 430).

Second Enoch, a work probably written early in the first Christian century, deplores "sin which is against nature, which is child corruption in the anus in the manner of Sodom"[14] and "abominable fornications, that is, friend with friend in the anus, and every other kind of wicked uncleanness which it is disgusting to report" (34:1–2). These references are significant in three respects: their use of Sodom to typify same-sex relations, the argument from nature that is an argument from how God created people to be, and the condemnation of apparently adult-to-adult consensual same-sex relations. The latter appears to be in mind in the *Apocalypse of Abraham*, written slightly later, which condemns men depicted not as engaging in anal intercourse but as standing naked, forehead to forehead (24:8).

Pseudo-Aristeas, written two centuries earlier, condemns male prostitution, which it alleges is a common practice in the wider world, depicting it as a perversion. It bemoans that same-sex relations would lead to population decline.[15] The notion of perverting one's natural state lies behind one of the arguments in Pseudo-Phocylides, a Jewish writing from the first century BCE, which seeks to pass itself off as a book of ancient

---

12. Sibylline Oracles, 3:185–87.
13. Ibid., 3:596–99.
14. Ms P 10:2.
15. Pseudo-Aristeas, 152.

wisdom penned by a seventh-century Greek sage. Like the Greek philosopher Plato, its author claims that one never finds same-sex relations among animals[16] (something we know now is untrue). Like others, he links the prohibitions of adultery and same-sex relations[17] and applies the prohibition also to same-sex relations between women.[18] He also warns parents not to braid their boys' hair lest it excite male sexual predators.[19]

The perversion theme occurs also in the *Wisdom of Solomon*, a first-century BCE text. Like Paul in Romans, the author argues that people with a perverted understanding of God often go on to have a perverted understanding of themselves, resulting in perverted sexual attitudes and behaviour.[20] A similar thought informs the condemnation of homosexual relations in the *Testaments of the Twelve Patriarchs*, which reached its current form in Christian hands in the second century CE but is substantially a Jewish text with much earlier material.[21] It draws an analogy between the Watcher angels of Genesis 6 and the men of Sodom.[22] It does so almost certainly on the basis that, as the angels sinned by denying their created order of being by engaging in sexual relations with women, human beings, so the men of Sodom similarly perverted their created order by engaging in sexual relations with men. This understanding of the Sodom incident is probably implied also in T. Levi 14:6; T. Benj. 9:1.

Mostly Sodom and Gomorrah serve as examples of violent inhospitality, explicitly or implicitly understood as sexual violence, but sometimes they clearly serve as examples of same-sex relations of a non-violent kind, such as characterised most pagan cities of their day. Some of the most grotesque images of sexual violence appear in the *Testament of Solomon*, which depicts the demon Ornias as raping boys,[23] the demon Onoskelis as perverting men from their true natures,[24] and Beelzeboul as promoting male anal intercourse.[25]

---

16. Pseudo-Phocylides, 191.
17. Ibid., 3.
18. Ibid.
19. Ibid., 210–14.
20. *Wisdom of Solomon*, 13:1; 14:12, 22–31.
21. On the Testaments, see *PJT* 368–435.
22. T. Naph. 2:2–4:1.
23. Testament of Solomon, 2:2–3.
24. Ibid., 4:5.
25. Ibid., 6:4; Ms P; *PS* 136–41.

Philo of Alexandria

We find similar concerns expressed in the voluminous writing of the Jewish philosopher Philo.[26] He was active in Alexandria around the time of Jesus and just after. His aim was to promote his Jewish faith to his fellow Jews in a way that would help them hold their heads high in the intellectual climate of their day. He gives us by far the most extensive repertoire of arguments against same-sex relations. The prohibitions in Leviticus, which he addresses directly in his discussion in *Special Laws*,[27] and his understanding of the making of male and female (Gen 1:27) as defining God's intended order for the nature of creation, underlie his stance. What is not according to nature is not according to God's creation and is to be condemned. He fills out these fundamental assumptions with arguments that must have been current in Jewish circles of his time. Some of them he shared with critics of same-sex relations in the Greco-Roman world, to which we return briefly below. In general terms he mostly addresses pederasty,[28] sexual exploitation of minors (predominantly slaves),[29] and depicts it as occurring in the context of wild parties where excess use of alcohol leads to excessive indulgence of passions and to illicit sexual relations, both heterosexual and homosexual.[30] He also condemns same-sex relations between women[31] and between men where the context is not pederasty but consensual adult behaviour. The latter seems to be reflected in his descriptions of the way some passive partners adorned themselves: "Mark how conspicuously they braid and adorn the hair of their heads, and how they scrub and paint their faces with cosmetics and pigments and the like, and smother themselves with fragrant unguents."[32] Philo notes how some such passive partners assume leadership in processions.[33] Adult consensual male-to-male sex is also to be assumed as characteristic of the behaviour of the men of Sodom.[34]

---

26. See *PJT* 2–258.
27. *Spec.* 3.37–42.
28. *Spec.* 3.37; *QG* 4.37, 39; *Contempl.* 50–52, 59; *Hypoth.*7.1
29. *Prob.* 124.
30. *Abr.* 135; *Contempl.* 53–56.
31. *QG* 2.49; *Virt.* 20–21; *Her.* 274; implied also in the rejection of Aristophanes's myth of sexual origins in *Contempl.* 57–63.
32. *Spec.* 3.37.
33. Ibid., 3.40–41.
34. *Abr.* 135.

While his judgments flow from the logic of his biblical starting points, his elaborations reach far and wide. His understanding of what a man was created to be is clearly shaped by the ideals of his world. There, maleness meant virility in contrast to femaleness, which is passive. God created woman but not as man's equal. Accordingly, any man playing a female role in allowing himself to be penetrated anally by another shames himself. Philo argues further that men who choose this part or have it forced upon them (such as slaves) become like women, lose their virility, and ultimately become impotent.[35] He calls this the "female disease," the feminisation of men. He sees not only feminised men but also masculinised women as an aberration, a perversion of what men and women were created to be.[36] He sometimes cites the biblical prohibition of cross-dressing in this context.[37]

Philo also condemns the active male partner who, while not losing his virility, wastes his semen, sowing his seed, as Philo puts, on infertile soil.[38] Semen might run out. There was genuine concern among both Jewish and Greco-Roman critics that homosexual practice could lead to the depopulation of cities.[39] This concern has perhaps more substance than we might allow, given the high rate of infant mortality. Accordingly, many argued that semen should be used only for purposes of reproduction, effectively ruling out not only same-sex intercourse but also masturbation, any form of contraception, and intercourse during menstruation or pregnancy or after menopause or with women unable to conceive. On the latter, Philo relents in the name of companionship and compassion, and grants the legitimacy of their having sexual relations.[40] Already Genesis had affirmed the value of companionship (Gen 2:18–25) alongside the command to procreate (1:28).

Philo's treatments of the story of Sodom go beyond Genesis 19.[41] Like others, he assumes that the intended act of sexual violence belonged to a wider malaise. He describes their "strange and monstrous practices of iniquity and all their heinous acts of impiety aimed at subversion of

---

35. Ibid.
36. *Spec.* 3.37; *Abr.* 136; *Contempl.* 60; *Spec.* 1.325; 2.50.
37. *Virt.* 18–21.
38. *Spec.* 3.37, 39.
39. *Spec.* 3.32–33, 39; *Abr.* 135–36; *Contempl.* 62.
40. Spec. 3.35.
41. His main discussion is *Abr.* 133–41.

the statutes of nature."[42] "Not only in their mad lust for women did they violate the marriages of their neighbours, but also men mounted males without respect for the sex nature which the active partner shares with the passive."[43] Here, again, we see the argument from nature, but also that such men were very likely engaging in illicit sex with both women and men, a common phenomenon in wild parties of Philo's time.

Philo not only alludes to the provision in Leviticus 20:13 that anyone caught engaging in such acts should be executed but adds that this should happen without delay.[44] Philo is aware of the argument that for some, homosexual orientation is their natural state and cites the speech of Aristophanes in *Plato's Symposium*.[45] There Plato has Aristophanes recount a myth that at one time human beings existed in three forms: male, female, and androgynous (male-female). The impiety offended Zeus, who therefore cut each in half, assigning a set of genitals to each. Ever since there have been three kinds of sexual attraction as the two halves seek each other. The two halves of the androgynous human, the male and the female, seek to join; but then so do the two male halves and the two female halves in homosexual union. Plato does not agree, and Philo disagrees emphatically, describing the account as "seductive enough, calculated by the novelty of the notion to beguile the ear," but to be treated by "the disciples of Moses trained from their earliest years to love the truth . . . with supreme contempt."[46] Philo knows from Genesis a very different version of events, according to which God created woman from the man Adam, not from an androgynous being, and did so as an act of caring, not anger. God then affirmed their union as male and female—both God-intended and good. For Philo, as for Paul, God made people heterosexual, male or female, not homosexual. Philo does know of eunuchs, including some born so,[47] but this relates to impotence, not to their sexual orientation. He criticises eunuchs who are obsessed with indulging their own and others' passions.[48]

---

42. *Spec.* 2.170.
43. *Abr.* 135.
44. *Spec.* 3.38.
45. Plato's *Symposium*, 189–93; Philo *Contempl.* 57–63.
46. *Contempl.* 63.
47. *Ios.* 58; *Somn.* 2.184; *Ebr.* 211.
48. *Deus* 111; *Mut.* 173.

Josephus

Josephus, the Galilean commander in the early years of the revolt against Rome, 66–70 CE, who subsequently became linked with the winning side and spent his final decades in Rome, writes little about same-sex relations, which, as Philo, he deplores.[49] Most references come in stories about key figures. He tells of Antony (of Antony and Cleopatra fame) and his failed attempt to lure both Herod's wife and her brother to Alexandria to exploit them for sex.[50] Josephus also tells us that in Herod's later years, "the king had some eunuchs of whom he was immoderately fond because of their beauty," and one was entrusted "with putting the king to bed,"[51] suggestive of a homoerotic relationship. The context of this information is the "disgraceful"[52] action of his son, Alexander, who lured the eunuchs with money to engage in intimate relations with him,[53] much as Absalom had done with David's concubines, and Abner with Saul's.

For Josephus, as for Philo, male-female sexual relations are enshrined in the order of creation.[54] Male-male relations had no place in it. He too cites the Leviticus prohibitions, explaining such behaviour as typical of "the pursuit of lawless pleasure."[55] He interprets the exclusions in Deuteronomy 23:1 of certain people from the assembly of Israel to apply to men, especially eunuchs playing the passive part in same-sex encounters, on the grounds that "by reason of the effeminacy of their soul . . . they have changed the sex of their body also and so with all that would be deemed a monstrosity by the beholders."[56] Political bias probably explains Josephus's claims that his rivals in the Jewish war, the Zealots, engaged in violation of women and effeminacy, cross-dressing, and copying women's passions.[57] Josephus is scathing of Greek cities which he accuses of tolerating homosexual behaviour,[58] which, like Romans of his time, he dubs a Greek disease.[59]

---

49. *Ap.* 2.199, 213; *PJT* 259–367.
50. *A.J.* 15.25, 30; *B.J.* 1.439.
51. *A.J.* 16.230.
52. Ibid., 16.229.
53. *A.J.* 16.232; cf. also *B.J.* 1.488–92.
54. *Ap.* 2.199.
55. *A.J.* 3.275.
56. Ibid., 4.290–91.
57. *B.J.* 4.561–62.
58. *Ap.* 2.273–75.
59. Ibid., 2.269.

Greco-Roman Attitudes

The consistently negative attitude of extant Jewish writings towards same-sex relations, based on the prohibitions of Leviticus and underlying assumptions about the nature of God's creation, is not without parallel in the Greco-Roman world.[60] As noted already, Plato does not approve and portrays Aristophanes's myth of the origins of sexual orientation as not a view he espouses. He emphasises that sexual intercourse should serve the purpose of propagation of the species and disapproves of it for all other purposes.[61] He does so over and against a background of Athenian society in which mentoring of youth by older men could sometimes become a sexual relationship, a practice which still had its supporters in New Testament times.[62] Plato has Socrates warn against unbridled passion and urges that a higher form of beauty be pursued.[63] Traditionally, Spartan society approved mentoring relationships which became sexual, and some Greek societies saw inter-male sexual relations as strengthening the bond, especially among soldiers, the butt of Josephus's critique in *Ap.* 2.273–75. Such sexual relations were expected to cease once the young man reached marrying age, around thirty. Roman law treated same-sex relations between citizens as a criminal offence,[64] but tolerated it between a Roman citizen and someone inferior, like a slave or a foreigner.[65] Romans sometimes deplored same-sex relations as a Greek disease and typically self-indulgent, to which Greeks responded by deploring the fact that Romans usually did not expect such relations to cease when a young man turned thirty.[66]

Greek and Roman critics of same-sex relations emphasised that no real man should allow himself to be penetrated by another, reducing his

---

60. See *NTS* 74–108.

61. *Leg.* 838E–839A.

62. See Bruce S. Thornton, *Eros: The Myth of Ancient Greek Sexuality* (Boulder, CO: Westview, 1997), 196–99; Martha C. Nussbaum, "*Eros* and Ethical Norms: Philosophers Respond to a Cultural Dilemma," in *The Sleep of Reason: Erotic Experience and Sexual Ethics in Ancient Greece and Rome*, ed. Martha C. Nussbaum and Juha Sihvola (Chicago and London: University of Chicago Press, 2002), 55–94.

63. *Phaedrus* 253D; *Symposium* 210–12.

64. Lex Scatinia.

65. See the discussion in Craig A. Williams, *Roman Homosexuality: Ideologies of Masculinity in Classical Antiquity* (Oxford: Oxford University Press, 1999), 96–104; Marilyn B. Skinner, *Sexuality in Greek and Roman Culture* (Oxford: Blackwell, 2005), 199–200; Johannes N. Vorster, "The Making of Male Same-Sex in the Graeco-Roman World and Its Implications for the Interpretation of Biblical Discourses," *Scriptura* 93 (2006): 447.

66. Skinner, *Sexuality*, 212–13, 266.

status to that of a woman.[67] The relationship between men and women was seen less in terms of different genitalia, where some saw women's genitalia simply as the outside-in version of men's genitalia, and more in terms of maleness as the norm. Thus femaleness was defective: inferior in physical strength, intellectual ability, and emotional control, and passive.[68] A man's sexual responses might range across a spectrum from female to male, but should never lead to his espousing a passive role. To become a "softy," effeminate, was a matter of great shame. Men should avoid the dangers of excessive passion, which might lead them to exceed established boundaries, such as sleeping with the wife or members of another man's household, but otherwise a man was free to exercise his power and rights to sexual gratification. Few objected to sexual exploitation of slaves or the dangers posed for both men and women by brothels. In contrast to the range of attitudes towards same-sex relations among men, such relations between women were widely condemned. Ovid, for instance, argued that no such thing occurs in the animal world.[69]

For Jews, including those who formed the Christian movement, same-sex relations were indications of the depravity of non-Jewish society. Not surprisingly, Paul singles out same-sex relations as a prime indicator of pagan depravity in writing to the fledgling Christian community in Rome, doubtless aware that he would find common ground with them in deploring such behaviour.

New Testament beyond Romans
New Testament beyond Paul

When we turn to the New Testament, Paul's letter introducing himself to the Romans is the main text and within it the few verses found in chapter 1. Before turning to it we may note some other texts which have sometimes been taken as also alluding to same-sex relations.[70] In Mark 9:42 Jesus declares, "If anyone causes one of these little ones—those who believe in me—to stumble, it would be better for them if a large millstone were hung around their neck and they were thrown

---

67. *Met.* 9.728–34; Skinner, *Sexuality*, 212, 249–51; Vorster, "Making of Male Same-Sex," 449.
68. Vorster, "Making of Male Same-Sex," 437–38.
69. Skinner, *Sexuality*, 187–90, 253.
70. See *NTS* 334–38.

into the sea." The Greek word translated "causes . . . to stumble," *skandalizo*, from whose root we get our word "scandal," was also used in contexts of sexual wrongdoing.[71] So Jesus may have been addressing child abuse. The words "who believe in me" may be addressing such abuse in the Christian community. The abhorrent nature of the crime, which has repeated itself, alas, right up to our own time, might account for the extreme language. The sayings that follow also employ extreme imagery: cutting off one's hands or feet or plucking out one's eyes (Mark 9:43–48). Matthew uses them to address sexual wrongdoing in 5:29–30. The extreme language is designed to confront and bring about change.

Other alleged allusions to homosexuality are usually read into texts which give them little support, such as seeing the centurion's slave in sexual terms (Matt 8:5–13; Luke 7:1–10; royal official's son in John 4:46–54)[72] or giving a sexualised interpretation to "the disciple whom [Jesus] loved" in John 19:26.[73] Jesus' saying about eunuchs makes the case that some people will see remaining unmarried as their calling, as did Paul in 1 Corinthians 7:7. "For there are eunuchs who were born that way, and there are eunuchs who have been made eunuchs by others—and there are those who choose to live like eunuchs for the sake of the kingdom of heaven. The one who can accept this should accept it" (Matt 19:12).[74] Being a eunuch is not about sexual orientation, but about sexual potency. Eunuchs were not asexual. Indeed, Philo complains that some exploited their state to engage in all kinds of sexual activity. We can only speculate about how people might have understood the reference to those who were born eunuchs. Possibly it included those born with incomplete or ambiguous genitalia, who fall into the broad category of people who these days might call themselves intersex. The saying does indicate awareness that gender identity can be complex.[75]

---

71. See, e.g., *Pss. Sol.* 16:7.

72. Daniel Helminiak, *What the Bible Really Says about Homosexuality* (Millennium Ed., updated and expanded; Estancia, NM: Alamo Square, 2000), 127–29.

73. Thomas Hanks, "Romans," in *The Queer Bible Commentary*, eds. Deryn Guest, Robert E. Goss, Mona West, and Thomas Bohache (London: SCM, 2006), 582–605, at 584.

74. On this, see *NTS* 436–44.

75. E.g., J. David Hester, "Eunuchs and the Postgender Jesus: Matthew 19.12 and Transgressive Sexualities," *JSNT* 28 (2005): 13–40, who suggests that "this logion of Jesus questions the privileged position of a heterosexist binary paradigm of identity," 37. See also Megan K. DeFranza, *Sex Difference in Christian Theology: Male, Female, and Intersex in the Image of God* (Grand Rapids: Eerdmans, 2015), 70–83.

Paul beyond Romans

We turn now to Paul.[76] Aside from the clearest expression of his views, namely in Romans, we do find two other possible references in the body of Pauline literature. In 1 Corinthians, in the context of warning against sexual wrongdoing, Paul draws the Corinthians' attention to what both he and they know: "Do you not know that the wicked will not inherit the kingdom of God?" (1 Cor 6:9 NIV 1984). He then lists typical kinds of wrongdoers, including those he designates in Greek as *arsenokoitai* and *malakoi*. There has been much debate about the meaning of these terms.[77] The latter means "softies," or effeminate, and is not itself a term for a homosexual person, for which there were plenty of terms available. The first word probably refers to men who bed men (literally, "male-bedders"). The balance of probability favours seeing here a reference to the active and passive participants in same-sex relations. The first word, but not the second, occurs in a similar list in 1 Timothy 1:10–11, immediately before reference to slave traders. This may well indicate that at least there it is being associated with those who purchase male slaves for sexual exploitation. Paul's least ambiguous statements about same-sex relations, however, are to be found in his letter to the Romans.

Romans
What and Why?

In writing to the Romans, whom he plans to visit, Paul makes the case for the validity of what he preached, because some questioned it. He states his understanding of the gospel in Romans 1:16–17 and returns to it in similar language in 3:22–26. In between he makes the case that all are in a broken relationship with God through sin, and therefore all need the restoration Christ brings. He begins with comments about same-sex relations, because he knows that in condemning these, he would find common ground with his audience with their strongly Jewish background. Any proud claims to superiority he might have evoked disappear when in Romans 2 he turns the judgment back on them. For they too must acknowledge that they have sinned and stand just as guilty before God's judgment as non-Jews, even though their sins may be of a

---

76. For what follows, see the detailed discussion in *NTS* 293–326.
77. See *NTS* 326–34.

quite different nature. Thus all needed salvation, not just Gentiles, and it is available to all. In one sense Paul set a trap, but nothing indicates he did not intend what he said about same-sex relations to be taken seriously, let alone that he dismissed its validity along with circumcision and food laws as Countryman suggests.[78]

It is possible that in writing to the Romans, he knows the gossip about wayward Stoic teachers, as Swancutt suggests,[79] and he may have known of the emperor Gaius Caligula's exploits, which finally end in his being stabbed through his genitals,[80] but primarily Paul stands firmly in Jewish tradition, such as we have noted above, where the prohibitions of Leviticus and an understanding of creation, including what it means to be honourable as a man, informs what he sees as attitude and behaviour contrary to nature as God made it.

Our detailed discussion will show that a number of the arguments already encountered reappear in Paul's account. The focus is very general. It is not just on heterosexuals and so not homosexual men;[81] nor on same-sex relations only in cultic contexts, which would make little sense of Paul's psychological explanations;[82] nor only on pederasty,[83] since Paul also mentions mutuality. Nor is it just on acts and not attitudes,[84] which

---

78. William Countryman, *Dirt, Greed, and Sex*, 108–23; similarly, Helminiak, *Homosexuality*; Hanks, "Romans," 586.

79. Diana M. Swancutt, "'The Disease of Effemination': The Charge of Effeminacy and the Verdict of God (Romans 1:18–2:16)," in *New Testament Masculinities*, eds. Stephen D. Moore and Janice Capel Anderson; SemeiaSt 45 (Atlanta: SBL, 2003), 193–234, at 205–206; "Sexy Stoics and the Rereading of Romans 1.18–2.16," in *A Feminist Companion to Paul*, ed. Amy-Jill Levine with Marianne Bickerstaff (London: T&T Clark, 2004), 42–73, at 43, 70–72.

80. James V. Brownson, *Bible, Gender, Sexuality: Reframing the Church's Debate on Same-Sex Relationships* (Grand Rapids: Eerdmans, 2013), 157, drawing on Neil Elliott, *The Arrogance of Nations: Reading Romans in the Shadow of Empire* (Minneapolis: Fortress, 2008), 79–82.

81. Cf. John Boswell, *Christianity, Social Tolerance, and Homosexuality: Gay People in Western Europe from the Beginning of the Christian Era to the Fourteenth Century* (Chicago: Chicago University Press, 1980), 111–14; Walter Wink, "Homosexuality and the Bible," in *Homosexuality and Christian Faith: Questions of Conscience for the Churches*, ed. Walter Wink (Minneapolis: Fortress, 1999), 33–49, at 34–37.

82. Cf. Boswell, *Homosexuality*, 108; M. Kuefler, *The Manly Eunuch: Masculinity, Gender Ambiguity, and Christian Ideology in Late Antiquity* (Chicago: University of Chicago Press, 2001), 255–60; Hanks, "Romans," 594.

83. Cf. Robin Scroggs, *The New Testament and Homosexuality: Contextual Background for Contemporary Debate* (Philadelphia: Fortress, 1983), 99–139.

84. Cf. Robert A. J. Gagnon, "The Bible and Homosexual Practice: Key Issues" and "Response to Dan O. Via," in Dan O. Via and Robert A. J. Gagnon, *Homosexuality and the Bible: Two Views* (Minneapolis: Fortress), 40–92, 99–105, at 81, 92; "Notes to Gagnon's Essay in the Gagnon-Via *Two Views* Book," accessed February 2009, http://www.robgagnon.net/2VOnlineNotes.htm, 82, 136.

would be very atypical of Paul's approach to sin, nor just on same-sex intercourse only when accompanied by excessive passion.[85]

Romans 1:18-25—From Perversion to Perversion

Paul begins his argument in support of his claims about his gospel in Romans 1:16-17 and 3:21-26 by focusing on God's anger against sin (1:18). As in Wisdom (13:1-14:31; similarly 1 Thess 4:5; 1 Cor 10:7-8), he immediately makes a link between the sin which does not acknowledge who God is but invents false gods and the sin that follows as a consequence. He is not rehearsing the story of Adam and Eve and their sin in Genesis 3 here,[86] but speaking more broadly of the sin of human beings whose perverted understanding of God resulted in perverted sexual attraction. In part it is a psychological argument. For Paul writes, "For although they knew God, they neither glorified him as God nor gave thanks to him, but their thinking became futile and their foolish hearts [minds] were darkened. Although they claimed to be wise, they became fools" (Rom 1:21-22). That is why, explains Paul, they "exchanged the glory of the immortal God for images made to look like mortal human being and birds and animals and reptiles" (1:23). Then Paul continues, "Therefore God gave them over in the sinful desires of their hearts [minds] to sexual impurity for the degrading of their bodies with one another" (1:24). The focus here is not ritual impurity, which is in itself unavoidable and not sin (such as impurity contracted from touching a corpse or having a sexual emission or after childbirth), but moral impurity. Paul means sin in what people do with their bodies among and between themselves. So, according to Paul, God abandoned people to perverse passions, and in 1:25 he repeats why this happened: they exchanged truth for a lie and failed to worship God as God. It is not just that they now had strong homosexual passions which they acted on but that they had homosexual attraction at all. This, he argues ran contrary to how God

---

85. Cf. Dale B. Martin, *Sex and the Single Savior: Gender and Sexuality in Biblical Interpretation* (Louisville: Westminster John Knox, 2006), 51-64, at 54, 56; Boswell, *Homosexuality*, 111-12; Brownson, *Sexuality*, 149-78.

86. Cf. Richard B. Hays, *The Moral Vision of the New Testament: A Contemporary Introduction to New Testament Ethics* (San Francisco: HarperOne, 1996), 384-85, 388; James D. G. Dunn, *Romans* (WBC 38AB; Nashville: Nelson, 1988), 62. Joseph A. Fitzmyer, *Romans* (AB 33; New York: Doubleday, 1993), writes, "The alleged echoes of the Adam stories in Genesis are simply nonexistent," unlike those to Genesis 1, 274.

made people to be, namely to be attracted to the opposite sex, not to the same sex.

Romans 1:26—Perverse Passions and Perverse Behaviour

It is not until Romans 1:26 that we have an explanation of what perverse passions these are and what behaviours they produce. Accordingly Paul explains, picking up what he had said in 1:24: "Because of this, God gave them over to shameful lusts" (1:26). He refers to sexual passion three times, using three different words: *epithymiai*, "desires" (v. 24); *pathe*, "lusts" (v. 26); *orexei*, "lust" (v. 27). On the third occasion in 1:27 he speaks of men burning with their urge or passion for one another. He also refers three times to exchange or perversion. Two are about exchanging a true understanding of God for a false one: *allaxan*, "exchanged" (v. 23); *metellaxan*, "exchanged" (v. 25). The other is found in 1:26 where Paul expounds his claim about perverted passions and perverted behaviour by referring to women: *metellaxan*, "exchanged." For Paul, desires are neutral in themselves as part of God's creation. It all depends on what one does with them. The desires to which he refers here, however, are not neutral, but are a manifestation of a state of perversion, according to Paul, because of their direction. Not just acting on them but having such wrongly directed desires in the first place is already something unacceptable, much as we might want him to have said otherwise. For they arise in his view from a perverted state of mind and are contrary to how we were made to be.

Explanations vary about why Paul first talks about women and then about men. Was it because same-sex relations between women were more widely condemned in the pagan world than relations between men? Or was it because he wanted to move in the opposite direction, beginning with women, considered lesser, and hence in a sense belonging to them (hence "their women," lit. "females"), and then turning to men? We may never know.

Romans 1:26: Perversion of "Females"

Paul's claim against such women states: "Even their women [lit. "females"] exchanged natural sexual relations for unnatural ones" (1:26). It is possible that Paul has sexual behaviours of women with men in mind that departed from what most then saw as natural (and for Paul that meant how God created things to be). It could refer potentially to any form of sexual intercourse which did not assume the male above the female engaging in vaginal intercourse,[87] such as anal intercourse, oral sex, and masturbation, or intercourse during menstruation or pregnancy (though not as dramatic as "exchange" suggests), or otherwise to have sex with animals. These possibilities cannot be ruled out. The more natural reading, given what follows, which is about male-male sexual relations, is that it refers to lesbian same-sex relations,[88] which by extension, as we have seen, one could understand the Leviticus prohibitions to include. It would be rather odd in the male-oriented culture of the time if Paul were suggesting that women rather than men were in control of the manner of sexual intercourse. Singling out women puts the focus on something women were doing apart from men. This makes best sense of the way Paul begins the following verse: "In the same way ..." What is the same is that both these women and these men are, contrary to nature and God's creation, being attracted to their own sex and acting on it. Both here and in what follows, Paul uses the terms "female" and "male," almost certainly alluding to the creation of "male" and "female" in Genesis 1:27, which is fundamental to Paul's understanding. This theme of perversion of the order of creation also makes best sense of seeing here an allusion to lesbian relations.

Romans 1:27—Perversion of "Males"

When Paul turns to men, he writes, "In the same way the men [lit. "males"] also abandoned natural relations with women [lit. "females"] and were inflamed with lust for one another. Men [lit. "Males"] committed shameful acts with other men [lit. "in males"], and received in themselves the due penalty for their error" (1:27). Clearly this refers

---

87. Brownson, *Sexuality*, 207–208; Swancutt, "Disease of Effemination," 200, who suggests it be read as referring to "various types of intercourse ranging from adultery and sex while pregnant to 'mutual intercourse' and a 'reversal of sexual roles,'" 209; similarly Swancutt, "Sexy Stoics," 63; James E. Miller, "The Practices of Romans 1:26: Homosexual or Heterosexual?" *NovT* 37 (1995), 1–11; Hans Debel, "'Unnatural Intercourse' in Rom 1,26–27: Homosexual or Heterosexual?" in *The Letter to the Romans*, ed. Udo Schnelle; BETL, 226 (Leuven: Peeters, 2009), 631–40.

88. Raymond F. Collins, *Sexual Ethics and the New Testament: Behavior and Belief* (New York: Crossroad, 2000); Robert Jewett, *Romans* (Hermeneia; Minneapolis: Fortress. 2007), 176; Bernadette J. Brooten, *Love Between Women: Early Christian Responses to Female Homoeroticism* (Chicago: University of Chicago Press, 1998), 239–53; Fitzmyer, *Romans*, 284.

to male homosexual desire and the actions to which it leads, and Paul sees both as manifestation of sin. Here the focus is not pederasty or the exploitation of one by another, but mutual passion ("for one another"), what we would call consensual adult homosexual acts. Such consensual activity is already implied in 1:24, when Paul speaks of men "degrading" their bodies in or among one another. "Males in males" may be meant quite literally and be referring to anal intercourse.

Romans 1:26 27 What Is "Natural"?

In Romans 1:26 and 27 Paul appeals to what is natural. It is possible that he thinks about this at a secular level of the observable, such as the way the penis and the vagina naturally combine as complementary, and he may have in mind the kind of argument promoted by Plato and repeated, for instance, in Philo that only what can lead to the propagation of the species is good and natural, but this is unlikely. He never uses such an argument elsewhere, for instance in discussing marriage. Paul can appeal to what appears natural to urge that women not remove their hair covering in assemblies of worship (1 Cor 11:13) and can speak of what is natural and unnatural in relation to tree grafting (Rom 11:24). But for Paul, what is natural has theological status because it is how God created things to be and so it is what is right (1 Cor 11:16).[89] As noted above, his use of the words "female" and "male" in Romans 1:26–27 in all probability reflects and is intended to reflect the story of the creation of humankind as "male and female" in Genesis 1:27. Thus the attitudes and actions which Paul depicts in Romans 1:26 and 27 are sinful because they pervert God's creation and are, as Paul argued, the consequence of a perverted response to God. Paul may have in mind that the male is created as the head of the female, as he enunciates this in 1 Corinthians 11:3, so that for men to take on the passive role traditionally associated with women would be shaming and dishonouring.[90] But Paul's concern with nature is about more than that, and, in any case, he sees the actions of both the active and the passive same-sex partners as shameful. His fundamental concern is that

---

89. On this, see *NTS* 311–15; Gagnon, "Notes," 82; Brooten, *Love Between Women*, 269–70; Andrie B. du Toit, "Paul, Homosexuality, and Christian Ethics," in *Neotestamentica et Philonica: Studies in Honour of Peder Borgen*, ed. David E. Aune (Leiden: Brill, 2003), 92–107, at 100–101.

90. Brownson, *Sexuality*, 204–15.

homosexual desire and its expression run contrary to how God made male and female to be and to relate.

Romans 1:26-27–"Male and Female" in Creation/Nature

As a Jew, Paul shares the belief we have encountered consistently in surviving Jewish literature of the time, namely that God made people male and female. There are only heterosexual people. We noted that the reference to some people being eunuchs from birth may indicate awareness that some fall into the broad category of being intersex, but neither Paul nor the other Jewish sources we considered indicated that they tolerated the notion which, for instance, in Plato's *Symposium*, the Aristophanes speech espouses, namely, that some people are by nature homosexual, men or women. Nor is there any indication that Paul contemplated that some are homosexual as a result of the fall. He does not use that language here. He accounts for the perversion of self-understanding and sexual orientation and behaviour as resulting not from Adam's fall, but from people's rejection of God and God's true nature. So Paul, here, cannot be said to address only heterosexuals and not homosexuals.

Romans 1:24, 26-27–Paul and Sexual Passion

Nothing indicates that Paul disapproves of sexual passion as such, as Martin suggests.[91] Paul sees it as sometimes difficult to contain and, on that account, urges those confronted with that challenge to marry (1 Cor 7:9), but then urges that they not think of doing so as sin (1 Cor 7:28). Sexual passion is not sin. Wrongly directing it clearly is sin. Paul may well have shared Philo's view that when men turned their passions toward their own, they did so as a result of excessive passion, perhaps fueled by excess alcohol, though the latter does not feature in his argument here, which is much more psychological. Paul would have disapproved of strong passions, especially where they resulted in people turning them in the wrong direction. Like the Jewish philosopher Philo, Paul may well have been aware of discourse about passions and their dangers in his day. His argument, however, is not that homosexually directed passions are tolerable as long as they are not excessive, but that homosexually directed passions are sinful because they are wrongly

---

91. Martin, *Sex and the Single Savior*, 59–60, 65–76.

directed, and even more so when acted upon. Something has gone wrong when people are being attracted to those of their own sex, and for Paul this happens because something has gone wrong with their relationship with God.

Romans 1:28–32—Paul's Perversion Psychology

It is hard to justify the view that Paul's concern was only with the Leviticus prohibition of the act and that he would have been neutral about people having such passions and desires toward their own sex, a view held by many today who thereby provide (what I believe is false) comfort for homosexual people as long as they remain celibate. That would be so atypical for Paul, for whom the focus is not just acts, but on attitudes as sinful; the corrupt tree, not just its fruits. His repeated negative references to passions directed in this way, and not only when excessive, and his psychological explanation of such passions being the result of perversion make such a conclusion unlikely. We see this again when Paul wraps up his argument in Romans 1:28 where he writes, "Furthermore, just as they did not think it worthwhile [lit. "fitting"] to retain the knowledge of God, so God gave them over to a depraved [lit. "unfit"] mind, so that they do what ought not to be done." Paul uses the same root twice (translated "worthwhile" and "depraved") to underline the connection: unfit understanding of God produces an unfit mind, one where sexual attraction and desire have gone in the wrong direction, perversion producing perversion.

For Paul, people with a perverse understanding of God, which produces in them a perverted understanding of both God and themselves, are "without excuse" (1:20). He continues his comments on an unfit mind in 1:29–32, showing that all kinds of sin result from a sin-perverted state of mind and concluding that such people deserve death, possibly an allusion to the death penalty in Leviticus 20:13 because for most of the sins in the list the death penalty does not apply.[92] The final verse suggests that Paul still has same-sex relations in mind when he speaks of people propagating and promoting such sin, recalling Philo's observations about the industry of sexual exploitation of the young, in particular, in both religious and secular contexts.[93]

---

92. Gagnon, *Bible and Homosexual Practice*, 122.
93. *Spec.* 4.89; *Contempl.* 53–56, 61.

Romans 1:27—Reaping What Consequences?

The comment in Romans 1:27 that men reap the consequences in themselves of their homosexual indulgence has puzzled commentators. Had we asked Philo to comment, the answer would have been along the lines that they make themselves feminine, but this would apply only to the passive partner. Robert Jewett suggests more plausibly physical soreness which might affect both partners.[94] Others have suggested, more vaguely, addiction, lack of a sense of fulfilment, or expense in terms of time and energy. Some, hearing it, may think of Emperor Caligula's assassination,[95] but the focus here is not on one person, but on all who engage in these activities. It may well reflect the common assumption, then and now, that same-sex relations are primarily about anal intercourse. However, until recent times, it was as much a practice between heterosexuals to avoid conception as between homosexuals, and not necessarily a part of either, as many gay people point out.

Conclusion: Listening in Our World to the Biblical Writers

In conclusion, where biblical writers address the issues of same-sex relations, the message is relatively clear. Leviticus prohibits the acts, which Jews read as equally applicable to female homosexual acts. Paul sees both the action and the attitude, homosexual passion, as sin. It is not the case that he sees only the act as sin, nor that he sees it as sin only when accompanied by excessive passion, as though moderate passion and its expression would be tolerable. Nor is it the case that he considers being gay and being sexually attracted to people of the same gender as in itself ethically neutral. Rather, Paul appears to assume, like other Jews whose discussions have survived, that all people are heterosexual. A homosexual orientation is contrary to nature as God created people. Thus he treats such attraction psychologically. A perverted understanding of God results in a perverted mind now sexually attracted to its own gender. Nor is it the case that Paul has only pederasty in view, because he includes mutual engagement. Nor is he concerned with acts in idolatrous contexts, because that makes no sense in his psychological arguments. Nor does he explain the state of having passion and expressing it toward

94. Jewett, *Romans*, 179.
95. Brownson, *Sexuality*, 157.

people of one's own gender as an inevitable consequence of the fall or as just a pathology. He sees it as sin generated by the sin of not acknowledging God's true nature. If we are serious about letting Scripture speak for itself and reading it in context, then we will avoid all such attempts from left and right to explain it away, however compassionately motivated our misreadings may be.

Repent and Repair?

What then is the believer for whom Scripture is a source of life and hope to do? One response, which is arguably the most longstanding response within the Christian tradition, is to uphold the biblical prohibition and, like Paul, see not only the act but also the desire as a manifestation of sin. This approach has integrity, and while some espouse it in a manner which is harsh and judgmental, others firmly believe it is true and so approach gay people with love and compassion, seeking to help them find ways out of their sin and its effects. They are advised to seek to have their orientation reversed so that they cease to be oriented to those of their same sex and are restored to how God made them to be. The strength of this option is that it takes seriously what Paul says, without compromise. Its weakness is that this option does not take the reality of human experience seriously enough, especially the widely accepted reality that some people, a minority, including highly respected individuals, seem to be naturally attracted to those of their own sex. In its wake are many sad stories of genuine and often traumatic failed attempts by gay people to seek to have their homosexual orientation reversed.

Accept and Refrain?

Another response, in part as a reaction to the first option, is an attempt to hold two things together: what Scripture says and what people observe in real life. The attempt to do so is often born of painful personal experience for individuals and their families who are faced with what seems to them to be not the result of perversion or sin but simply the way they are. For some this response comes after years of tormenting themselves with having tried so hard to change. How then can they reconcile their reality with what they read in Paul? One way is to suggest that Paul did believe some people were naturally attracted to those of the same sex, but was concerned only when they acted on those feelings. This, it can be argued, is the same as when a married man might find another woman attractive. Feelings are natural. It is what one does with them that counts as sin, both in intent and in action. Similarly, I may find food tempting, but I need to take responsibility for how I respond. Some, then, might see being gay as similar to having a disability and explain it as one of the results of Adam and Eve's sin. All these explanations help people to accept being gay as nothing to be ashamed of. They just must not act on it, but instead remain celibate.

This option, however, is vulnerable to critique as an unsatisfactory compromise between Scripture and human experience that fails to do justice to either. While this option may be very brave, it can also be tragic and potentially dangerous to impose on oneself and, by implication, on others the rule to never give full expression to one's sexuality. It seems very unfair and inconsistent to tell people that it's OK to be gay, but not OK to give natural expression to their sexuality. This does not really do justice to gay people.

This option's re-reading of Paul fails, as I see it, to do justice to what he was saying, in contrast to option one. Like other Jews, whose works have survived, Paul does not appear to embrace the notion that some people are gay, but rather explains same-sex attraction as the result of a state of mind perverted by sin. His and their assumptions are shaped by Genesis 1:27, which declares that God made people male and female. Paul does not explain same-sex attraction as a disability resulting from Adam's fall, but as something that ought not to be, a state of mind resulting from a perverted understanding of God: "Their thinking became futile and their foolish hearts [= minds] were darkened" (Rom 1:21); "God gave them over in the sinful desires of their hearts [minds]" (1:24); "God gave them over to a depraved mind" (1:28). It is not like the prohibition of adultery and adulterous attitudes, where being attracted is not a sin but becomes one when one pursues it, because for Paul, having attraction to the same sex, unlike attraction to the opposite sex, is unnatural, contrary to how God made us as male and female.

Accept and Affirm?
A third option is like the first, but one that is often misunderstood and lampooned as giving up on Scripture. At its best it derives, on the contrary, from deep reverence for the Scripture. It shares common ground

with the first option in recognising what the text actually says and in avoiding attempts, in effect, to water it down, however well intentioned. Thus, this stance too allows itself to feel the full force of the prohibitions of act and attitude, which gives it great integrity. It argues at the same time that we do Paul (and other biblical writers) an injustice when we expect them to have said all there was to say about an issue and to have known all there was to know. The reason why Paul argued as he did is that he, like other Jews of his time whose writings survive, believed that all people were heterosexual, male or female. Given that assumption about human reality, his conclusions make sense. It is contrary to the divinely created order when heterosexuals start being attracted to people of their own sex.

The question our current observations compel us to confront is: What if there really are people who are homosexual? The wider community and governments in many of our countries have come to acknowledge that there are genuinely gay people, and many governments have therefore removed barriers to gay people marrying. As noted in the introduction, among the many who now feel safe from persecution, shaming, and prosecution, and able to be open about their orientation, are outstanding citizens, including fine Christians. If, then, we need to acknowledge that Paul's understanding about the nature of human sexuality was limited, we cannot simply apply his judgments to the situations where people are genuinely gay.

People following option three argue therefore that gay people should be treated in the same way as heterosexual people and not be discriminated against, and this is a conclusion based on the biblical principle of informed love. It can only do so by acknowledging that the assumptions about human sexuality which underlie the approach of Paul and his fellow Jews needs supplementing with the insights and observations about human sexuality we have gained since. This is just one of many areas where it has been necessary to supplement first-century understandings of reality with twenty-first-century understandings. To do so is not to show disrespect for biblical writers, but to stand alongside them in their commitment to truth and willingness to change as essential to their faith.

Weighing the Options

Weighing all three options, I would see the first as the least satisfactory. It shares with option three the strength that it more accurately interprets

Paul in Romans than does option two. Its weakness is that it fails to take into account present understanding of reality and assumes that everyone is heterosexual, so gay people need help to reverse their state. Option two's strength, which it shares with option three, is that it recognises that there are genuinely gay people. Its weakness is twofold. First, it claims that Paul would have believed that there are genuinely gay people despite lack of evidence, and Paul's psychological argument appears to rule that out. Second, it bars genuinely gay people from ever expressing their sexuality, something which seems unfair and inequitable if their state of being gay is in itself acceptable. Ultimately the ground for option two's prohibition of gay people seeking to express their sexuality lies in a strict adherence to the prohibitions in Leviticus, which similarly are based on limited understandings of human sexuality. Option three's strength is that it recognises that there is an issue of fairness and human rights at stake and that Christian tradition has always needed to grapple with situations where, because of new understandings, biblical commands needed to be revisited.

Engaging Scripture and Experience—Foundational for Our Faith

The need to engage both Scripture and experience, including setting some parts of the former aside or overriding some parts of Scripture with others, goes back to the beginnings of the Christian movement. On each occasion there was controversy, usually between those wanting to uphold literal commands of Scripture and those arguing that core scriptural values warranted change. To some degree this already played a role in Jesus' conflicts with his contemporaries where his focus on love, leading him to mix with sinners, was met with disapproval by the pious. Jesus' argument that the Sabbath was made for people, not people for the Sabbath (Mark 2:27), typifies his putting people first in discerning priorities in interpretation of Scripture. While arguably he never set scriptural commands aside, this changed when believers faced the issue of Gentiles joining the Christian movement. Genesis 17 required that they be circumcised. The majority of believers, however, reached the conclusion that God's new initiative of love in Christ meant that this should not be required. In the eyes of some believers, to set aside a clear biblical command was heresy. Paul argued that all provisions which discriminated against Gentiles should be set aside and was hounded all through his ministry by other believers who argued that Scripture must never be set aside. Mark portrays Jesus as not only setting aside biblical food and purity laws but also arguing that they never really made sense because food cannot make people unclean (Mark 7:1–23).

Over the centuries a number of other issues have been contentious, like slavery, the role of women, the place of divorce. It is understandable that in each instance there were some who were concerned that biblical commands not be set aside and who therefore opposed change. There were also some who tried to explain away the force of the biblical commands. The better way forward was to acknowledge with respect the views of biblical writers and why they held them, and then acknowledge what were grounds for making changes, based both on new understandings and driven by the same focus on love that informed Jesus' stance. For Paul and Jews of his time, the social status of women, who usually married men twice their age, meant that they were seen as inferior to men and, aside from some exceptions, were therefore not to exercise leadership, but to remain silent in church (1 Cor 14:34–36; 1 Tim 2:9–15). Society has rightly changed in this regard. The same is true of slaves. It took centuries for the church to move from Paul's affirmation of slaves as persons to actually abolishing slavery. Divorce, clearly forbidden (Mark 10:9–12), is seen by many, including some churches, as in some situations the more caring option for all concerned.

It is not disrespectful of writers of Scripture and, in particular, of Paul, to suggest that their understanding of human reality needs to be supplemented. This will surely also be true of a wide range of ideas that they would have held about the nature of reality. These include belief that the universe was only a few thousand years old, that it came into being over seven days and in the sequence set out in Genesis, that there was a single original man, that woman was created from his rib, and that increased pain in childbirth and thorns and thistles came about because of Eve's sin. One could add what would have been their assumptions about cosmology: belief in a three-tiered universe or in the earth as a sphere which the sun orbited. Indeed, faith in God is what has inspired new understandings. Acknowledging that the universe is billions of years old, for instance, does not mean that we dismiss all the rest of Scripture. Similarly, acknowledging that human beings may be heterosexual and homosexual and not just male or female does not mean dismissing all the Bible says about humanity. If we accept the need for a revised understanding of human sexuality, as do the proponents of both options two and three, then it is hard to justify imposing laws which were grounded on the understanding of human sexuality which we acknowledge needed supplementing. We can too easily find ourselves on the wrong side of the pattern of conflicts that have characterised the development of faith over the centuries, rather than on the side pioneered by Jesus. In many ways, it comes down to our approach to Scripture.

There are many truly loving same-sex partnerships (and in some countries, marriages) among highly respected citizens and deeply committed Christians. Some find it highly offensive when others assume that they are obsessed with sexual orgasm or are constantly engaging in anal sex. For many, the latter plays no part. They claim the same kind of mutual commitment and affection that characterises the best of heterosexual marriages. Ultimately it is people like this who are the most influential argument for acknowledging the legitimacy of their relationships, much more than any intellectual arguments, and when it is seen in this way, then the sexual aspect ceases to be the central focus and finds its proper place as simply one aspect of deep human intimacy, where it belongs.

MEGAN K. DEFRANZA

It has been an honor to write alongside such scholarly men in this volume, not least of which is Dr. William Loader. Dr. Loader's numerous volumes have provided contemporary students of the Bible resource upon resource for gaining a better understanding of attitudes toward sexuality in ancient contexts. Like all of the contributors to this volume, Dr. Loader has a high regard for Scripture, a regard which demands we do not force the Bible to say what we want or expect it to say. Respect for Scripture requires not skating over difficulties—a flat earth, global flood, genocide, patriarchy, or divine regulation of slavery. Rather, he calls for Christians to allow biblical authors to speak in their own voices, only then bringing them into conversation with our own perspectives, shaped (as we are) by the last 2,000 years of Christian history. This is the task of biblical study for Christian ethics.

According to Loader, modern arguments that separate orientation from acts (condemning only the latter) or those that suggest biblical authors denounce only exploitative relationships (not those marked by mutuality and fidelity) do not respect the "otherness" of the Bible. In this, his arguments challenge Wesley Hill's proposal as well as my own. Trusting that Dr. Hill will respond to the argument about desire, I will focus my attention on the other half of his thesis (p. 19).

Where biblical texts in themselves may appear ambiguous, thus open to more than one interpretation, Loader looks to extrabiblical Jewish literature from the same period to close the debate. I find material from the tradition helpful but do not think it closes off alternative interpretations. Ultimately, I will argue that the tone of biblical prohibitions may point us in another direction.

Weighing the Tradition: Adam, Eve, and Nature

In his argument that biblical authors would have condemned not only same-sex actions but also desire, Loader returns us, once again, to natural law arguments built upon the figures of Adam and Eve. He argues that ancient authors would have viewed same-sex desire as different from adulterous heterosexual desire, since in the latter case "being attracted is not a sin, but becomes one when one pursues it." By contrast, "attraction to the same sex . . . is unnatural, contrary to how God made us as male and female" (p. 44).

Dr. Loader does not argue that Adam and Eve were in the mind of the author of Leviticus. Positing a number of potential reasons for the prohibitions, he admits, "The text gives no rationale for the prohibition beyond its offence against divine will" (p. 22). Instead, he looks to the reception of the text in later Jewish literature for clues as to how these may have been understood by Paul and the authors of the New Testament. "Once the prohibitions of Leviticus 18:22 and 20:13 were read as a whole within the Pentateuch (the first five books), hearers might well have made a connection with the creation story, understood as limiting sexual union to heterosexual intercourse. Whatever rationale people might have brought to the prohibitions, these prohibitions were certainly understood subsequently as absolute and, as we shall see, extended also to same-sex relations between women" (pp. 22–23). Where the text (or, in this case, the logic behind the text) is unclear, tradition can provide clues. Nevertheless, one must exercise caution so as not to assume that biblical authors always mirror their contemporaries.

Loader has marshaled sufficient evidence that some of Paul's contemporaries argued from Adam and Eve to the natural order of heterosexuality against all forms of same-sex behavior. The first-century Jewish writer Philo makes explicit connections between the Levitical prohibitions and "the making of male and female (Gen 1:27) as defining God's intended order for the nature of creation" (p. 27). A little after Philo, the Jewish author of 2 Enoch would connect a "sin which is against nature" with "child corruption in the anus in the manner of Sodom" and would go on in another passage to censure "friend with friend in the anus" that Loader interprets as "apparently adult-to-adult consensual same-sex relations" (p. 25). The description of men "standing naked, forehead to forehead" in the *Apocalypse of Abraham*, another contemporary Jewish text, is taken as corroborating evidence that every kind of same-sex sexual act was viewed as a violation of God's order inscribed in the creation of Adam and Eve (p. 25).

These passages certainly illustrate that some ancient writers condemned not only exploitative same-sex relationships (such as the pederasty described in 2 Enoch above) but also consensual relations, and some grounded their arguments about nature in Adam and Eve. Still, unlike Philo, Paul does not explicitly link his reading of natural sexual orientation to Adam and Eve. The first parents are conspicuously missing from Romans 1 where Paul seems to be building a case from nature which could be understood by those not schooled in Hebrew creation stories.[1] Despite the apostle's ambivalent statements on the status of women, Paul comes nowhere near the misogyny of Philo. It is hard to imagine Philo arguing, as Paul did, that "the husband does not have authority over his own body but yields it to his wife" (1 Cor 7:4b).

Paul's theological interpretation of Adam and Eve also differs from the author of the *Apocalypse of Abraham*, who blends the Genesis account with the legend of the Watchers in 1 Enoch, describing Eve as sexually seduced by the fallen angel Azaz'el.[2] Reworking the narrative so that Eve appears more culpable for the fall of humankind, the *Apocalypse* stands in sharp contrast to Paul, who traces responsibility for sin back to Adam in Romans 5:12–19 and upholds the tradition of Eve's deception, rather than seduction, in 2 Corinthians 11:2–3.[3]

Where there is evidence, it is safe to assume shared perspectives. Paul's censure of "effeminate[s]" (*malakoi* in 1 Cor 6:9 KJV) appears to affirm the ancient association between virtue and virility on the one hand and effeminacy and vice on the other. But he was also quick to praise virtuous women and partner with them for the advance of the gospel.[4] We must be careful not to suggest more certainty than texts support.

---

1. Dale Martin, *Sex and the Single Savior* (Louisville: Westminster John Knox Press, 2006), 52–57.

2. The Watchers were described as fallen angels who mated with human women, an ancient interpretation of the "sons of God" in Gen 6:4.

3. Megan K. DeFranza, "The Transformation of Deception: Understanding the Portrait of Eve in the *Apocalypse of Abraham*, ch. 23," *Priscilla Papers*, 23.2 (Spring 2009): 21–28.

4. Note the women Paul commends in Romans 16:1–15.

Weighing the Tradition: Sodom

Another place where one finds a difference between Pauline arguments and those of his contemporaries is the apostle's failure to use Sodom as a paradigm for all same-sex relations. As Loader has shown, every kind of same-sex act began to be associated with Sodom: pederasty in *2 Enoch*, a perversion of nature in the *Testament of the Twelve Patriarchs*, and adult consensual sex in Philo (pp. 25, 26, 28 respectively). The persistence and universality of this tradition can be traced through the ages to sodomy laws still on the books in the twenty-first century.[5] The strict definition of sodomy is "anal or oral copulation with a member of the same or opposite sex," but in colloquial use, sodomy is understood to refer to same-sex acts of any kind regardless of the fact that Genesis 19:4–9 describes only attempted gang rape.[6]

The widespread association of gay love with gang rape in the Western tradition reveals a powerful bias which does not clarify the Scriptures but actually keeps people from an honest reading of the biblical text and from genuine listening to people who are gay, lesbian, or bisexual. Long before children ever learn what sodomy means, they have already been enculturated to fear for their lives by the story of a city burned to the ground, the wrath of God poured out on people who do wicked things. Is it any wonder our adolescents are terrified to come out to their families? Loving Christian families though they may be, these are the same families who have taught them that the name Sodom should incite fear of the wrath of God.

Paul may not have used Sodom as paradigmatic for same-sex relations, but his language is not any softer. In 1 Corinthians 6:9 he lists the *arsenokoitai* with "wrongdoers [who] will not inherit the kingdom of God," hardly an improvement on the tradition of Sodom. It is this tone that moves me to ask if Paul's concern was same-sex activity in general or if it could have been more narrowly focused.

Pastoral Tone Then and Now

It is possible that Paul's comments were directed at all same-sex acts, but it is not beyond reason that the apostle was speaking to the

---

5. "12 States Still Ban Sodomy a Decade After Court Ruling," (April 4, 2014) Associated Press, *USA Today*, http://www.usatoday.com/story/news/ nation/2014/04/21/12 -states-ban-sodomy-a-decade-after-court-ruling/7981025/.

6. http://www.merriam-webster.com/dictionary/sodomy.

majority of same-sex sex activity found in the Roman Empire. As Stephen Holmes admits, "Lifelong, exclusive, equal same-sex partnerships are virtually unknown to human history and anthropology outside the contemporary West. Same-sex sexual activity is common, but it almost never takes this cultural form" (p. 26). The forms which were common in the first century were sexual relationships with significant power differentials—upper-class men over lower-class men, boys, eunuchs, slaves; wealthy "johns" exploiting the poverty of those pressured into prostitution through economic need; aristocrats grown tired of the ordinary, searching for more exotic pleasures, and supplied by those looking to profit from human trafficking. These were the more common forms of same-sex sexuality in Paul's day. And it is these kinds of exploitative relationships which make the best sense of the tone which Paul uses in his warnings to the Christians in Corinth, Ephesus, and Rome.[7]

Commenting on the task of moving from exegesis to ethics, Robert Song cautions, "We cannot assume that faithfulness consists in the bald repetition of what has been said in the past; to say the same word in a different context is to say a different word."[8] Here I must agree with Dr. Loader that where sexual acts arise from "deliberate perversion and sin . . . the condemnation remains; but where [they do] not, we must find a new way of responding" (p. 179).

If Paul were confronted with same-sex-attracted Christians unable to change their orientation, I do not believe that he would respond with the same words we find in Romans, 1 Corinthians, and 1 Timothy. I suspect, if he did want to limit sexual activity to heterosexual marriage, he would speak as Jesus did when our Lord faced the woman charged with adultery. Despite her clear violation of the law, we do not read warnings of hellfire and brimstone, but compassion, gentle exhortation to "go, and sin no more" (KJV), alongside stern warnings for those so eager to condemn (John 8:2–11). I believe the apostle Paul would respond with empathy, recalling the war within his own flesh (Rom 7:7–25), because he would recognize that the context is different. It requires a different word.

---

7. See my chapter in this volume (p. 69) for the larger argument and supporting evidence.
8. Robert Song, *Covenant and Calling: Towards a Theology of Same-Sex Relationships* (London: SCM, 2014), xii–xiii.

Could it be that Paul's strong language *was* pastorally appropriate because it addressed different kinds of behaviors? As I argued in my own chapter, I believe the strong warnings we read in these "texts of terror" would have been completely appropriate if addressed to the sexual exploitation of the ancient world—the common abuse of enslaved persons by their masters and mistresses, the slave trade which captured and at times mutilated male children in order to create more exotic living sex toys for those with the means to pay, the misuse of women destitute or enslaved as prostitutes. As Christians have become more aware that such horrific sexual exploitation continues to this day, we have come to feel his righteous indignation.

Dr. Loader may be right; I may be inadvertently softening the biblical text in my attempts to make sense of the tone of these passages and my awareness of the diversity of sexual behavior—acts born of love and devotion as opposed to selfishness and greed. But what if the text is not as clear as we thought? What if we could imagine a context in which the force of Paul's words makes perfect sense? Reimagining the apostle to say what I want him to say would be bad exegesis . . . but asking, "What would a good Christian pastor say? How would he say it? How would Jesus have responded to a Christian college student struggling to understand her same-sex desires?" That is the task of Christian ethics.

WESLEY HILL

William Loader's essay is marked by deep learning and sensitive, painstaking exegesis. Much of my disagreement with the essay lies more at the hermeneutical level than the exegetical. On many (though not all)[9] of the exegetical points, Loader and I agree. Fundamentally, Loader sees the biblical prohibitions of same-sex sexual behavior as no longer binding because we now know more than Paul did—specifically, about the instance of people who appear to be "hardwired" to be attracted to members of the same sex and capable of expressing that attraction with fidelity and virtue. To follow Paul in condemning what we now know to be an innate and more or less fixed psychological orientation would be to consign a whole class of people to a life without (sexual) intimacy—which seems to fly in the face of Paul's own most central insights about the priority of love and mercy (Rom 13:8–10).

Toward the end of his essay, Loader attempts a fair summary of something that resembles my own view, which he describes this way: "Some . . . might see being gay as similar to having a disability and explain it as one of the results of Adam and Eve's sin. All these explanations help people to accept being gay as nothing to be ashamed of. They just must not act on it, but instead remain celibate." He then makes three lines of criticism, to which I would like to respond in turn.

First, according to Loader, this (what we might call) "accommodationist" view—the "accept being gay but refrain from gay sex" view—"claims that Paul would have believed that there are genuinely gay people despite lack of evidence, and Paul's psychological argument appears to rule that out." Loader's problem with the accommodationist view is twofold: First,

---

9. To highlight only one instance, I do see "echoes of Adam" in Romans 1, who in turn prefigures Israel's "fall" as well (Rom 7), and this affects my reading of Romans 1. Paul is not targeting specifically Gentile cultural practices but rather painting on a broad scriptural canvas and working primarily, I think, with less culturally specific references (e.g., Gaius Caligula).

Paul probably thought of all people as "heterosexual," and, second, Paul therefore opposed not just same-sex sexual acts but also the psychological disposition of having same-sex sexual desires. (Loader repeats this latter point several times in his essay, insisting that Paul believed "homosexual orientation is contrary to nature as God created people.") In response to this, I would want to make two points. First, it is most probable that Paul—like other ancient authors of his time—thought of people neither as "heterosexual" nor "homosexual."[10] He did not think of a normative "sexual orientation" because he did not think at all in terms of sexual orientations in the modern sense of that term. And in any case, regardless of what Paul knew or didn't know, the text which Loader finds condemning of the experience of "being gay" (as opposed to only condemning of same-sex sexual acts) may be read more straightforwardly as condemning a limited part of what modern psychology and cultures understand as "gay experience." Paul inveighs against "the lusts of their hearts" (Rom 1:24 NRSV), "degrading passions" (1:26 NRSV), and men's "passion for one another" (1:27 NRSV). All of these references, I suggest, are best read in light of the text's immediate focus, which is on the sexual acts in which these passions culminate. If Paul focuses on the interior psychological experience of same-sex attraction, in other words, he is focusing on one particular part—but not the whole—of that interior experience. He is highlighting lust and its culmination, not the sort of "pre-behavioral" inclination toward one sex or another, which still exists even in the absence of passionate fantasizing and genital intimacy.

Contemporary understandings of "sexual orientation," while often inclusive of what Loader describes in relation to Romans 1, cannot be reduced to "passions" or "lusts." The American Psychological Association, for example, defines sexual orientation as "an enduring pattern of emotional, romantic, and/or sexual attractions to men, women, or both sexes," whereas sexual behavior is how one's sexual orientation is "expressed."[11] Likewise, gay people's descriptions of their sexual orientations often focus as much on the emotional and romantic as they do the narrowly "sexual." Gay people speak not just of an inclination to have sex

---

10. See David M. Halperin, *One Hundred Years of Homosexuality: The New Ancient World* (New York: Routledge, 1990), ch. 1; Holt N. Parker, "The Myth of the Heterosexual: Anthropology and Sexuality for Classicists," *Arethusa* 34 (2001): 313–62.

11. American Psychological Association, "Sexual orientation, homosexuality and bisexuality," accessed March 8, 2016, http://www.apa.org/helpcenter/sexual-orientation.aspx.

with people of the same sex (which inclination may be experienced, in Christian terms, as temptation before it is experienced as a consciously cultivated pattern of lust) but also of a heightened sensitivity to and gifting for non-genital, same-sex friendship. They speak of a preference for or special interest in the emotional and intellectual company of people of the same sex. They speak of a kind of "knack" or genius for seeking out and maintaining such company. And they imagine that their experience of all these things is not simply equivalent or reducible to the desire for same-sex genital contact, but also is not always neatly separable from that desire either. In other words, they imagine that their experience of this broad desire for same-sex friendship and intimacy would not exist in the same way for them if all their sexual desires were for sex with people of the opposite sex. As one lesbian woman writes:

> Sexual desire [cannot] be easily tweezed away from nonsexual longing and love and adoration. . . . That's not how *eros* actually works! My lesbianism is part of why I form the friendships I form. It's part of why I volunteer at a pregnancy center. Not because I'm attracted to the women I counsel, but because my connection to other women does have an adoring and erotic component, and I wanted to find a way to express that connection through works of mercy. My lesbianism is part of why I love the authors I love. It's inextricable from who I am and how I live in the world.[12]

Similarly, a gay man writes:

> A homosexual inclination is a form of same-sex desire or *eros*, but to reduce *eros* solely to sexual desire is to forget its richer meaning. *Eros* is the form of love that desires intimacy not in a reductively sexual sense, but in the broader sense of exclusive and committed companionship. It is a longing for physical and emotional closeness. *Eros* is often experienced as sexual desire, but cannot be identified with it.[13]

---

12. Eve Tushnet, "Order from Confusion Sprung," eve-tushnet.blogspot.com, accessed March 8, 2016, http://eve-tushnet.blogspot.com/2010_06_01_archive.html#1921445070183139.

13. Aaron Taylor, "Can One Be Gay and Christian?" *First Things* website, accessed March 8, 2016, http://www.firstthings.com/web-exclusives/2013/04/can-one-be-gay-and-christian.

Given such a complex experience on the part of gay people, it seems important to recognize that Romans 1 both does and does not speak *directly* to them. I continue to maintain that Paul's description of same-sex genital behavior does rule out certain contemporary forms of homosexual behavior, including sex, as incompatible with life in Christ. But it is not at all clear that Paul is condemning the larger *sensibility* of same-sex attraction, the drive that marks out (but is not limited to) gay people, insofar as neither Paul the historical person nor Paul the author as given to us in his texts seems to have had such a concept of a "gay sensibility" at all.

Loader's second line of criticism is that an "accept the orientation but condemn the behavior" sort of view "bars genuinely gay people from ever expressing their sexuality, something which seems unfair and inequitable if their state of being gay is in itself acceptable." Elsewhere in his essay he puts the point forcefully: "Choosing celibacy is one thing. Obliging it by implication on all who are gay, so that they must never give natural expression to their sexuality, is another." But I worry that this way of putting the matter once again assumes or implies that what Scripture and the Christian tradition have historically condemned is *orientations*. As I've already indicated, I think that is not the case. Romans 1 has lust and sexual behavior in view, and when the church has historically turned its attention to homosexuality (which is itself an anachronism), it has focused on acts, not orientations. In short, traditional Christianity has not condemned "being gay" nor "having a homosexual orientation" nor "the expression of gay sexuality" not only for the simple reason that it hasn't had access to those concepts in those forms but also because it has positively celebrated much of what we have chosen to locate under the rubric of "being gay." For many decades, the Roman Catholic Church, while maintaining its stricture against same-sex sexual coupling, also provided a haven for the expression of much of what goes under the banner of "homosexuality."[14] There are many ways one may sublimate one's sexual energies, activating what the Catholic Church regularly describes as one's "affective capacity," and celibate people too may make "an embodied and spiritual response to the innate dynamics of human sexuality to connect, to belong, and to give life."[15]

---

14. This is the argument of a book like Frederic S. Roden, *Same-Sex Desire in Victorian Religious Culture* (New York: Palgrave Macmillan, 2002).

15. Louis J. Cameli, *Catholic Teaching on Homosexuality: New Paths to Understanding* (Notre Dame, IN: Ave Maria Press, 2012), 65.

I also find reason to question Loader's notion that celibacy must always be a "free" choice if it is to be seen as properly Christian. What would he say about a heterosexual friend of mine, known to me for many years and now in her eighties, who has never married despite wishing to and has chosen to remain sexually abstinent? Has her celibacy, insofar as she has accepted it as an unwelcome cost of her Christian discipleship and viewed it as "un-free" in that sense, been unfair? Throughout Scripture and in the history of the church, many of the most beautiful vocations have been laid on believers against their wishes (see, for instance, Ex 4:1–17). As Eve Tushnet has put it in contemporary terms:

> We have important elements of freedom in our vocations—you can choose your spouse, you can choose your friends. But we also live in conditions of constraint. Many of our vocations are the result of circumstances rather than a perceived call from God—and often these are not circumstances we would choose. If you're in recovery, for example, and you serve others struggling with addiction, you probably wouldn't have chosen that path for yourself but you may find it's a real path of love. Caring for an ailing relative can be harrowing, but it can also be a path of sanctification (as marriage is). The example I always use is one taken from my work with women in crisis pregnancies: That second line comes up on the little plastic test and suddenly you're staring down the barrel of your call from God.[16]

In short, to say that celibacy is an obligation gay people must embrace and *therefore* it can't be humane or loving or life-giving represents, I think, a misunderstanding of what kind of freedom traditional Christianity envisions for believers.

Loader's final criticism is that this "accept and refrain" view of gay Christians ultimately depends upon "a strict adherence to the prohibitions in Leviticus, which will be similarly based on limited

---

16. Eve Tushnet, "The Three False Gods of Marriage, Freedom, and Morality," February 25, 2016, accessed March 9, 2016, http://www.patheos.com/blogs/evetushnet/2016/02/the-three-false-gods-of-marriage-freedom-and-morality.html.

understandings of human sexuality." Since my essay below is an extended effort to show that refraining from gay sex is based much more in a broadly Augustinian reading of the entire biblical canon on marriage, sexual difference, and procreation, I will simply say here that I don't recognize my own view as based on a narrow reading of Leviticus or Romans 1 (or the other "proof texts") in isolation.

RESPONSE TO WILLIAM LOADER

STEPHEN R. HOLMES

Professor Loader's essay is characteristically erudite and careful. His knowledge of ancient texts on the theme of same-sex sexual activity may be unparalleled in the world today, and the fruit of that learning is amply on display here. I cannot pretend to be equipped to engage with him exegetically (although I have one minor query); instead I will raise three substantial points, one concerning broader themes of sexuality, one concerning what we do with the fruits of our exegesis, and the last concerning the doctrine of Scripture.

To put aside my one minor query first, Loader twice suggests that the audience for Paul's argument in Romans 1:18–32 is Jewish, speaking once of their "strongly Jewish background" (p. 34). I do not follow contemporary scholarship on Romans closely, but this seems a very strange assumption. Romans 11:13–24 is absolutely explicit that (at least a substantial proportion of) Paul's audience is non-Jewish: "I am talking to you Gentiles," he begins. I am not sure that this makes any substantial difference to Loader's exegesis, but I note it simply out of puzzlement.

My first significant point is that Loader focuses on texts about same-sex sexual activity without locating them at all in a broader biblical theology of marriage/sexuality. We have passing references to Genesis 1–2 as the background to other texts, nothing at all (I think) on the Song of Solomon, nothing on Matthew 19, one quick aside on 1 Corinthians 7, and so on. This seems to me to be important, inasmuch as most of Loader's argument turns on the idea of the perversion of what is natural/normal. Some analysis of the biblical account of norms in the area of sexuality would seem to be necessary to make this argument work.

As Loader points out, we have no real insight into Paul's concept of "natural" from the letters; we have to propose a plausible reconstruction of what he might have been thinking. I suggest that the rich account of the goodness of human sexuality rightly ordered in the Hebrew

Scriptures really should be a significant part of that reconstruction, and so needs to be explored if we are to understand Paul correctly. I assume that a set of assumptions like this underlies Loader's arguments, but it is nowhere explicit, and unless it is stated, it is difficult to engage with.

Second, I turn to what we do with our exegesis. Loader argues that Romans 1:26–27 teaches not only that same-sex sexual activity is wrong but that homoerotic desire is disordered, and this seems to me to be plausible. However, he makes two moves on the basis of this, both of which seem to me to be open to challenge: he suggests that Paul thought heterosexuality is normal; and he assumes that other desires are not also disordered. Let me consider these in turn.

Loader suggests repeatedly that Paul would have regarded all people as heterosexual (to take only one quotation: "God made people male and female. There are only heterosexual people" (p. 40). This seems wrong to me, and importantly so. Loader acknowledges that Paul could have had no concept of sexual orientation, as it is a modern Western way of thinking unknown in Paul's day. If this is true, it self-evidently applies to heterosexual orientation as much as homosexual orientation. Either is an assertion that a person is erotically attracted only to people of one sex. This has become our normal experience in the West in recent decades, but—as I argued in my own essay—there is essentially no evidence that it was/is normal experience for anyone except late-modern Westerners, and plenty of evidence that it was/is not.

I assume Paul was familiar enough with Greco-Roman cultures that he understood that for at least many adult males in his world, sexual interest was aroused by certain body shapes and characteristics possessed by both adult females and adolescent males; he also held tenaciously to an account of properly ordered sexuality that led to either celibacy or disciplined heterosexual monogamy; this does not yet allow the assumption that he thought people were naturally heterosexual. To put the point bluntly, Paul no doubt knew directly of Roman aristocrats who habitually raped their slaves, both male and female. To say he regarded them as "heterosexual" is to say that he regarded the rape of female slaves as somehow more acceptable, or at least more natural, than the rape of male slaves. I suppose Paul would have regarded both with equal horror as marks of disordered sexuality.

This leads to the second assumption noted above, that heterosexual desires are not wrong. Again, the point is made more than once, but to highlight one direct assertion, Loader speaks of "the prohibition of adultery and adulterous attitudes, where being attracted is not a sin" (p. 44). This seems to stand as assumption or assertion in the essay—it is nowhere argued—and it seems wrong. The obvious response is the words of Jesus in Matthew 5:27–28, where the contrary point seems explicit: it is not just the act of adultery that is wrong; looking "lustfully" is equally wrong. I suppose Loader's response would be to point to the distinction he has made between "adulterous attitudes" and "being attracted," but "looking lustfully" sounds to me like merely "being attracted" (in the Greek as well as in our English translations).

In Christian theology, ideas of the fall and original sin teach us that all our desires are in some sense wrongly directed. This doctrine finds its origins in Paul's letters, of course (e.g., Rom 3:10–18; 7:14–25; 8:7–9; Eph 2:1–3), but as Chesterton once memorably quipped, it is the one doctrine that can be proved empirically. We might say that we can conceive in principle of a pure heterosexual desire—Eve's desire for Adam, perhaps—but, east of Eden, every actual desire is warped, including all heterosexual desire.

This point gets to the heart of Loader's argument: he offers us three alternatives in conclusion, which each turn on his identified distinction between sinful homosexual desire and pure heterosexual desire. His exegetical reason for rejecting the "accept and refrain" position is that in its acceptance of gay and lesbian people, it does not adequately reflect Paul's teaching that homosexual desire is wrongly directed. But every desire of every person is wrongly directed; the church is a company of sinners. The acceptance offered to lesbian and gay people is exactly the same as the acceptance offered to straight people: we are all invited through the mercy of God and the sacrifice of Christ to come as we are, desiring wrongly in multiple ways, and to find ourselves gradually transformed to desire rightly through the work of the Spirit.

Similarly, Loader's pastoral reason for rejecting his "accept and refrain" position is that it is "very unfair and inconsistent to tell people that it's OK to be gay, but not OK to give natural expression to their sexuality" (p. 44). But that is exactly what we say to all people: it is not OK to give natural expression to our sexuality—or indeed to any other natural desire we have. Instead, the gospel calls every one of us to repentance and transformation in every area of our lives. Christian marriage is not permission to indulge our sexual desires, but an ascetic discipline through which our wayward desires are transformed (just as celibacy is).

My third substantive point is on the doctrine of Scripture. Loader closes his essay with an invitation "to engage both Scripture and experience, including setting some parts of the former aside . . ." (p. 46). I just cannot accept that we should ever set Scripture aside, on the basis of experience or anything else. We will sometimes be forced by experience to reexamine our understanding of Scripture and discover that we read it wrong; we always have to read Scripture well, in context, in the light of the whole story of the Bible, through the lens of Christ; we always have to be careful not to invest our own interpretations of Scripture with the authority that only the text itself carries; but we must never set it aside.

Loader tries to suggest that such setting aside is unexceptional, that it is something the church has done repeatedly, from Jesus on down. His examples are, however, repeatedly unconvincing, and in at least one case apparently self-contradictory (he states Jesus "never set scriptural commands aside" and then in the same paragraph asserts "Mark portrays Jesus as . . . setting aside biblical food and purity laws" (p. 47). Unless he intends us to understand that the evangelist invented the story of Jesus he tells in Mark 7:1–23, these two statements stand in straight contradiction.

The examples he offers are familiar: slavery, the status of women, divorce, young-earth creationism. The responses to each are equally familiar and have been rehearsed at great length in the literature.[17] The church was tragically slow to take a stand on slavery, but (despite some arguments around 1800) never taught that slavery was supported by Scripture. We read texts for centuries through the lens of a false Aristotelian biology, which taught that women were deficient males, and so read them wrong (something we can all agree on even if some disagreement on how to read them right remains). On divorce, as I argued in my own essay, we have made space to live with pastoral messiness,

---

17. See particularly William J. Webb, *Slaves, Women, and Homosexuals: Exploring the Hermeneutics of Cultural Analysis* (Downers Grove, IL: IVP, 2001); Richard B. Hays, *The Moral Vision of the New Testament: A Contemporary Introduction to New Testament Ethics* (London: T&T Clark, 1997).

not set aside biblical teaching (I did explore the possibility of doing the same thing for gay and lesbian couples). It is not news that early readers of Genesis 1 (e.g., Philo, Origen, Augustine) did not hear it as teaching creation in six literal days; Philo also explicitly denies that it is possible to date creation. None of these examples demonstrates that the church has "set aside" Scripture.

Loader never articulates a doctrine of Scripture in his essay. He speaks of "respect and reverence" for the text, but then immediately notes that he (rightly!) applies such principles very widely (p. 21). Christian theology depends on ascribing a unique status to Scripture; we simply have no place to stand without so doing. We might disagree on how to articulate that unique status ("inerrant," "infallible," "authoritative," "inspired") and on the conditions for interpretation that it imposes, but somehow it must be there. I assume Loader is indeed committed to the authority of Scripture and that his language of "setting aside" the text is an inexact way of referring to a hermeneutical principle that I have not been able to identify; it would be good to achieve clarity on this point, however.

Finally, I note and celebrate Loader's proper pastoral concern that frames his essay at beginning and end. It is vital that we are attentive and responsive to people's lives and experiences. That said, I have dealt with pastoral questions and concerns at length in my own essay, so will not add more here. Loader gives us much to be grateful for in his discussions of history and in his exegesis. That said, as I have argued above, I find his reasons for rejecting his "accept and refrain" position finally unconvincing, not because I disagree with his exegesis of Romans, but because he sets that exegesis in the context of an assumption which is just wrong.

REJOINDER

WILLIAM LOADER

As a person of faith, I welcome the increasing recognition both in the wider community and in the church that being gay is not something from which one needs to be healed. This does justice to those concerned. As a biblical scholar, I am less convinced that the modern attempt to claim that this was what Paul meant all along does justice to Scripture.

I have greatly valued our respectful exchange of views. I remain committed to seeking to listen to what Paul and others were saying in their world, whether we like it or not. I do not have an approach to Scripture as infallible or equivalent which would put me under pressure to defend what Paul said or read it in ways that more closely conform to my views. Paradoxically, while the latter approach will often claim a high view of biblical authority, the former view treats Scripture with greater respect. When we see divorce, for instance, as sometimes the compassionate way forward despite Scripture's prohibition, we are also acting in a way that is nevertheless soundly scriptural and modeled by Jesus, namely by allowing informed love to determine what we do, not just law, just as he did in sometimes overriding Sabbath law.

I respect that Stephen never wants us to set Scripture aside and perhaps that language should be avoided and we should talk instead of recognising priorities. Doing so was controversial from the very beginning, not only in Jesus' ministry but also when the first believers permanently overrode biblical laws on circumcision, food, and purity laws in the name of prioritizing biblical values of inclusivity and removal of barriers. New knowledge leads to new understandings of the universe, humanity, and sexuality, and new insights generated by gospel values have led us to challenge the institution of slavery and not least the patriarchal understandings of women and marriage, a point Megan makes so well.

For each of us, limited space left some aspects unaddressed or unclear. I offer a fuller treatment in *The New Testament on Sexuality*. To Stephen I need to confirm that in speaking of the Roman churches' strongly Jewish background, my intent was not to deny the obvious Gentile constituency. Also gospel studies have long recognised diversity among the Gospels' portraits of Jesus' attitude towards the Law, which cannot be reduced simplistically to an allegation that writers "invented" stories. Nor was it my intent to suggest that Paul believed that everyone was heterosexual in the sense that he had no knowledge of people attracted to their own sex (in our terms, "homosexual"). Otherwise his argument in Romans 1 would make no sense. His response was that such attraction was a distortion of how God made people to be. To Stephen I need also to emphasise that, far from ignoring Genesis 1:27 behind Paul's argument, I assume it (especially in the language "male" and "female"), and to Megan I want to insist that allusion is there, though I never suggest Adam and Eve are alluded to.

Both Megan and Wesley seem not to give sufficient weight to reading Paul in his Jewish context. I chose to focus on the detailed exegesis of Romans 1, reading it within both its literary context and its cultural religious context because I believe that must be the basis for approaching Scripture. When one does so, Paul's psychological argument seems to me to be clear, and his stance coheres with what we know of attitudes of fellow Jews of the period. Alternative readings need to be argued on the same basis.

Historical reconstruction of meaning is about degrees of probability. Thus it is not impossible that Paul in Romans 1 was thinking only of certain kinds of same-sex attitudes and behaviour, overly passionate ones, and that he might have thought quite permissively about less intense gay relations. Those who argue like this are, however, in danger of unraveling their own argument and effectively dismissing the relevance of Paul's arguments for contemporary discussion, leaving us with only the Leviticus prohibitions. Stephen finds my reading of Romans "plausible," and I suggest that it is much more plausible historically than the notion that Paul was targeting only intensity.

The issue was not just act, nor just intensity, but direction, misdirection. My reference to Jesus' prohibition of lusting after another's wife, to which Stephen alludes, was to make the point that in that case there was nothing implicitly sinful in finding someone of the opposite sex attractive. The issue was whether this became intent (Greek *pros* plus the infinitive in Matthew expresses purpose), let alone action. Same-sex attraction was seen as more than that. Genesis implied that males are to be attracted to females and vice versa. Something had gone wrong, they believed, where that was not the case. This might not be our conclusion, but it has made sense for centuries for those whose sexual anthropology is informed primarily by how Genesis and Romans 1 were understood. Mentioning that eunuchs existed does not disprove this, since they were still seen as males.

Until recently on the basis of the biblical understanding, many people concluded that gay people needed healing to restore them to being heterosexual. Knowledge and experience have helped people move away from that understanding to affirm that being gay is not something to feel bad about or to change. Many who embrace this new understanding try to read Paul differently, especially if they fear setting Scripture aside, as I am convinced they are doing. Yet to truly honor Scripture and respect Paul, we do better to acknowledge respectfully that we see Paul's understanding of human sexuality as no longer adequate. My faith does not commit me to first-century views about the universe, humanity, and sexuality which Paul and others assumed. As Megan notes, gender is one of the areas where updating has become unavoidable. Having this kind of flexibility belongs to the DNA of Christian faith.

Once we accept same-sex orientation as the way some people are, then to forbid them responsible expression of their sexuality is to fail to follow the biblical principles of justice and compassion, especially if the basis for doing so is a prohibition generated by understandings of sexuality which we no longer share. Do we not then find ourselves more among those who in the name of biblical law opposed Jesus and Paul? Whether this is so—and it need not be—will be something, hopefully, to which our shared work in this book will contribute.

CHAPTER TWO

JOURNEYING FROM THE BIBLE TO CHRISTIAN ETHICS IN SEARCH OF COMMON GROUND

MEGAN K. DEFRANZA

My Unexpected Journey

I never would have anticipated writing a chapter arguing for a more inclusive theology of Christian marriage in a volume of this kind—not when I attended my little Christian college in the Bible Belt, or after finishing my master's work at an evangelical seminary, or my doctoral studies in theology, not even after having completed my dissertation on the complexity of biological sex/gender differences. The Bible had always seemed clear to me on this point. Male-female marriage was assumed. Same-sex sexual acts were condemned. Case closed.

Still, I could not ignore the growing number of Christian voices—voices from heterosexual pastors and theologians, even from my evangelical tradition—calling for a reconsideration of what I had always believed to be self-evident. And I had been learning that some things we think are self-evident are less so upon closer study.

It was my growing awareness of the complexity of biological sex development that opened my mind to consider the possibility that I could be missing something. I had learned that not all people are fully or clearly male or female. While most humans seem to be clearly sexed, there is a significant minority for whom being male or female is not obvious or uncomplicated.[1] What was even more surprising to me

---

1. Intersex persons or persons with Differences of Sex Development (DSDs; historically "hermaphrodites") have bodies with both male and female physical features. Approximately

was the discovery that ancient Christians and Jews were very familiar
with people who could not be neatly categorized as male or female and
had language to describe them and laws governing their place in the
community. Jesus uses one of these terms in the first part of Matthew
19:12 when he tells his disciples, "There are eunuchs who have been
so from birth, and there are eunuchs who have been made eunuchs by
others, and there are eunuchs who have made themselves eunuchs for
the sake of the kingdom of heaven" (NRSV). "Eunuch from birth" was
one of four additional categories which later rabbis coined to describe
bodies that did not fit the typical male/female pattern—labels under
which some kinds of intersex would have been categorized.[2] Persons
with differences of sex development were old news but, until I started
my doctoral studies, this was news to me.

As I scoured the Scriptures and Christian history for help in thinking about intersex from a Christian perspective, I kept returning to
Genesis 1—a text I had taken for granted as self-evident proof that
God makes only two kinds of people, male and female. But as I examined that opening chapter of the Bible, I discovered that this was not
a comprehensive account of all of God's good creation. For example,
amphibians are not named in the narrative. They do not fit neatly into
any of the categories of creatures God made (of the air, sea, and land)
because they "mixed" the categories of land and water animals. I have
never read an Old Testament scholar argue that frogs are clear evidence

---

one out of every 2,500 live births is intersex. Susannah Cornwall, ed., *Intersex, Theology, and
the Bible* (New York: Palgrave, 2015), 1. Intersex persons are currently differentiated from
transgender persons because transgender bodies appear clearly male or female, but their gender
identity does not match what appears to be their bodily sex. As urgent as it is to consider the
ethics and experiences of transgender people, these remain beyond the scope of this volume.
See also Megan K. DeFranza, *Sex Difference in Christian Theology: Male, Female, and Intersex
in the Image of God* (Grand Rapids: Eerdmans, 2015), ch. 1.

2.   Naturally born eunuchs were called "eunuchs of the sun" (*saris khama*) because from
the first day the sun shone upon them, they knew these babies were different. In addition to
male, female, and eunuchs, rabbis recognize *aylonith* (persons with underdeveloped genitalia
which nevertheless appeared more feminine than masculine), *androgynos* (equally male and
female), and *tumtum* (whose sex was unclear but thought to reveal itself in time). See John
Hare, "Hermaphrodites, Eunuchs, and Intersex People: The Witness of Medical Science in
Biblical Times and Today," in *Intersex, Theology, and the Bible*, 83–87. Despite the fact that
these terms have no precedent in the Old Testament, Jesus felt free to use "eunuchs from
birth" and Augustine acknowledges the reality of hermaphrodites. Augustine, *The City of God
Against the Pagans*, vol. 5, Loeb Classical Library, trans. Eva Matthews Sanford and William
McAllen Green (Cambridge: Harvard University Press, 1965), 16.8, 47. See also DeFranza,
Sex Difference, chs. 1–2.

of the fall since they do not fit into one of the three categories of animals which God created in Genesis 1, but I have heard this explanation of humans who mix the categories of male and female. Simply because persons of mixed sex are not listed in the creation account does not prove that they are therefore not good or not part of God's plan. Genesis 1 is a theological account describing creation in broad categories, not a scientific inventory of all of God's good creatures.[3] I began to think that it might be better to read Genesis 1 as the beginning of the story, Adam and Eve, male and female, could be interpreted as the majority, the broad categories, rather than the exclusive model for all humankind.[4]

A simple reading of Genesis revealed only two kinds of human beings, which many have interpreted as representing an idealized male and an idealized female. But when I read Genesis in the context of the whole Bible, at the beginning of a story that later welcomed those who did not fit into either of these categories (such as eunuchs from birth), I began to see space opening up between these two, between male and female—space for others.[5]

Moving from Sex Difference to Sexuality: What Does the Bible Say?

Some might object that intersex persons and eunuchs are not the same as persons with same-sex or bisexual attraction. This is true. Yet our growing knowledge of sex development does point to biological influence on everything from genital formation, to gender identity, to sexual orientation.[6] Many kids come to feel "different" before they understand what it means to be sexual. As their bodies enter puberty, sometimes they experience desires they were not expecting, sexual desires different from the majority.

As I studied eunuchs in the Bible and the ancient world to find wisdom for thinking about persons who do not fit neatly as either male

---

3. Allister McGrath, John Polkinghorne, Karen Strand Winslow, N. T. Wright, et al., "The Book of Genesis," BioLogos Foundation (April 27, 2012), http://biologos.org/resources/audio-visual/the-book-of-genesis. Excerpted from "From the Dust: Conversations in Creation," directed by Ryan Pettey (Mountain View, CA: Highway Media, 2012).

4. DeFranza, Sex Difference, 175–81.

5. The welcome of eunuchs and foreigners prophesied in Isa 56:3–8 is fulfilled in Acts 8 with the baptism of the Ethiopian eunuch.

6. Sheri A. Berenbaum and Adriene M. Beltz, "Sexual Differentiation of Human Behavior: Effects of Prenatal and Pubertal Organizational Hormones," Frontiers in Neuroendocrinology 32 (2011): 183–200.

or female, I discovered that ancient expectations about masculinity and femininity influenced arguments about sexuality. Virtues were considered manly—in Latin, *virtue* was said to come from *vir* ("male")—so sexual virtue, sexual self-control, was considered a manly quality. Because women and eunuchs were unmanly, they were caricatured as being sexually out of control.[7] Assumptions about sex and gender bled into arguments about sexual ethics. I realized I needed to dig deeper into ancient understandings of sexuality in order to better understand biblical instructions.

Corinthians and Timothy—Their Background in Leviticus, Genesis, and Judges

Learning about eunuchs in the ancient world, particularly Jesus' second type of eunuch (eunuchs made by people), I was reminded of the gulf between the ancient world and our own. Most eunuchs were enslaved persons in aristocratic households. Any enslaved person in the ancient world could be used as a sex slave, since they had no power to refuse the sexual demands of their masters. But eunuchs who were created specifically for this purpose were expensive luxury sex toys. Traffickers stole or bought boys, cut off or mutilated their testes to preserve a prepubescent beauty, and sold them to wealthy individuals and pimps who prostituted their bodies for money. Many ancient men lusted after the "soft," effeminate bodies of these castrated males because androgynous features were considered by many to be more alluring than feminine beauty.[8] As I returned to some of the biblical passages which have been understood to condemn sexual acts between persons of the same sex, the context of sexual slavery and the effeminacy or softness of certain bodies proved significant.

Historians estimate that as many as "one in five of the residents of Rome was a slave."[9] Given the extent of the slave trade in the first century, it seemed reasonable to me that the apostle Paul would have been concerned to address the rampant sexual abuse which affected many in

---

7. DeFranza, *Sex Difference*, 76–77.

8. Piotr O. Scholz, *Eunuchs and Castrati: A Cultural History*, trans. John A. Broadwin and Shelley L. Frisch (Princeton, NJ: Markus Weiner, 2001), 113–18.

9. Everett Ferguson, *Backgrounds of Early Christianity, 2nd ed.* (Grand Rapids: Eerdmans, 1993), 56.

the early church. Closer inspection of 1 Corinthians 6:9 and 1 Timothy 1:9–10—passages which, in some English translations, appear to condemn same-sex sexuality in general—reveals this as a possibility. The problem is that there is much scholarly debate around how to translate these passages because one term (*arsenokoitai*) occurs only in these two passages while the other (*malakoi*) appears rarely in the Bible but refers to sexual matters only here.[10] Even more difficult, this combination of terms is never used in Greek literature before Paul as a way of speaking about same-sex sex.

Malakoi literally means "the soft ones" but is sometimes translated as "effeminate"—to which we will return later. Meanwhile, a number of scholars have argued that *arsenokoitai* is a compound of the Greek words for "male" (*arsen*) and "bed" (*koite*—which recalls the English "coitus"); thus, "male-bedders." They believe Paul joined two words from the Greek translation of Leviticus 18:22 and 20:13—passages also relevant to the current discussion.[11]

> Do not sleep with a **man** (*arsenos*) as one **beds** (*koiten*) a woman; that is detestable. (Lev 18:22)
>
> If a man sleeps with a **man** (*arsenos*) as one **beds** (*koiten*) a woman, both of them have done what is detestable. They must be put to death; their blood will be on their own heads. (Lev 20:13)[12]

Because all four of these prohibitions occur in sin lists—devoid of a narrative which could illuminate exactly what is banned and why—they are particularly difficult to interpret. Even those who think Paul

---

10. David F. Wright, "Homosexuals or Prostitutes? The Meaning of *Arsenokoitai* (1 Cor 6:9; 1 Tim 1:10)," *VC* 38 (1984): 125–53; idem, "Translating *Arsenokoites* (1 Cor 6:9; 1 Tim 1:10," *VC* 41 (1987): 396–98. Preston Sprinkle provides a helpful summary of this scholarly debate in chapter 7 of *People to Be Loved: Why Homosexuality Is Not Just an Issue* (Grand Rapids: Zondervan, 2015), 103–20.

11. Thomas E. Schmidt, *Straight and Narrow? Compassion and Clarity in the Homosexuality Debate* (Downers Grove, IL: InterVarsity, 1995), 33–34, 95–96. Wright, "Homosexuals or Prostitutes?," 126–29.

12. I have chosen to translate the Greek terms more literally to show that the terms differ in the Greek Old Testament (LXX). In English, the euphemism "sleep with" carries the connotation of mutuality, but "bed" more accurately reflects the ancient assumption that sex is something a man does to someone else. To bed a man was to treat him as a woman. In the Hebrew, "bed" is used in both halves of the verse.

derived *arsenokoitai* from Leviticus disagree on the rationale behind the prohibitions: Were the Mosaic commands general condemnations of all same-sex acts regardless of context, or did they refer to rape? Could they have arisen from ancient patriarchal concerns to protect the honor of masculinity? It was considered shameful for a man to be penetrated by another man.

In his commentary on Leviticus 18 and 20, Philo (the first-century Jewish contemporary of the apostle Paul) does raise concerns about male honor and shame. He names the practice of pederasty (the sexual use of boys by adult men) among the violations of these Mosaic laws. But unlike contemporary Christians who would be concerned with the age of consent, Philo worried that such a boy would suffer "the affliction of being treated like women," being turned into a "man-woman who adulterates the precious coinage of his nature." Philo believed the adult shares in the blame since he proved to be "a guide and teacher of those greatest of all evils, unmanliness and . . . effeminacy."[13] Clement of Alexandria, a second-century Christian pastor, shared similar concerns, warning his congregation that a man who removed body hair by day (e.g., who shaved) was likely to "prove himself manifestly a woman by night."[14] Bedding a man as one beds a woman was believed to ruin the passive (penetrated) male and indicted the active man for bringing about the former's demise—replacing the honor of manliness with the shame of femininity.

This concern to preserve male honor can also be observed in the only Old Testament narratives associated with same-sex sexual acts. The story most often connected to same-sex sexuality is the tale of Sodom and Gomorrah, such that "sodomy" came to mean "homosexuality" in English. However, the men of the city of Sodom were not inviting Lot and his guests to an orgy—they were threatening gang rape. To rescue his angelic visitors, Lot offers to send his virgin daughters outside in their place. Thankfully, the angels intervene (Gen 19:1–8), but in a parallel story in the book of Judges, the victim is not so lucky. In Judges, "some of the wicked men of the city surrounded the house"

---

13. Philo, *The Special Laws*, vol. 3; cited by Matthew Vines, *God and the Gay Christian* (New York: Convergent, 2014), 87.

14. Clement of Alexandria, *The Instructor* (*The Paedagogus*), bk. 3; cited in Vines, *God and the Gay Christian*, 88.

where a Levite was staying. "Pounding on the door, they shouted to the old man who owned the house, 'Bring out the man who came to your house so we can have sex with him'" (19:22). Once again the host offers his virgin daughter as a substitute, but the Levite sends out his wife/ concubine to the mob instead (19:24–25). "They raped her and abused her throughout the night," so that she died on the doorstep of the house at dawn (19:25–28).

"Homosexuality" was not the sin of these mobs. These gangs threatened rape. Ironically, the only person actually raped was not a man but a woman, a concubine—the lower-class wife of the Levite. Both hosts appear to respect the ancient values which could undergird the laws of Leviticus 18:22 and 20:13; they do not want their male guests to be treated as women. In their patriarchal perspective, it seemed better to offer up their own daughters to rape than allow a man to be treated as a woman.

These ancient patriarchal values feel far from Christian ethical sensibilities today. For this reason many scholars give greater weight to New Testament passages since it is on these that many decide whether Leviticus 18 and 20 remain binding for Christians today.[15]

With this background in mind, how should Christians interpret the warnings in 1 Corinthians and 1 Timothy?

1 Corinthians 6:9–11 (NIV 1984): Do you not know that the wicked will not inherit the kingdom of God? Do not be deceived: Neither the sexually immoral nor idolaters nor adulterers nor *malakoi* nor *arsenokoitai* nor thieves nor the greedy nor drunkards nor slanderers nor swindlers will inherit the kingdom of God. And that is what some of you were. But you were washed, you were sanctified, you were justified in the name of the Lord Jesus Christ and by the Spirit of our God.

1 Timothy 1:9–10 (NIV 1984): We also know that law is

---

15. Lev 18 and 20 do not provide a comprehensive sexual ethic for Christians. The only sexual instruction given to women is not to present themselves for sex with an animal (Lev 18:23). Many scholars point to the law prohibiting men from having sexual relations with a menstruating woman in Lev 18:19 to illustrate the fact that at least one of these Old Testament sexual prohibitions is not considered universally binding. Most Christians overlook the fact that Abraham also violated Lev 18:9 and 20:17 by marrying his half-sister, and Jacob violated 18:18 by marrying the sister of his wife. Jennifer Wright Knust, *Unprotected Texts: The Bible's Surprising Contradictions about Sex and Desire* (New York: HarperOne, 2011), 141–42.

made not for the righteous but for lawbreakers and rebels, the ungodly and sinful, the unholy and irreligious; for those who kill their fathers or mothers, for murderers, for adulterers and **arsenokoitais**, for slave traders and liars and perjurers—and for whatever else is contrary to the sound doctrine.

Whatever these terms mean, the contexts of both passages indicate they are grievous sins.[16] The interpretive debate begins to manifest when comparing English translations. In the New International Version (1984) and the Revised Standard Version, the translation of *arsenokoitai* differs even from one passage to the other:

	MALAKOI 1 Cor 6:9	ARSENOKOITAI 1 Cor 6:9	ARSENOKOITAI 1 Tim 1:10
King James Version (1611)	effeminate	abusers of themselves with mankind	them that defile themselves with mankind
Revised Standard Version (1952)	sexual perverts	sexual perverts	sodomites
New King James Version (1982)	homosexuals	sodomites	sodomites
New International Version (1984)	male prostitutes	homosexual offenders	perverts
New Revised Standard (1989)	male prostitutes	sodomites	sodomites
New American Standard (1977 & 1995)	effeminate	homosexuals	homosexuals
New International Version (2011) translates both terms with one phrase	men who have sex with men		those practicing homosexuality

A number of commentators have argued that these words form a pair: the passive penetrated (*malakoi*) and active penetrator (*arsenokoitai*) in male same-sex sexual acts.[17] A man who chose or was forced into the

16. Several scholars note a parallel between the list in 1 Tim 1 and the Ten Commandments: (5) honor father and mother, (6) do not murder, (7) do not commit adultery, (8) do not steal, (9) do not give false testimony. The author of 1 Tim may be illustrating how these ancient commands are being violated in the first-century context—expanding the category of adulterers (*moichoi*) to include *pornois, malakoi,* and *arsenokoitai*. Sprinkle, *People to Be Loved,* 117–18, n. 36, 216.

17. Dale B. Martin, *Sex and the Single Savior: Gender and Sexuality in Biblical Interpretation* (Louisville: Westminster John Knox, 2006), 38.

passive position was considered "feminized" or "softened" because he was treated "like a woman."[18]

Other scholars have argued for a more narrow interpretation—suggesting the "soft ones" could be prepubescent boys in pederastic relationships with their mentors—a common practice among ancient Greeks but criticized by Romans, Christians, and Jews. Some scholars object that if pederasty was the only meaning Paul had in view, he would have employed one of the more specific terms for this practice, such as "child-corruption" (*paidophthoria*).[19] But early Christian vice lists omit *malakoi* and *arsenokoitai*, substituting "child-corruption" where one might expect the pair—what could be interpreted as a strategy similar to the NIV 2011.[20] Unfortunately, the phrase in the updated NIV ("men who have sex with men") suggests adult behavior, whereas the Greek does not specify age.

Eunuchs were also considered "soft ones," described by one first-century Roman as "unhappy youth, softened by the blade, their manhood cut out."[21] Despite the fact that these enslaved persons had no choice in their mutilation and no power to resist the sexual advances of their masters, they were criticized both for their gender differences and their "passive" sexuality.[22] Lack of choice did not protect an individual from ridicule or moral censure.

Surprisingly, ancient literature reveals that men could be accused of being "softies" (*malakoi*) for things that had nothing to do with lack of muscle or same-sex eroticism. Men who were lazy or lacked courage in battle or failed to control themselves when faced with the temptations of rich food or beautiful women were criticized as "softies." A man who displayed excessive interest in sex (either with men or with women) could be called a "softie."[23] The vice of "softness" went well beyond sexual excess. It was a broad term of moral failure associated with weakness which could be summed up "in one ancient category, the feminine. For

---

18. Roy E. Ciampa and Brian S. Rosner, *The First Letter to the Corinthians* (Grand Rapids: Eerdmans, 2010), 241.

19. Sprinkle, *People to Be Loved*, 116.

20. *Didache* 2.2; *The Epistle of Barnabas* 19.4; Michael W. Holmes, ed., *The Apostolic Fathers: Greek Texts and English Translations*, (Grand Rapids: Baker, 1999), 252–53, 320–21. I am indebted to Roy Ciampa for directing me to these sources.

21. Sprinkle, *People to Be Loved*, 107; citing Lucan, 10.133–4.

22. DeFranza, *Sex Difference*, 77.

23. Martin, *Sex and the Single Savior*, 44–45.

the ancients, or at least for the men who produced almost all our ancient literature, the connection was commonsensical and natural."[24] David Fredickson suggests a better translation of *malakoi* would be "those who lack self-control."[25]

The New International Version (1984) and the New Revised Standard Version reveal an older suggestion that *malakoi* could have referred to "male prostitutes." Joining the two terms, 1 Corinthians 6:9 would thus indict both the male prostitute and the one who pays for his service.[26] However, as we have seen, *malakoi* is far too broad a term to be limited by this narrow translation. On the other hand, if we separate the terms, allowing *malakoi* to indict those who lack self-control and courage, the lazy and the decadent, and then look at *arsenokoitai* in its own right, we may still find evidence of the apostle's concern to curb sexual exploitation in the first century.

Dale Martin has argued against reading *arsenokoitai* as a reference to Leviticus 18 and 20, reminding us that compound words do not always mean what the sum of their parts suggests. English speakers do well to remember that "understanding" has nothing to do with "standing" or location "beneath."[27] He provides evidence that in Greek literature, *arsenokoitai* did not always speak of sexual misconduct, but was often included in ancient vice lists with sins of economic exploitation. Of course, if the ideas of sexual sin and economic exploitation are combined, we find ourselves faced, once again, with the sexual use of enslaved persons and prostitutes.[28]

Other factors in 1 Timothy 1:10 may also support the idea that sexual slavery was the target of the apostle's exhortation since "kidnappers"

---

24. Ibid., 44.

25. David E. Fredrickson, "Natural and Unnatural Use in Romans 1:24–27: Paul and the Philosophic Critique of Eros," in *Homosexuality, Science, and the "Plain Sense" of Scripture*, ed. David L. Balch (Grand Rapids: Eerdmans, 2000), 197, 218–21; cited in Vines, *God and the Gay Christian*, 122.

26. Cultic prostitution has also been suggested, but there is little to no historical evidence of sacred prostitution in Corinth. However, at feasts in temple districts, prostitutes were available not for religious ritual but as "part of the festivity" (Ciampa and Rosner, *First Letter to the Corinthians*, 248–49). Ciampa and Rosner note that the connection between prostitutes and temple feasts ties together what can appear to be unrelated topics in 1 Cor 6, particularly the apostle's concerns about food (v. 13), and the concluding exhortation: "Your bodies are temples of the Holy Spirit . . . therefore honor God with your bodies" (vv. 19–20); ibid., 261.

27. Martin, *Sex and the Single Savior*, 39.

28. Ibid., 41.

(sometimes translated "slave traders") is listed right after *arsenokoitai*. In 1 Timothy we find three terms: *pornois* (translated "sexually immoral" but derived from *pornē*, "prostitute"), *arsenokoitai*, and *andrapodistais* ("kidnappers," "slave traders").[29] Placed in order, this could be a grouping of the sexually immoral, or prostitutes, or those who visit prostitutes (e.g., the KJV "whoremongers"), followed by those who use male prostitutes more specifically or those who sexually exploit others for money, along with traffickers who kidnap and sell human beings for their own gain.[30] Krenkel notes that male prostitutes fetched a higher price than their female counterparts, and when supply ran low "beautiful boys were captured, imported . . . sold . . . and prostituted."[31]

Differentiating prostitution from sexual slavery in the first century is difficult since most prostitutes were enslaved persons or formerly enslaved.[32] Unfortunately, both served an important purpose in the patriarchal economy of the first century. Given that men were encouraged to wait until they had established their financial independence, the age of thirty was recommended as the ideal age for men to marry in both Roman and Jewish circles. Enslaved persons, those formerly enslaved, concubines, and those without vocational options were used by men who did not want to risk their own economic advancement in preparation for marriage.[33] Even when married, husbands were encouraged to have sex with their wives solely for the purpose of procreation and to find other outlets for their erotic passions; sex with slaves and prostitutes was considered a "moral" alternative.[34]

---

29. *Pornois* (masculine plural) is derived from *pornē* ("prostitute" in the feminine) and could have designated male prostitutes or the men who visit them. Over the centuries *porneia* was expanded to encompass sexual sins beyond prostitution; thus, translated "sexually immoral" or "fornicators." Gerhard Kittel, *Theological Dictionary of the New Testament, vol.* 6, trans. G. W. Bromily (Grand Rapids: Eerdmans, 1969), 580, 584, 587. Only a few verses later in 1 Cor 6, Paul argues that men should not "take the members of Christ and unite them with a prostitute" (v. 15). He concludes, in verse 18, "Flee *porneia!*" Most modern versions translate *porneia* as "sexual immorality," but the nearest verses describe prostitution.

30. James V. Brownson, *Bible, Gender, Sexuality: Reframing the Church's Debate on Same-Sex Relationships* (Grand Rapids: Eerdmans, 2013), 274.

31. Walter A. Krenkel, "Prostitution," in M. Grant and R. Kitzinger, eds., *Civilization of the Ancient Mediterranean: Greece and Rome* (New York: Scribner, 1988), 2: 1296; quoted in Robert Jewett, *Romans: A Commentary*, ed. Eldon Jay Epp (Minneapolis: Fortress, 2006), 181.

32. Lynn H. Cohick, *Women in the World of the Earliest Christians: Illuminating Ancient Ways of Life* (Grand Rapids: Baker, 2009), 281.

33. Concubinage functioned in a similar way. Cohick, *Women in the World*, 105–106.

34. Ciampa and Rosner, *First Letter to the Corinthians*, 250.

It is impossible to prove beyond a shadow of a doubt that sexual exploitation, slavery, and prostitution were the apostle's intent, but these do provide important context for understanding the kinds of sexual sins which early Christian pastors would be concerned to address. From a contemporary point of view, the sexual sins of the slave trade certainly deserve the strong censure found in both passages.

Studying these passages in depth surprised me. Verses that had seemed quite clear in their English translations were not as clear when studied in their original languages and contexts. Translating *malakoi* and *arsenokoitai* as "effeminate" and "homosexuals" respectively does not accurately reflect the use of these terms in Greek literature of the same period. Contemporary readers will recognize the importance of speaking against the vices of decadence, lack of self-control, laziness, and sexual excess associated with the *malakoi*, but modern Christians should reject the cultural packaging which summarized these evils as femininity or effeminacy. On the one hand, *arsenokoitai* may be translated as "males who bed males," but not without noting the regular practice of masters exploiting enslaved boys, eunuchs, and men. On the other hand, *arsenokoitai* may refer to exploitation—those who take advantage of the poverty and vulnerability of others for their own pleasure and/ or gain—a category into which the use of slaves and prostitutes would certainly fit.

It is only very recently that Christians are coming to reassess the "sins" of prostitutes. Growing awareness of human trafficking and its roots in global economic disparity is changing how we consider the culpability of those who have been forced into selling the use of their bodies or the bodies of their children. Such dire economic pressures certainly fit the majority of prostitution in the ancient world.[35]

There is a significant ethical difference between lack of self-control, decadence, laziness, exploitation, prostitution, and sexual slavery on the one hand and same-sex marriage on the other. I realized I needed to consider the possibility that not all same-sex acts are morally equivalent.

Still, my mind was not made up. Although Leviticus can be read through the lens of rape and/or the patriarchal shaming of men by treating them like women, and while 1 Corinthians and 1 Timothy could

---

35. William Loader, *The New Testament on Sexuality* (Grand Rapids: Eerdmans, 2012), 15–18.

refer to a number of vices, including decadence, exploitation, sexual slavery and trafficking, the study was not conclusive. And there were other passages to consider. In my mind, the warnings in the first chapter of Romans appeared insurmountable. At least here, one could look to the literary context for more direct interpretive clues.

Romans: Rereading the Rhetoric

New Testament scholars on both sides of the debate agree that the first chapter of Romans was not written to address questions about sexual ethics. Paul makes a lengthy argument about the universality of sin—the sin of the Gentiles who turned their backs on God to worship idols (Rom 1:18–24) which resulted in greater moral degradation (1:24–32), but also the sins of the Jews who believed they were morally superior to these Gentiles (2:1–29). The apostle calls out their hypocrisy, insisting that "all have sinned and fall short of the glory of God, and all are justified freely by his grace through the redemption that came by Christ Jesus" (3:23–24).[36] Still, the sins listed in Romans 1—presented as a result of the Gentiles' rejection of the true God—must be examined to see whether they also give insight into Paul's sexual ethic.

Because Paul is making an argument that he hopes will be persuasive to both Jews and Gentiles, he builds his case from nature—assumptions about nature coming from Stoic philosophy and first-century Jewish culture. "God's . . . eternal power and divine nature—have been clearly seen, being understood from what has been made, so that men are without excuse" (Rom 1:20 NIV 1984), but people "exchanged the glory of the immortal God for images" (v. 23). "Therefore God gave them over in the sinful desires of their hearts to sexual impurity for the degrading of their bodies with one another" (v. 24). Paul then cites two more exchanges: People "exchanged the truth of God for a lie" (v. 25); "women exchanged natural sexual relations for unnatural ones. In the same way the men also abandoned natural relations with women and were inflamed with lust for one another. Men committed indecent acts with other men, and received in themselves the due penalty for their perversion" (vv. 26–27 NIV 1984).

Much ink has been spilt unpacking Paul's use of "natural" and

---

36. Richard Hays, *The Moral Vision of the New Testament: Community, Cross, New Creation* (San Francisco: Harper, 1996), 389; Brownson, *Bible, Gender, Sexuality*, 150–51.

"unnatural." Some scholars insist that nature refers to male and female reproductive complementarity. Others counter that arguments from "nature" are laden with cultural baggage—as can be seen in another of Paul's epistles when he asks, "Does not the very nature of things teach you that if a man has long hair, it is a disgrace to him, but that if a woman has long hair, it is her glory? For long hair is given to her as a covering" (1 Cor 11:14–15). This latter use of nature gives us insight into first-century Greco-Roman and Jewish gender norms, not a universal Christian ethic. Rather, commentators try to make good sense out of the logic beneath Paul's concern about hair lengths and head coverings. For example, was it a concern for modesty and decorum so as not to bring undo criticism of the early church? Modesty seems to be a universal value but one which plays itself out in various ways in different cultural contexts.

In her detailed study, *Love Between Women: Early Christian Responses to Female Homoeroticism*, Bernadette Brooten explains how "natural" and "unnatural" sexual relations were typically understood among first-century Jewish and Roman Christians:

> The shapers of Paul's culture saw any type of vaginal intercourse, whether consensual or coerced, as natural, such as between an adult man and woman married to each other, an adult man and free woman not married to each other, an adult man and a slave woman or slave girl, an adult man and his daughter, or an adult woman and her son. The type of sexual relations engaged in by women most often called "contrary to nature" (*para physin*) in the Roman world is sexual relations between women. . . . The "natural relations" that women gave up include a wide variety of heterosexual relations, such as marital relations, adultery, rape, incest, prostitution, and sexual relations between an adult male and a minor girl.[37]

This passage illustrates how arguments from first-century understandings of nature are hardly sufficient to ground Christian sexual ethics.

---

37. Bernadette J. Brooten, *Love Between Women: Early Christian Responses to Female Homoeroticism* (Chicago: University of Chicago Press, 1996), 251–52.

Brooten believes that Paul is referring to female homoeroticism in this passage, but James Brownson argues against this interpretation, noting that many early commentators interpreted Romans 1:26 as referring to non-procreative "oral or anal intercourse between women and men."[38] Brooten provides evidence for reading "against nature" as lesbianism from another early Christian text, the *Apocalypse of Peter*, in which one finds the same close connection between idolatry and homoerotic behavior as appears in Romans 1.[39] Particularly salient, the *Apocalypse* describes both the active and passive female partners being tortured in hell for acting "as a man [does] with a woman." Meanwhile only the passive male partner is punished because it is only he who acted contrary: "like women."[40] Surprisingly, Romans 1 may support a similarly imbalanced view of punishment in verse 27: "Men . . . received in themselves the due penalty for their perversion" (NIV 1984). Scholars struggle to make sense of the penalty, but some take Paul quite literally as focusing on the passive reception of the male member, indicating the shame of feminization and/or physical soreness in the anus.[41] If they are right, it is only the passive partner who experiences punishment because it is only he who has perverted "nature."

Studies of "natural relations" in the early centuries of Christianity warn us against moving too quickly from what we see as "natural" to a supposed "natural law." In the first century, rape, prostitution, and the sexual use of enslaved people were all considered natural, while non-procreative sex of any kind, passive male sexuality, and active female sexuality (women taking sexual initiative toward men or women) were considered "unnatural." More often than not, what we find "in nature" are the social conventions of our own context.[42]

Debate continues as to what these women were doing, but there is no question as to the men's activity. "Men also abandoned natural relations with women and were inflamed with lust for one another. Men committed indecent acts with other men" (v. 27 NIV 1984).

Despite the obvious condemnation of male same-sex relations in this

38. Brownson, *Bible, Gender, Sexuality*, 207–208. Augustine, *Of Marriage and Concupiscence*, 2.35.
39. Brooten, *Love Between Women*, 305–308.
40. Ibid., 307.
41. Loader, *New Testament on Sexuality*, 318–19.
42. Knust, *Unprotected Texts*, 110–12. Brownson, *Bible, Gender, Sexuality*, 232–37.

passage, some scholars still do not believe that all same-sex relationships are therefore censured. Brownson reminds contemporary readers
that the language "inflamed with lust" reflects ancient explanations of
homoerotic desire. Men whose lust was not slaked by women sought less
common conquests.[43] First-century historian Dio Chrysostom explains
their logic:

> The man whose appetite is insatiate in such things, when he
> finds there is no scarcity, no resistance, in this field, will have
> contempt for the easy conquest and scorn for a woman's love, as
> a thing too readily given—in fact, too utterly feminine—and will
> turn his assault against the male quarters, eager to befoul the
> youth who will very soon be magistrates and judges and generals,
> believing that in them he will find a kind of pleasure difficult
> and hard to procure.[44]

This is why many scholars argue that the idea of homosexual orientation was foreign to people in the first century. "It was not a question of
'disoriented desires' but of legitimate desires that were allowed illegitimate freedoms."[45] Chrysostom compares it to greed—the natural desire
for food that "will not remain within its usual bounds."[46] What was
unnatural was the desire of a man "to demean himself by enthusiastically
assuming the despised, lower position appropriate for women."[47] Robert
Jewett exhorts his readers to pay attention to "the correlation between
homosexuality and slavery," believing that "those members of the
Roman congregation still subject to sexual exploitation by slave owners
or former slave owners who are now functioning as patrons" would have
welcomed Paul's critique.[48]

The idea of excess and exploitation fits with the movement of the
passage from the rejection of God to out-of-control passions to "evil,
greed and depravity. . . . envy, murder . . . heartless[ness], ruthless[ness]"

43. Brownson, *Bible, Gender, Sexuality*, 166.
44. Martin, *Sex and the Single Savior*, 57; citing Dio Chrysostom 7.151–52.
45. Ibid., 58.
46. Ibid., 57; citing John Chysostom, *Homily IV on Romans*.
47. Ibid., 58.
48. Robert Jewett, *Romans: A Commentary*, ed. Eldon Jay Epp (Minneapolis: Fortress Press,
2006), 181.

(vv. 29–31 NIV 1984). The second-century pastor Clement of Alexandria makes similar connections between luxury (which he describes as an effeminate passion and disease) and sexual excess, assuming that those who indulge in fineries (dying their hair to hide the grey and shaving their beards) are clearly prone to sexual licentiousness of every kind.[49]

Neil Elliott believes this passage cannot be describing the actual practices of ordinary Roman citizens but the excesses of the aristocracy since, as "a description of conventional Gentile morality, the passage is an inexcusable exaggeration."[50] Richard Hays would excuse Paul's hyperbole as part of his rhetorical ploy—"whip[ping] up the reader into a frenzy of indignation."[51] But Elliott counters that as "a description of the horrors of the imperial house," Paul's words are not an overstatement. They may even "seem restrained."[52]

Elliott suggests that Paul may have been alluding to sins of the Roman aristocracy who kept eunuchs, men, and women as sexual slaves or to particular Roman rulers who embodied both the idolatry condemned in this passage and the excessive lust, depravity, and violence censured in the latter verses of chapter 1—such as the Emperor Gaius Caligula, who set himself up as a god and even ordered a statue of himself to be erected within the Jewish temple.[53] Caligula was accused of "perpetual incest with his sisters" along with "sexual liaisons with the wives of dinner guests, raping them in an adjoining room and then returning to the banquet to comment on their performance. Various same-sex sexual encounters between Gaius and other men are similarly recounted. Finally, a military officer whom he had sexually humiliated joined a conspiracy to murder him . . . ," a successful assassination crowned by stabbing Gaius repeatedly in the genitals.[54] This, Elliot proffers, could explain the obscure reference to "received in their bodies the due penalty for their perversion," thinly veiled by a shift to the plural.[55]

---

49. Clement of Alexandria, *Paedogugus*, III.3.

50. Neil Elliott, *Liberating Paul* (Maryknoll, NY: Orbis, 1994), 195; cited in Brownson, *Bible, Gender, Sexuality*, 159.

51. Hays, *Moral Vision*, 389.

52. Elliott, *Liberating Paul*, 195; cited in Brownson, *Bible, Gender, Sexuality*, 159.

53. Elliott, *Liberating Paul*, 112.

54. Brownson, *Bible, Gender, Sexuality*, 157.

55. As one might complain about Washington politicians who take advantage of interns in closets—a veiled reference to former president Bill Clinton—suggests that corruption can be found throughout the political center.

But the epistle could also be aimed at the current emperor Nero, "whose rapes of Roman wives and sons, brothel-keeping, incest with his mother, and sexual submission to various men and boys prompted his tutor, the philosopher Seneca, to conclude that Nero was 'another Caligula.'"[56]

Whether or not this passage alludes to the misdeeds of the imperial house or to more general sexual excess, exploitation, slavery, promiscuity, and sexual violence in first-century Rome, the overall force of the passage illustrates in graphic detail the downward spiral of sin which begins with a rejection of the true God. Drawing on ancient assumptions among Jews and Romans familiar with Stoic philosophy, heterosexual and same-sex excess are both explained as resulting from a turn away from God. Contemporary students of sexuality will find this explanation of same-sex desire inadequate.

Even after studying the extended literary context of the book of Romans, I did not find the clear-cut universal condemnation of all same-sex relations that I had expected. The ancient context mattered—a context which shaped what was considered "natural" and explained same-sex desire as "excessive lust." As a whole, the passage is meant to describe the depravity of those who have rejected God, not faithful gay, lesbian, and bisexual Christians seeking to solemnize their relationships with the vows of Christian marriage. While "nature" might have grounded the ancient assumption of male-female marriage, the fact that nature was also used to defend slavery (including sexual slavery), prostitution, and rape should caution us against moving from ancient ideas about nature to Christian moral teaching. Once again, I was left looking for a more direct answer to the possibility of same-sex marriage for Christians.

Mark Achtemeier, in *The Bible's Yes to Same-Sex Marriage*, warns that when Christians cite a few verses from Scripture, even a few verses that appear to be clear, "obvious" readings, coinciding with centuries of church teaching, this does not necessarily put them on solid ethical footing, since these have also been used to support slavery, Aryanism, and the subordination of women.[57] In *Changing Our Mind*, Baptist ethicist David Gushee makes a similar argument when he compares

---

56. Suetonius, *Nero*, 26–29; cited in Elliott, *Liberating Paul*, 195.
57. Mark Achtemeier, *The Bible's Yes to Same-Sex Marriage: An Evangelical's Change of Heart* (Louisville: Westminster John Knox, 2014), 17–20.

the traditional position on same-sex relationships to the almost 2,000 years of contempt for "the Jews"—a contempt based on a handful of verses supported by Christians throughout the tradition, which was not challenged until it was too late, until the world saw the direct line from Christian anti-Semitism to Auschwitz.[58] Instead of piecing together a handful of verses, both insist that we look to the overarching emphases of Scripture to ground our ethics. Theirs is an important point (to which I will return), but one could easily counter that it is not simply on the basis of these proof texts that Christians have rejected same-sex marriage. The unanimous picture of marriage in the Bible is heterosexual. While polygyny and marriage to women captured in war were regulated by Old Testament law, the consistent witness of marriage is nevertheless heterosexual. Even more significant, the covenant between a husband and wife was chosen by the prophets and apostles to illustrate the relationship between God and God's people. Surely, I asked myself, if anything represents an overarching witness of Scripture, doesn't this?

Genesis to Revelation: Heterosexual Marriage as Theological Truth

Baptist theologian Stanley Grenz summarizes major streams of Christian theology which view heterosexual marriage as communicating fundamental truths about God and humankind. The creation of male and female in God's image (Gen 1:27) and the statement "[these two will] become one flesh" (Gen 2:24) provides the primitive form of the image of God which is more fully revealed in Christ, "the image of the invisible God" (Col 1:15), but ultimately points to the marriage of Christ and church (Eph 5:21–32):

> "For this reason a man will leave his father and mother and be united to his wife, and the two will become one flesh." This is a profound mystery—but I am talking about Christ and the church.

Christ's marriage to the church is a "mystery" (sacramentum in the Latin), a mystery that has grounded a sacramental view of marriage. According to Grenz, the marriage of two differently sexed persons is

---

58. David P. Gushee, *Changing Our Mind*, 2nd ed. (Canton, MI: Read the Spirit, 2015), 126–45.

sacramental in that it reveals the Trinitarian nature of God (who is a plurality-in-unity), illustrates God's promise of faithfulness to humanity (Isa 54:5–7), and prefigures the union between God and creation (Rev 21:1, 9).[59] In Grenz's opinion, same-sex couples may be able to give themselves to one another in love and mutual submission—thus fulfilling one of the meanings of sex in marriage—but he believes their unions will never represent the "unity in difference" that heterosexual marriage symbolizes as the union of God and church.[60]

I believe Grenz is right to argue that heterosexual marriage offers a theological metaphor for the relationship of the church to Christ in a way that same-sex marriage does not. What is ironic, and unfortunate, is that Grenz did not acknowledge the difference between the biblical patterns of marriage which undergird the theological metaphor and the vision of Christian marriage toward which he urged contemporary evangelicals.

The marital metaphor found throughout the Bible is based on ancient patriarchal marriage, not the egalitarian marriage which Grenz, most Protestants, and the Catholic Church now defend, nor even the soft patriarchy of many complementarians. Patriarchal marriage is based on ancient gender assumptions which viewed women as "naturally" inferior, soft in body, mind, and morality; thus in need of a husband's strong, wise, virtuous rule.[61] Stereotypical sex differences, such as average physical size, were exaggerated by differences in education and guaranteed by age at marriage. Thus, when each sex married at the ages recommended in the first century—fifteen to twenty for a girl (although sometimes as young as twelve) and thirty for a man—"natural" sex differences were compounded by the fact that men had twice as many years of education, worldly experience, and vocational training.[62] Of course, women's "lack of wisdom" was assumed to be "natural"; thus marriage "naturally"

---

59. Stanley J. Grenz, "The Social God and the Relational Self: Toward a Trinitarian Theology of the *Imago Dei*," in *Trinitarian Soundings in Systematic Theology*, ed. Paul Louis Metzger (London and New York: T & T Clark, 2005), 87–100.

60. Stanley J. Grenz, *Sexual Ethics: An Evangelical Perspective* (Louisville: Westminster John Knox Press, 1990), 238. Grenz has been criticized on this point by those who argue that the traditional names of the First and Second Persons of the Trinity do not provide a basis for sex or gender difference in the Trinitarian union. Some have argued on this basis that gay or polyamorous marriages more fully reflect the Trinity. I have offered my own critique of both the sexualizing of Trinitarian relations and the assumption that sex/gender are paradigmatic of "otherness" in *Sex Difference*, chs. 5 and 4 respectively.

61. DeFranza, *Sex Difference*, 108–32.

62. Loader, *New Testament on Sexuality*, 17.

pointed to a wife's obedience and a husband's rule. A millennium and a half later, John Calvin was still arguing that woman was "by nature . . . formed to obey."[63]

Patriarchal marriage, the union of an inferior person to one who is superior and to whom one owes obedience, is much more suited to illustrate the relationship of the church to Christ than contemporary heterosexual marriage. It is the imbalance of power between humanity and divinity that led ancient writers to see a parallel in the imbalance of power between wives and husbands which was assumed by them to be natural and secured by law. "Biblical marriage" was heterosexual, but it was also patriarchal, often uniting an adult man to a child or teenage girl with little education and fewer legal rights. Patriarchal marriage is the basis for the theological metaphor illustrating the relationship between God and God's people, not contemporary Christian marriage supported as it is by equal education and modern law.

Patriarchal marriage is not the only ancient legal structure employed to teach the right relationship between God and God's people. The institutions of kingship and slavery are similarly employed. Christ is both "King of kings" (Rev 17:14) and our Master who "bought [us] at a price" (1 Cor 7:22-23). Kingship and slavery both illustrate how humans should honor and obey God. And yet, despite their foundation in Scripture, many Christians see no problem leaving monarchy and slavery in the past. In fact, Christian values motivate these changes. These ancient forms of government are now read as descriptive of past culture rather than universally prescriptive.

In a similar way, many Christians believe that the pattern of marriage between two unequal partners, while it provided a useful metaphor for teaching the relationship of the church to Christ, does not reflect the biblical teaching that men and women are equally made in the image of God. Early Christians struggled to work out the implications of their theology with respect to women, slaves, and the class system—a struggle evident in Paul's epistles.[64] A number of church fathers argued that men

---

63. John Calvin, *Commentaries on the Epistles to Timothy, Titus, and Philemon* in *Calvin's Commentaries, vol. 21*, trans. William Pringle (Grand Rapids: Baker, 2003), 68; 1 Tim 2:12.

64. One can see the tension and slow progress in Pauline literature when comparing the radically egalitarian argument that a wife has authority over her husband's body (1 Cor 7:4) with calling wives to submit to their husbands in Col 3:17—a passage without the overarching exhortation to mutual submission found in Eph 5. Similar tensions appear in the commands

are more fully made in the image of God since they ruled while women (and slaves) obeyed.[65] A contemporary theology of marriage which acknowledges the equal value of the sexes had developed to support not only equal access to education and equal protection under law but also a vision of mutually submissive love between persons of equal value.[66] Our models of government and marriage have grown to better reflect biblical teaching about the value of all human life.

Contemporary Christian marriage is not "biblical marriage" of the Old or New Testament. The biblical teaching of the image of God in all people has come to supersede ancient patterns of marriage. The question before Christians today is whether "biblical marriage" can be revised *yet again* to better honor the humanity of gay, lesbian, and bisexual people and the biblical truth that they too are made in the image of God and equally capable of ordering their relationships and sexual lives in ways that honor God, benefit the common good, and promote their own growth in health and holiness.

Allow me to summarize the biblical interpretations offered above:

1. Genesis 1 and 2 do not need to be read as providing an exclusive model of what it means to be human. The creation narratives speak in broad categories. Just as most animals fall into the classification of land animal, sea creature, or creature of the air; so most humans fit into the category of male or female. Nevertheless, there are animals that are creatures of both water and land and there are humans who exhibit characteristics of both male and female. Adam and Eve can be understood as the majority story rather than the exclusive model for what it means to be human. By extension, heterosexual marriage can be seen as the majority story, not the exclusive model.

---

that slaves obey their masters (Col 3:22) and the exhortation to one particular master to receive his runaway slave as a brother (Phil 1:16). Even though Paul appears to be moving away from the radical dehumanization of women found in literature of his day, he still employs patriarchal categories when he talks about marriage.

65. On men as more fully images of God, see Frederick G. McLeod, S.J., *The Image of God in the Antiochene Tradition* (Washington, DC: Catholic University of America Press, 1999), 191–92.

66. It is only very recently that Christians have been shifting their interpretation of Eph 5 so that the call to "mutual submission" in verse 21 (grammatically tied to 5:22 in the Greek) is read to support egalitarian human marriage, while the ancient vision of patriarchal marriage remains an analogy for Christ and church. Churches have been changing traditional marriage vows—removing the wife's vow to obey—to underscore their evolving theology of marriage. "Church Omits 'Obey' from Marriage Vows to Tackle Domestic Abuse" (Oct. 3, 2006), http://www. christiantoday.com/article/church.omits.obey.from.marriage.vows.in.efforts.to.tackle .domestic.abuse/7843.htm.

2. The story of **Sodom and Gomorrah in Genesis 19 and its parallel in Judges 19** describe gangs threatening to rape men and angels when in fact it is only a woman who suffers sexual violence at their hands, violence which led to her death. While Lot may have been declared "righteous" in 2 Peter 2:7, no Christian today would argue that we should follow his patriarchal ethic by offering our daughters to an angry mob at our door. These stories warn of judgment upon sin—certainly the sin of sexual violence.[67] They teach nothing about marriage.

3. There were many different ways of practicing "heterosexuality" and "homosexuality" in the ancient world, and many of them were not the ways we are familiar with today. Just because the Bible declares some heterosexual sex as sinful does not mean that all heterosexual sex is sin. In the same way, just because the Bible condemns *certain kinds* of same-sex sexual acts does not mean that *all* same-sex sexual acts are therefore out of bounds. It is possible to read the prohibitions in **1 Corinthians 6 and 1 Timothy 1** as proscriptions of decadence, lack of self-control, and exploitation, including the sexual exploitation of enslaved persons and prostitutes.

4. Leviticus 18 and 20 may stand behind the creation of the term *arsenokoitos* in 1 Corinthians and 1 Timothy. Nevertheless, we cannot assume the universality of this Levitical prohibition, given that not all of the Levitical commands are considered binding by Christians today. It is difficult to discern the rationale behind the prohibition, given how same-sex relations were understood to dishonor a man by treating him as a woman and the lack of understanding of sexual orientation as we are beginning to understand it today.

5. The condemnations in Romans 1 are part of a rhetorical "sting operation" intended to stir up judgmental ire against "godless" Gentiles which turns on those doing the judging, proving all need redemption in Christ.[68] Given the epistle's audience and rhetorical force, the apostle could very well have had in mind the excesses of the Roman aristocracy and imperial court, including the sexual exploitation of enslaved persons, as examples of the extreme forms of sin to which one can fall when one rejects God. Paul seems to be drawing on Stoic philosophy to make an argument from "nature" which could serve as common ethical

---

67. Ezekiel lists other sins of Sodom as arrogance, gluttony, lack of concern for the poor and needy (16:49).

68. Hays, *Moral Vision*, 389.

ground for Jewish and Gentile Christians. Stoics valued moderation, a moderation which ran against the ancient understanding of same-sex desire as heterosexual desire which has run beyond its natural bounds. Female same-sex behavior was considered "against nature" in early Christian and Roman sources, as was passive male sexuality, and any form of non-procreative sex (even between husband and wife).[69] At the same time, prostitution, rape, the sexual desire of men for boys, and the sexual use of slaves were considered "natural." Romans 1 was not written to provide a universal natural law to ground Christian sexual ethics. More importantly, it provides no guidance for those Christians who have not rejected God but nevertheless experience same-sex attraction.

6. Contemporary Christian marriage is not "biblical marriage" of the Old or New Testament. In both testaments, **heterosexual marriage functions as an analogy based on ancient patriarchal marriage illustrating God's covenant faithfulness, sovereignty, and condescending love for "his" creaturely "bride."** Over the last two thousand years, Christians have altered laws to better reflect biblical teaching that all people are made in the image of God and that we should love our neighbors as ourselves—even when our neighbors are enslaved people, the poor, and women. These Christian values have led us to move away from ancient social structures (monarchy and slavery) and ancient models of marriage (raising the legal age of marriage for girls, improving education, equalizing protections under law, etc.). Christians can learn what metaphors based on ancient social structures teach about our relationship to God while working to reshape those same structures to better reflect Jesus' ethic of neighbor love.

This brief survey of the biblical record on sexuality and marriage illumines the complexity of trying to construct a Christian sexual ethic today. Careful study reveals movement from the Old Testament to the New; slow but steady improvement of ancient laws too often focused on the rights of men toward an ethic of neighbor love.[70] In the ancient world, heterosexual and same-sex sexuality were too often practiced in contexts of exploitation and domination (men over women, masters over

---

69. Knust nuances this point, recalling that in Greek thought the passive male partner was not censured as long as the active partner was of higher social status. *Unprotected Texts*, 88–89.

70. For example, Jesus' stricter view on the Mosaic provision of divorce served to protect women from being discarded for "any and every reason" (Matt 19:3–9).

slaves, those with means over impoverished prostitutes, higher-ranking males over lower-ranking males)—sexual practices worthy of Christian censure. No biblical passage indisputably condemns loving, same-sex marriages of equal-status partners; therefore, it is reasonable to consider whether Christians can once again add to the growing tradition of Christian marriage in order to include our gay, lesbian, and bisexual neighbors seeking to solemnize their unions in holy matrimony.

How would we add to the growing tradition of Christian marriage? That is the question to which we now turn.

Moving from the Bible to Christian Ethics

When N. T. Wright describes how the Bible communicates God's authority, he compares the movement in the canon—from creation, fall, Israel, and Jesus to the church—to five acts in a Shakespearean play. According to Wright, the fifth act begins with the New Testament church but extends until the return of Christ—the promised conclusion to the biblical drama. As such, it is the unfinished story in which we live. But in order to move the narrative to its final conclusion, we are not called to simply repeat lines from earlier sections of the script as if all Christians are first-century Jews and Gentiles living in the Roman Empire. Rather, by following the major themes of earlier acts, we are to push the plot forward by faithfully improvising in our own time.[71]

Recognizing movement in the Bible helps us account for twists and turns in the plot—such as the surprising inclusion of Gentiles without insisting they be circumcised. Circumcision was described as an "everlasting covenant" (Gen 17:1–14); so when the Jerusalem Council, by the leading of the Spirit, ruled that Gentiles no longer needed to be circumcised, it came as quite a shock to many members of the early church (Acts 15:1–31). A number of contemporary Christians have begun to view the inclusion of gay, lesbian, and bisexual persons into the tradition of Christian monogamy as similar to the surprising grafting of the "wild" Gentiles into the "cultivated olive tree" of Israel—a grafting which Paul himself described as "contrary to nature" (Rom 11:24).[72]

---

71. N. T. Wright, "How Can the Bible Be Authoritative," *Vox Evangelica* 21 (1991), 7–32.
72. Eugene F. Rogers Jr., "Sanctification, Homosexuality, and God's Triune Life," in *Theology and Sexuality: Classic and Contemporary Readings* (London: Blackwell, 2002), 225–26; J. R. Daniel Kirk, "Homosexuality and the Church Debate: Dr. Robert Gagnon vs. Dr. Daniel Kirk" October 17, 2015, https://www.youtube.com/watch?v=m-Y1WpXmfso.

But how are we to know when we are hearing something surprising from the Holy Spirit or when we are unduly influenced by other voices? There is no recognized ecumenical council to deliberate on such matters for us. Instead, we must listen to the voice of the Spirit as we study the Scriptures and sift other sources of wisdom from the tradition(s) of the church, human experience, and our growing knowledge of the human body and sexuality gained from science, psychology, sociology, etc. The good news is this conversation is already under way—in this volume and elsewhere in the church—and a number of common themes are emerging.

Spirit-Led Christian Sexual Ethics: Finding Common Ground and Tending Fences

Common Ground

Looking to the Scriptures and the history of the church, we find themes which ground a Christian vision of marriage and sexual ethics— themes which can be found in the writings of evangelical and mainline Protestants, Catholics, Anglicans, and Eastern Orthodox Christians. They represent the wisdom of the church through the ages as faithful people have reflected on the Bible and the sources above.[73]

Human beings are created for communion with God and with other people. We are born into families, raised in communities, and are called to join the family of God—the church. Human sexuality points to a particular kind of bodily communion which has come to be placed within marriage. While singleness is also honored in Scripture, espe- cially in the New Testament, it is considered a rare calling, recognized by the one being called, not a general rule for communities of Christ- followers. "It is not good that the human should be alone. I will make [the human] a suitable partner" (Gen 2:18).[74]

Because of sin, we need help to keep our promises. Human sexual- ity points to sexual relations in general rather than directly to marriage, but most cultures have found it wise to limit sexual activity to publicly

---

73. I compare John Paul II's *Theology of the Body* to Grenz's evangelical theology of marriage in *Sex Difference*, chs. 4–5. These Anglicans note similarities between Anglican and Eastern Orthodox theologies of marriage: Deirdre J. Good, Willis J. Jenkins, Cynthia B. Kittredge, Eugene F. Rogers Jr., "A Theology of Marriage Including Same-Sex Couples: A View from the Liberals," *Anglican Theological Review*, 93:1 (Winter 2011): 51–52.

74. My translation.

recognized (legal) relationships in order to reduce community conflicts which tend to arise from jealousy, quarrels over paternity and responsibility, etc. In the Bible, marriages were sometimes viewed through the ancient legal category of "covenant." Marriage covenants include promises of fidelity and particular obligations. As C. S. Lewis wisely quipped, "Eros is driven to promise what Eros of himself cannot perform."[75] Marital promises and the witness of our communities hold us accountable to do the work of love.

In the history of the church, marriage came to be viewed as a sacrament or sacramental. Traditionally, a sacrament has been understood as a means of grace, a visible sign of invisible realities. Marriage has come to be seen as a means of sanctifying grace and making visible God's love.

Marriage provides a means of sanctification, particularly of human sexual desire (which, for many, naturally outruns the bounds of marriage). Our vows "for better, for worse, in sickness and in health, 'til death do us part" call us into the daily discipline of love which, with practice, transforms so much more than our sexual selves. As gay theologian Eugene Rogers argues, "Marriage is a sacrament because it gives desire time and space to stretch forward . . . into things that are *more* desirable. Marriage allows sex to mean *more*. . . . Marriage is a place where our waywardness begins to be healed and our fear of commitment overcome—that, and much more."[76]

As spouses grow in sanctification, marriages are able to witness to the character of God who is faithful, self-giving love. Reflecting on Ephesians 5, Mark Achtemeier writes, "The clearest picture we have of the love that fills God's heart comes to us in the love Jesus shows as he reaches out to us. For this reason, the passage identifies the goal of marriage as growing into the kind of love that unites Jesus to the church. This growth in self-giving, Christ-like love is what it means for human beings to realize the potential of our own creation in the image of God."[77]

Rather than viewing marriage as the proper place for sexual indulgence, Rogers argues that marriage (like celibacy) should be understood as ascesis . . .

---

75. C. S. Lewis, *The Four Loves* (Orlando: Harcourt Brace, 1960, 1988), 114.
76. Rogers, "Sanctification, Homosexuality, and God's Triune Life," 223.
77. Achtemeier, *The Bible's Yes*, 51.

an ascetic discipline, . . . a school for virtue, where God prepares the couple for life with himself by binding them for life to each other. Marriage, in this view, is for sanctification, a means by which God can bring a couple to himself by turning their limits to their good. And no conservative I know has seriously argued that same-sex couples need sanctification any *less* than opposite-sex couples do.[78]

As spouses love and forgive, remain faithful and persevere under trial, they are each transformed into the image of Christ, and together their marriage can become an icon of the faithful covenant love of God for God's people. "Marriage bears witness to both of the great commandments: it signifies the love of God and it teaches love of neighbor."[79]

A Christian theology of marriage recognizes that humans are made for communion and that our sexuality brings us into particular relationships which, because of sin, need to be governed by public vows which hold couples accountable and enable communities to support their unions and arbitrate when vows are broken. In the Christian tradition, marriage has also come to be understood as a particular way of growing in the sanctifying love of God—inviting each spouse to become more like Christ and calling each marriage to point to the faithfulness of God. Considering this shared theology of marriage, Achtemeier concludes,

A same-gender marriage appeared to afford the same or very similar opportunities for growth in love and grace and mutuality and for learning to give the whole of oneself to another person. And if God's purpose for marriage could be fulfilled in a gay marriage as well as a straight one, it made absolutely no sense to tell gay people that God's will for them could be fulfilled only in a heterosexual context or in celibacy.[80]

---

78. Eugene F. Rogers Jr., "Same-Sex Complementarity: A Theology of Marriage," *Christian Century* (May 11, 2011), http://www.christiancentury.org/article/2011–04/same-sex-complementarity. With gratitude to Wesley Hill for drawing my attention to this work in his blog post "The Future of Asceticism," http://spiritualfriendship.org/2015/11/27/the-future-of-asceticism/#more-6202.

79. Good, et al., "A Theology of Marriage," 70.

80. Achtemeier, *The Bible's Yes*, 58.

Of course, many do argue that celibacy or heterosexual marriage are the only options for those with same-sex attraction. Disagreements over how to interpret the contested passages are like fences built nonetheless on the common ground of Christian marriage as outlined above.

Fences Remain

Aside from interpretations of the biblical texts, there are two main theological objections to same-sex marriage: procreation and some notion of sex/gender complementarity.

There are those who argue that God intended only male and female to join in marriage because only heterosexual sex produces children. The legal status of marriage has served in most cultures as a way to designate legitimate offspring, supplying social pressure on husbands to care for their wives and children. The Bible does present children as a blessing (Ps 127:3–5) and yet "no regulations appear anywhere in Scripture suggesting that infertile people or persons past the age of childbearing should refrain from getting married."[81] Augustine argued that the Jews fulfilled the command, "Be fruitful and multiply . . . fill the earth" (Gen 1:28 NRSV) when the Messiah was born. Therefore, Christians should invest their energy in evangelism—the adoption of people into the family of God—not procreation.[82]

Those who argue that infertile couples or those past the age of childbearing may still marry tend to base their exclusion of same-sex couples on some form of complementarity: physical or psychological. The physical argument focuses on the "fit" between male and female genitalia.[83] Others have argued that masculine and feminine psychology (the difference in the ways men and women think, desire, and live) undergirds the "unity-in-difference" which marriage can symbolize.[84]

These are arguments from nature, not from Scripture.[85] As such they

---

81. Ibid., 60.

82. Augustine, *De bono coniugali. De sancta uirginitate*, ed. and trans., P. G. Walsh (Oxford: Clarendon Press: 2001), XVII, 37.

83. Gagnon argues for procreative, psychological, and anatomical complementarity. Robert A. J. Gagnon, *The Bible and Homosexual Practice: Texts and Hermeneutics* (Nashville: Abingdon, 2001), 488.

84. Dennis P. Hollinger, *The Meaning of Sex: Christian Ethics and the Moral Life* (Grand Rapids: Baker Academic, 2009), 16.

85. For more robust discussions of gender complementarity, see Brownson, *Bible, Gender, Sexuality*, 26–38; and DeFranza, *Sex Difference*, ch. 4.

must stand up to other arguments from nature. Psychological complementarity is the least persuasive when one considers scientific studies of gender which conclude, "Although most of us appear to be either clearly male or clearly female, we are each complex mosaics of male and female characteristics."[86] Procreative complementarity (and the "fit" required to make this possible) is necessary for the survival of the species and seems to correspond with the fact that the majority of the human race (and the majority of mammalian sexuality) is heterosexual. What is not obvious is that this statistical majority should be interpreted as the exclusive moral model. Given that many different kinds of sexual activity can also be found in the animal kingdom, Christians should be cautious about attempting to argue for heterosexual ethics on the assumption of reproductive complementarity grounded in "nature."

On the other hand, some theologians have argued that we should hold onto the idea of sexual complementarity but expand our understanding beyond reproduction or "fit" to a complementarity of sexual orientation. "Reproductive complementarity will not be a possibility in the case of homosexual couples, but genital complementarity—understood in an orientation, personal, and integrated sense, and not just in a biological, physical sense—will be."[87]

Biblical authors never defend marriage on the basis of procreative, physical, or psychological complementarity. In contrast to Augustine, who believed the only sinless sexual acts were those within marriage "undertaken to beget children," the apostle Paul exhorts spouses, "Do not deprive each other except perhaps by mutual consent and for a time, so that you may devote yourselves to prayer. Then come together again so that Satan will not tempt you because of your lack of self-control" (1 Cor 7:5).[88] In this lengthy defense of marriage, children are never used to justify sex or marriage. They are only mentioned with respect to mixed marriages—the union of a believing and unbelieving spouse—assuring Christian spouses that their children are not unclean but holy (1 Cor 7:14).

86. Melissa Hines, *Brain Gender* (Oxford: University Press, 2004), 18–19.

87. "This personalist interpretation of genital complementarity, which sees the physical genitals as organs of the whole person, including his or her sexual orientation, allows us to expand the definition of a natural, reasonable, and therefore moral sexual act to include both homosexual and heterosexual nonreproductive sexual acts." Todd A. Salzman and Michael G. Lawler, *The Sexual Person: Toward a Renewed Catholic Anthropology* (Washington, DC: Georgetown University Press, 2008), 67.

88. Augustine, *De bono coniugali*, VI, 15.

In 1 Corinthians 7 marriage is presented as the answer to human passion, a concession to those who do not have the gift of celibacy which Paul believes is ideal but admits not all have (vv. 6–7). Within marriage, he speaks of sex as the debt each spouse owes the other—a shockingly egalitarian challenge to the patriarchal assumptions of the first century (vv. 3–4). The duties which Paul fears will distract a person from devoting themselves to God's service are not the time-consuming obligations of parenthood, but duties of the heart—pleasing one's spouse (vv. 32–35).

None of Paul's comments in this chapter depend on the complementarity of male and female—procreative, physical, or psychological. His counsel could be applicable to heterosexuals as well as to same-sex attracted couples and singles who do not experience the gift of celibacy. Burning with passion for a sexual partner, they yearn for the kind of union wherein they too can sanctify their desires, directing their energies toward the good of their spouse, wherein they too can model the faithfulness of God's covenant love and know joy.

Standing on Common Ground and Tending Fences

Given the common ground beneath these fences, is it possible for Christians to "agree to disagree" on same-sex marriage? Given the hurt that many gay Christians feel as a direct consequence of non-affirming interpretations of the Bible, not all people will be able to remain in fellowship with those with whom they disagree. But it is long past time that lesbian, gay, and bisexual Christians learn that there are Christian congregations who will welcome them as they are and that there are faithful Christians—pastors, theologians, church leaders—who are unashamedly Christian and unashamedly gay. They do not have to choose between their sexual identity and their Christian faith. They do not need to question the love of God on account of sexual desires they cannot change. They can engage, *as Christians*, in this conversation—disagreeing or agreeing without having to question their place in the community.

Evangelical pastor Ken Wilson believes we find wisdom studying Paul's arbitration of similarly fraught arguments among early churches.[89] In 1 Corinthians 8 the apostle is working to reconcile believers who feel free to eat food sacrificed to idols (knowing that "an idol is nothing"

---

89. Ken Wilson, *A Letter to My Congregation* (Canton, MI: Read the Spirit, 2014), 94–110.

v. 4) and those who refuse to eat such meat (because their "conscience is weak" v. 7). In Corinth, he leaves the decision to individuals so long as their choices do not cause others to sin and are guided not by indulgence but by the desire to bring glory to God (v. 13). In his letter to the Romans, he exhorts believers not to judge one another "over disputable matters" (Rom 14:1) but allow "each [to be] fully convinced in their own mind. Whoever regards one day as special does so to the Lord. Whoever eats meat does so to the Lord, for they give thanks to God; and whoever abstains does so to the Lord and gives thanks to God" (14:5–6). But in Galatians he worries that he has "wasted [his] efforts" on those who continue to observe the "special days . . . and seasons" of the old law (Gal 4:10–11). Paul seems to be giving different pastoral advice in different contexts—possibly out of patience for congregations still trying to comprehend Jesus as the "end of the law" and possibly in recognition of other factors—a pastoral sensitivity Wilson believes is required in many moral debates, including this one.[90]

Christians *have* learned to agree to disagree over other weighty moral concerns: just war vs. pacifism, women's ordination, infant vs. believers' baptism. All of these disputed matters still matter—some still cause pain. And yet we are finding ways to debate and disagree without adding the pain of persecution, or accusing our opponents of abandoning the faith, or rejecting the authority of the Bible.

How have we begun to move past some of the bitterness of these differences? I believe it happened as we began listening to one another; when we recognized that those who disagree with us are still making arguments from Scripture, from the wisdom of the tradition, from humble, prayerful struggles to follow Jesus faithfully—loving God and neighbor.

Things changed as we began to recognize our common ground; still, fences remain. Mennonites may occasionally attend churches that support a "just war," but they will not make their home in a congregation which they believe tolerates and even honors violations of the sixth commandment. I will occasionally attend a church that does not ordain women, but I will not raise my daughters in an environment where they may experience themselves as second-class citizens, evaluated first on their bodily sex and only then by their character and spiritual gifts.

---

90. Wilson, *Letter*, 30–35.

Baptists may visit Presbyterians, but they will not settle down in a church that baptizes those who have not reached the age of accountability. Despite our common ground, these fences still divide us.

Yet some of our fences have worn down over the years. Protestants no longer drown one another over different baptismal practices as they did in the sixteenth century. Christians have stopped using the Bible to defend slavery. Some of the painful splinters on these rough beams have worn smooth. Other beams have fallen and not been replaced. In a few spots only the foundation stones remain, memorials of past sins, warnings of the ways in which we can injure one another, and the gospel, as we differ on how to faithfully follow Jesus, the Bible, and our consciences.

In light of these controversies of old, I do not believe Christians will come to complete agreement on the matter of same-sex marriage, but I do hope that we will continue to listen to one another, that we will remain open to the leading of the Holy Spirit, and that we will see more and more churches welcoming, blessing, and supporting lesbian, gay, and bisexual Christians, those committed to celibacy and those who bind themselves to another, to God, and to their communities through Holy Marriage.

WILLIAM LOADER

I appreciate Megan's sharing her personal journey of reflection on the issues of homosexuality. I have also valued her research that focused on the rarely acknowledged or spoken-about reality that there are people who are not unambiguously male or female, in particular, intersex people.[1] It is not the same as acknowledging that there are also people who are gay, but it at least makes it easier to do so when one understands that the claim that all people are either male or female is too simple, indeed, inaccurate. Increasingly people are, indeed, acknowledging that some people are gay, sexually attracted to those of their own gender, and this has posed a challenge to people of faith who then seek to reconcile what they find in Scripture with what they find in reality—let alone, what they do about it. It is certainly time for careful and sensitive conversation.

Given the reference in Matthew 19:12 to people who were eunuchs from birth, the possibility must be acknowledged that when the people of the time read in Genesis 1:27 that God created humankind male and female, that would not have been understood as a hard-and-fast rule admitting no exceptions. In all probability, however, people understood eunuchs still to be males who lacked an ability which normally belonged to maleness.

I appreciate the way Megan is sensitive to the significant cultural gap which exists between contemporary Western society and first-century society, noting in particular the prevalence of slavery and its context for sexual exploitation. As she notes, the list of wrongdoers in 1 Timothy 1:9–10 may well deliberately associate slave traders with those who engaged in same-sex relations with males, reflecting this context. She also notes that the term *malakoi*, while not a technical term for the passive partner in such relations, nevertheless reflects a common disdain

---

1. Megan K. DeFranza, *Sex Difference in Christian Theology: Male, Female, and Intersex in the Image of God* (Grand Rapids: Eerdmans, 2015).

for effeminacy among men since men were meant to be strong and virile, not soft and passive, attributes seen to be characteristic of women. To treat a man as a woman was to humiliate him and worse, in contexts of war, to assert one's superiority by destroying the other's honor and dignity. The matter of how the terms are translated in 1 Corinthians 6:9–10 and 1 Timothy 1:9–10 is contentious, as she shows, though I see the balance of probability favoring an allusion to the active and passive partners in same-sex relations.[2] She wisely, however, points beyond these to Romans where Paul says more.

I find some points of disagreement with her discussion of Romans. This is partly because my research into Jewish literature of the time which has survived has persuaded me that Paul must be read as someone who remains committed to his Jewish ethical heritage and is not only influenced by Stoic thought about what is natural but also by cultural concerns about passivity or philosophical strictures about excess passion.[3] This is also true of Philo despite his extensive engagement with Hellenistic philosophy of his era. For Philo, like other Jews of his time—and like Paul—all people are male or female because God created them that way, and to act otherwise is more than unnatural in a Stoic sense; it is to act contrary to God's created order.[4] It is also clear that both Paul and Philo assume the prohibitions of Leviticus and apply them broadly to include both pederasty, which features large in Philo's work, and consenting adult same-sex relations, both male-to-male and female-to-female relations. I find extension to lesbian relations in Romans 1:26 as something to be expected more persuasive than women engaging in non-vaginal sex with men, since males, not females, would be deemed responsible for that, or than women engaging in bestiality.

I have no argument with Megan's observation that *we* might see Paul's claims about head attire as only social convention. I am not, however, persuaded that Paul saw it like that. Paul differs from Philo (and Plato) in not using the argument that same-sex relations are unnatural because they are not procreative, which he could have grounded

---

2. William Loader, *The New Testament on Sexuality* (= *NTS*) (Grand Rapids: Eerdmans, 2012), 326–34.

3. Ibid., 22–33, 293–326.

4. William Loader, *Philo, Josephus, and the Testaments on Sexuality* (=*PJT*) (Grand Rapids: Eerdmans, 2012), 204–17.

in Genesis 1:28, but is one with Philo in seeing it as unnatural because it goes against how God ordered creation. Similarly, without taking into account Paul's Jewish theological frame of reference, one can see his statements about shamefulness and dishonor as simply peddling popular male values of his time, but for Paul, as for Philo, something more is at stake: God's creation. Paul's awareness of Genesis 1:27 is reflected in the fact that in his discussion he chose to speak of "male" and "female."

Similarly, I see it as very likely that Paul shares and reflects concerns about excess of passion and may well have explained its wrongful direction as resulting from such excess where it runs out of control. Philo frequently points to drunken parties as the context for such excess. Paul's argument is, however, not primarily about the wrongfulness of excess, let alone the promiscuity of wild parties, but psychological. Misdirected and perverted responses to God produce minds that are perverted and so misdirected. This has been difficult to accept by those who feel compelled to declare that the direction itself is ethically neutral, and they have my sympathy. But Paul's argument is typical of his anthropology elsewhere. Something has gone wrong with the mind. It is in a state of sin and from that state arise misdirected passions, condemned not primarily because of their intensity or only when they issue in intent and action, but because of their direction. It is also important to see that Paul's argument is not that this is a consequence of the fall of Adam, but that it is a consequence of having a distorted understanding of God, producing in turn a distorted, messed-up mind. This traditional analysis of what has gone wrong produced the condemnation with which people have lived in history and led to the call to restore such people back to how God made them. There is an inner logic to this stance as long as one embraces Paul's analysis.

Taking Paul's analysis seriously has been increasingly difficult for people who have been convinced that not all gay people are in a state of sin like this. It is understandable that people have reexamined Paul and tried to find some way in which he could be interpreted as saying something less. I can very much identify with their intent, though I believe the better way is to allow what seems the most natural meaning to stand and then take responsibility for how to respond to it. This is not to say that in recent times further light has not been shed on the text.

Paul may well have had in mind hypocrisy among Stoics who rejected same-sex relations but then engaged in them with their students or the goings-on in the imperial household, perhaps even Caligula's being stabbed through his genitals. Clearly, assumptions about male honor and about excess passion play a role, but we need to see that Paul is generalizing here. He is not just talking about exploitation of slaves or about pederasty. He is talking also of those whose passion is mutual, of consenting adults (with or for one another; Rom 1:24, 27). He is employing an established argument that seeks to make a causal link between a broken relationship with God through idolatry that denies God's true being and a broken relationship with oneself that denies one's own true being, in particular as male or female.

When Megan writes, "Drawing on ancient assumptions among Jews and Romans familiar with Stoic philosophy, heterosexual and same-sex excess are both explained as resulting from a turn away from God," I find this falls short of the evidence because it suggests that the problem is only "excess." The problem is not primarily excess, but direction. When she writes, "Contemporary students of sexuality will find this explanation of same-sex desire inadequate," I would apply it more broadly. I value then the way she unpacked that inadequacy. This volume is not about same-sex marriage, although much of what deals with it has implications in this regard. It is particularly relevant if one sees marriage as the only legitimate context for sexual relations, or, at least, their genital expression. My own research confirms the observation she makes that biblical marriage cannot simply be identified with modern Western understandings of marriage. This complicates the discussion in ways not always recognized.

First-century marriage in both Jewish and Greco-Roman cultures was bound up with the household, and the household was the cornerstone of society and the welfare of its citizens. Fathers negotiated with fathers about the best pairings. Self-negotiated marriage or romantic engagements were frowned upon. What was at stake was the future of the household and all its members. Greatly unequal in age, the partnership was not equal, but one in which the husband was head of the household and the woman subordinate and, by a flawed logic, seen as less mature and intelligent not just because of her age but because of her being. The model leant itself well to describing the unequal relation between the church and Christ, its head; never, of course, in reverse: Christ as the bride and the church as the husband!

Megan rightly notes that our understandings of marriage have changed. Not only would we want to affirm equal partnership and ground it in a reading of Genesis 1:26–27 of seeing both male and female in the image of God, but a good deal else has changed. My response to Stephen will address this in more detail because he raises the question of whether we should ever call Augustine's understanding of marriage into question. Among other major changes is the advent of effective contraception, which means that we must rework traditional *mores* relating to pre-marital and extramarital sex where fear of pregnancy was one major strand of the argument. More significantly, it has made it easier for us to differentiate sexual intercourse as primarily for the propagation of the species from sexual intercourse as an expression of intimacy in companionship. These two aspects were largely inseparable in the ancient world.

The rationale for the existence of marriage as the procreation of children could lead, and often did, to the assumption that sexual intercourse has only procreation as its end and is otherwise sin or self-indulgence. Philo shared this focus, but then suggests that the pleasure of union has its place because it facilitates procreation.[5] But Philo, like Plato before him, had to come to terms with marriages where the woman was infertile or post menopause. In a rare moment of generosity, Philo acknowledges that to demand that companions for life cease to engage in intercourse in such instances, let alone dissolve their marriage, is unwarranted.[6] Plato had reached a similar conclusion in his otherwise highly regulated scheme for breeding the best citizens.[7]

One could argue that patriarchal marriage, whether as assumed in New Testament times or as elaborated by Augustine, should be upheld or even restored. But marriage has evolved, shaped by changing circumstances. The industrial revolution changed marriage from being household-based with both partners working with roles internal and external and managing the household's craft and agricultural output together to a situation where the man went outside the home to work to support the household and the woman was confined to domestic support

---

5. *Opif.* 151–52, 156.
6. Spec. 3.35.
7. *Leg.* 784E3–785A3, 783E4–7, 784B1–3.

roles. This was stereotypically a 1950s model of marriage, reasserted in the West after the slippage of World War II, when many women had gone out to work for the war effort and were then replaced by returning soldiers and sent back to domesticity. The advent of women's voting and educational rights combined with the availability of effective contraception transformed our societies and their marriages, so that at least since the 1960s in many Western societies, the grumblings about women going out to work have given way to acknowledgment of women in leadership and, despite retardant tendencies, an affirmation of women's leadership roles, even in the church.

One then must face the question, If it is healthy that some marry without the prospect of procreation, in other words marry for lifelong companionship, and want that formally and legally recognized, why can this not be the case for same-sex couples? Of course, the answer must be no if one shares Paul's sexual anthropology. And if one does not? I see no barrier. Megan reminds us that opinions still diverge, but that we must now learn to live with the fences and talk to each other across them.

WESLEY HILL

Megan DeFranza's essay begins in the right place: with real aching, yearning human beings seeking to come to grips with their uniqueness before God. Scripture isn't "timeless truth"; it is, as the Reformers and many before them recognized, God's Word *pro nobis*, "for us"—it is gospel, "good news" for actual sinners. So DeFranza's determination to start with the lived experiences of intersex, bisexual, gay, and other "non-heterosexual" persons—and to then ask how those experiences can be surrendered to God in discipleship—is, in my judgment, simply right.

But I find myself disagreeing with how she goes about achieving that goal. Her first approach to the question of how lesbian and gay people and other sexual minorities ought to live well is to claim that the biblical portrayal of marriage in Genesis 1 and 2 is descriptive of the majority of human experience—most human beings fit into the categories of "male" and "female" and most experience opposite-sex attraction, freeing them to marry and procreate (though not always in that order)—but not *normative*. She claims that the gaps in the text—for instance, the creation of amphibians, who confound the neat sea-land dichotomy of Genesis 1:20–25—leave room for us to understand that while male-female marriage may be the majority practice, it need not be understood as an exclusive one that all people must embrace.

This leads DeFranza into the further claim that biblical marriage is *pluriform*. Her essay emphasizes the diversity of ways marriage in the Bible has been understood and how entangled its practice was with the various patriarchal cultures of the biblical authors. She sees this diversity of ancient experience as a sign that the Bible is not interested in delivering a once-for-all model of marriage and that the appropriate Christian response is to form contemporary practices of marriage that "honor the humanity of gay, lesbian, and bisexual people and the biblical truth that they too are made in the image of God and equally capable of ordering their relationships and sexual lives in ways that honor God, benefit the common good, and promote their own growth in health and holiness." In short, given the Bible's inability to deliver a definitive model of marriage, believers today are to *improvise* a humane Christian practice of marriage in light of the Bible's overarching story.[8]

In my judgment, both of these approaches err. I will discuss them each in turn.

First, with regard to the claim the Bible presents a regular, typical practice of marriage without making that practice authoritative for the church's ongoing ethical teaching, DeFranza downplays certain features of the Genesis text in order to make her argument work better. The first of these is the climactic nature of Genesis 1:26–27, which presents God's creation of "male and female" not only as the crowning moment in the creation sequence[9] but also, most likely, as the mirror of a shadowy divine relationality that will not be fully unveiled until the I-Thou relationship of Father and Son in the New Testament.[10]

Furthermore, DeFranza does not discuss the fact that the creation story in Genesis 2 climaxes with an affirmation of its goodness (2:25) that is subsequently overturned (3:7, 10–11). In other words, already built into the narrative itself is a recognition that its features are *not* to be understood as straightforwardly descriptive of ongoing human life. The creation of "male and female" is now to be understood in a very real sense as "a half-remembered dream and an inchoate longing" rather than something we have unmediated access to now, after the "fall" of Genesis 3.[11] And, on the flip side of this, God's creation of "male and

---

8. At this point DeFranza adverts to N. T. Wright's five-act play model of improvisation in Christian ethics. For a fuller treatment of this way of thinking about the ethical life, see Samuel Wells, *Improvisation: The Drama of Christian Ethics* (Grand Rapids: Brazos, 2004).

9. Gerhard von Rad, *Genesis: A Commentary*, trans. J. H. Marks, OTL (Philadelphia: Westminster, 1961), 57: "The high point and goal has been reached toward which all of God's creativity from v. 1 on was directed," as evidenced by the divine self-address (1:26), the declaration after the creation of humanity that's God work is "very good" (as opposed to only "good"; 1:31), and the fact that this story is expanded in ch. 2 of Genesis, among other things.

10. There is an analogy "between this mark of the divine being, namely, that it includes an I and a Thou, and the being of man, male and female" (Karl Barth, *Church Dogmatics III/1* [Edinburgh: T&T Clark, 1958], 196).

11. I borrow this language from Stephen Holmes's comments in an interview with Vicky Beeching, accessed March 8, 2016, http://faithinfeminism.com/feminist-conservative -on-sexuality-2/. In a blog post on DeFranza's book, Holmes commented similarly: "True maleness and true femaleness are, theologically considered, a memory and a hope, not a present possession. East of Eden, in our present fallen, broken state, we are all inadequately sexed," accessed March 8, 2016, http://steverholmes.org.uk/blog/?p=7538.

female" *is* to be understood as normative in a way that our current access to it in actual human life is not. Putting that point slightly differently, I would say that the placement of Genesis 1 and 2 before Genesis 3 is already an indication of the former's theological primacy and normativity. "Male and female" is the creational intention not because we can see that clearly in our present contexts but rather because it is given to us in the pre-fall, pre-sin-and-death narratives of Genesis 1 and 2.

And finally, DeFranza does not adequately address Jesus' own prioritization of these texts in Matthew 19:1–12 (cf. Mark 10:1–12). When Jesus is asked about divorce, he does not appeal to contemporary human behavior, whether of the majority culture or of those on the margins. He explicitly repudiates current practice, which goes back to a concession to human fallenness embedded in the Mosaic law (Matt 19:8). In light of the eschatological arrival of the kingdom of heaven, Jesus appeals over against contemporary experience to Genesis 1 and 2—intertwining both 1:27 and 2:24—and treats "the created order [as] a guide for the moral order." Crucially, this is not, as W. D. Davies and Dale Allison point out, an appeal to the "natural order as it is (corrupted by sin) but the natural order as intended by God."[12] Jesus, in other words, treats Genesis 1 and 2 both as something to guide and norm the moral life of his followers and also as something that has been lost or obscured by human "hardness of heart." DeFranza's reading omits both of these emphases: She does not recognize Jesus' giving special theological priority to "male and female" with his appeal to Genesis, and she appears also not to recognize his understanding that the Genesis text is describing a reality which in a crucial sense does not correspond to present human life, majority "heterosexual" culture included.

With regard to her second point—that much of the biblical portrayals of marriage are patriarchal and need to be chastened or superseded by the "biblical teaching of the image of God in all people"—I would agree that we must be taught by Scripture how to read Scripture. But rather than say there is an egalitarian strand of the Bible that we can use to critique the Bible's own depictions of marriage, I would rather say there are signs in the canon itself of what might be called canonical self-criticism, and it is these elements that direct our own reading of

---

12. W. D. Davies and Dale C. Allison, *Matthew 19–28: Volume III*, ICC (London: Bloomsbury T&T Clark, 1997, 2004), 10, n. 30.

what to prioritize in the canon.[13] Consider, for example, DeFranza's comments on Ephesians 5. She claims, "It is only very recently that Christians have been shifting their interpretation of Ephesians 5 so that the call to 'mutual submission' in verse 21 (grammatically tied to 5:22 in the Greek) is read to support egalitarian human marriage, while the ancient vision of patriarchal marriage remains an analogy for Christ and church." Her view seems to be that the Old and New Testaments offer patriarchal visions of marriage that we now, in light of certain elements of Christian teaching, rightly endeavor to move beyond, and our doing so involves us in criticizing Scripture's moves—such as the command for wives to submit—by means of our grasp of what the gospel's essential teaching is.

But this neglects what I described in my essay as the Augustinian consensus—the understanding that there is "a trajectory in the canonical Scriptural portrayal of marriage," one that culminates in an understanding of the spousal union as procreative, permanent, and transparent to the love of God in Christ. Certainly alternative portrayals abound in the pages of the Bible—think of Solomon (1 Kings 11:1–3)—but, for Christians, not every passage in the Bible is equally prescriptive or determinative for a Christian ethical life. Rather, the Old Testament must be read in light of the New, the Mosaic legislation must be read in light of its fulfillment in Christ (Rom 10:4), and so on. The point is simply that one must look for Scripture's Christological center and read all of its various parts in light of that center. When one does that, one finds that the canon has itself already given priority to a Christ-shaped view of marriage.

Consider how a marital text like Ephesians 5 seems to envision the qualification[14] or even subversion of the patriarchal marriage that is found in the Old Testament (and elsewhere in the ancient and contemporary worlds). By the time wives are enjoined to submit to their husbands in 5:22, men and women alike have already been told to submit to one another (5:21), and when men are told to love their wives (5:25), they are

---

13. Further on this, see Ellen F. Davis, "Critical Traditioning: Seeking an Inner Biblical Hermeneutic," *Anglican Theological Review* 82 (2000): 733–51.

14. Richard Bauckham, "Egalitarianism and Hierarchy in the Bible," in *God and the Crisis of Freedom* (Louisville: Westminster John Knox, 2002), 116–27, argues that while some biblical passages oppose hierarchy outright, it is more common to find "a strategy of relativizing and transforming hierarchy" (p. 118).

simply receiving the same command that their wives too received at the beginning of the passage (5:2). And the Christ whose role the husband bodies forth is one who has already descended to the uttermost place of humiliation (4:9). Certainly the language and form of submission and hierarchy remain in place (5:22, 24), and yet "behind the façade, its substance is subverted and transformed. The bridging of the gulf between above and below by Christ the reconciler [4:8–10] is, if not the abolition, at least the *deconstruction* of patriarchal marriage."[15] Paul "attempts to transform relationships of dominance and subordination into relationships of *mutual* subordination."[16] And thereby the canon itself rules its own reading: If Christ's self-giving shapes the practice of marriage in this way, then marriage itself is elevated, sanctified, and rendered full and true in a way that should guide our reading of other alternative views of marriage we see even in the Bible (like Solomon's, for instance).

What does all this mean for the discussion of the inclusion of LGBT persons in the church? DeFranza's aim, I take it, is to undermine the notion that there is one normative picture of marriage in the Bible, so as to make sure lesbian and gay believers may enter into marriage on equal footing with their "straight" sisters and brothers. But on my reading, however else we think about the place of LGBT people in the body of Christ, we cannot do so by "expanding" the definition of Christian marriage in a way that distorts its biblical contours.

---

15. Francis Watson, *Agape, Eros, Gender: Towards a Pauline Sexual Ethic* (Cambridge: Cambridge University Press, 2000), 234.

16. Bauckham, "Egalitarianism and Hierarchy in the Bible," 126.

RESPONSE TO MEGAN K. DEFRANZA

STEPHEN R. HOLMES

I am grateful to Dr. DeFranza for her careful, irenic, and honest essay. I particularly welcome her closing comments on finding common ground, and I hope that the conversations we have in this book can be a means of doing that.

DeFranza begins her essay with an extended autobiographical reflection that describes how her experience of discovering theological strategies to more adequately discuss intersex led her to reflect on the texts that (she had been taught) led to negative ethical judgments about lesbian, gay, and bisexual people in the church. She begins arguing that Genesis 1 does not necessarily teach a simple binary account of sexuality and concludes with the suggestion that Romans 1:26–27 is a key text; in between, she deals more briefly with other texts.

I find DeFranza's omission of Genesis 2 in these opening exegetical comments puzzling, particularly as she suggests in her summary of her exegesis (pp. 70–71) that the readings she derives from Genesis 1 should be taken as readings of Genesis 2 also. She uses the example of amphibians inhabiting a space between "land animals" and "sea animals" in Genesis 1 to propose that, similarly, the human male/female binary in the text might have concealed space for intersex people. The narrative of Eden in Genesis 2 has no hint of such generalisations, however. Adam appears as an individual, not a class. No suitable companion for Adam can be found amongst the animals, so God creates Eve, another individual, and the two find delight in their union.

This is important, because DeFranza's argument at this point relies on a parallel between the existence of intersex people in the apparent male-female binary and the opening up of marriage to same-sex couples (on p. 90 she states this explicitly: "*By extension*, heterosexual marriage can be seen as the majority story, not the exclusive model"—my italics). There is no exegetical reason offered to make this "extension." Indeed, once we recognise (as all responsible biblical scholarship does) the relative independence of the two creation narratives, there would seem to be good exegetical reason not to.

When we turn to Romans, DeFranza offers us an extended rhetorical reading which is illuminating in several ways, but I am again not convinced by her exegesis. She claims Paul is constructing an argument that will "be persuasive to both Jews and Gentiles" (p. 81), a point which I assume most readers of Romans will agree with—and indeed will want to stress as fairly central to the logic of the early chapters of the letter. Then, however, with the help of Brooten, she deconstructs exclusively Gentile notions of "nature" that cannot have been in Paul's mind because no Jew would ever have entertained them. Whatever Paul might have been meaning by "natural" in Romans 1:26–27, it cannot have been this because—on DeFranza's own reading—this undermines the entire logic of his argument.

DeFranza uses her exegetical reflections to argue that there is no blanket biblical prohibition against same-sex sexual activity; she recognises, however, that this is not yet an argument for extending Christian marriage to couples of the same sex (she does not consider the possibility of a "third vocation" route, permitting sexually active same-sex partnerships that are not marriages). She acknowledges that "the unanimous picture of marriage in the Bible is heterosexual" (p. 87), but argues that we can nonetheless open up our understanding of "Holy Marriage" (her capitals) to same-sex couples.

The argument begins with some engagement with Grenz on marriage as an image of Christ's love for the church which, Grenz suggests, is not possible for same-sex marriages. DeFranza appears to accept that point, but argues that "the marital metaphor found throughout the Bible is based on ancient patriarchal marriage, not [modern marriage]" (p. 88). This is important for her argument, because she bases the plausibility of her proposal for changing our understanding of marriage to open it to same-sex couples on the claim that we have changed our understanding of marriage already, from patriarchy to (relative) equality.

I suggest that the theological reality of marriage is in fact fairly stable—a point I argued in my own essay by pointing to the unchanging liturgical definitions. (Dr. Hill's essay in this volume argues this same point at length exegetically and very convincingly.) So I do not accept that there has been a change in our understanding of marriage, just many and repeated changes in its cultural expressions. We need to distinguish, I suggest, between the theological reality of marriage and its ever-changing cultural trappings. We need to do this because the biblical texts make no sense if we do not. To take only one example, the idealised visions of human marriage in Genesis 2 (and indeed the Song of Solomon) are significantly different from the realities of particular marital relationships—including Solomon's—narrated in the Old Testament.

We might compare the reality of the church: although prosperous American megachurches look very different from the house churches of Paul's day (and from underground churches in contemporary Iran, and from rural European medieval gatherings, and . . .), there is a stable theological definition ("one, holy, catholic, and apostolic" and/or "the pure preaching of the Word and the right administration of the sacraments") that makes these (astonishingly) varied cultural artifacts expressions of the same unchanging reality. In just the same way, I believe that the marriages within my local congregation are theologically the same, if culturally wildly different, from the marriages which Paul knew in the churches in Ephesus and Corinth.

For this reason, I do not accept the logic of DeFranza's claim that, having changed marriage once, we are free to change it again. When she says, "The question before Christians today is whether 'biblical marriage' can be revised *yet again*" (p. 90; italics original), the force of her position relies on our accepting the claim that it has been "revised" before; as I have argued, she has not shown this to be true.

I see no problem in holding to the above position if, as DeFranza asserts, "The marital metaphor found throughout the Bible is based on ancient patriarchal marriage" (p. 88). Many biblical metaphors are culturally specific. The shepherd metaphor of Psalm 23 and John 10 assumes ancient practices of animal husbandry that we need to uncover and translate to understand. That said, as indicated above, I think there is good reason to question whether the metaphor works as DeFranza suggests. She herself describes Paul's account of marriage in 1 Corinthians 7 as "shockingly egalitarian" (p. 99). Yet Paul offers the most thorough development of "the marital metaphor" in the whole of Scripture in Ephesians 5 and uses it in 1 Corinthians as well (11:3).

If the metaphor assumes a hard patriarchy, as DeFranza suggests, then Paul is being quite astonishingly inconsistent in his teaching on marriage. It is very hard to imagine Paul offering the subversively egalitarian teaching on marriage of 1 Corinthians 7 and then assuming his readers will understand that in 1 Corinthians 11:3 he is wanting them to assume the culturally normative hard patriarchal model.

First Corinthians 11 is a notoriously difficult text to interpret,[17] but the very difficulty of the passing reference to marriage may be of help to us. Paul appears to line up three examples of "headship": God the head of Christ; Christ the head of man; and the husband as the head of the wife. If we read this as hard patriarchal marriage defining the Christ-human relationship, then we cannot read "God is the head of Christ" in any way that is not Arian (John Chrysostom already knew this in the fourth century; see his *Homily* 26 on 1 Corinthians). We make most sense of the text, and of the broader scriptural use of the marriage metaphor, when we are attentive to Christology. The Incarnate One is truly human as well as truly divine, and so properly spoken of as our friend and brother as well as our Lord and God.

The marital metaphor in Scripture seems to me to play with this dual relationship in sophisticated ways that vary in the different contexts in which it appears (just as there is more emphasis on the authority of Christ in the "body metaphor" in Eph 4 than there is in the use of the same metaphor in 1 Cor 12). I believe the marital metaphor is capacious enough in its biblical deployment to encompass fully egalitarian understandings of marriage, and, indeed, that there is a good argument that Christians down through history have heard the metaphor in a surprisingly egalitarian, and so generally counter-cultural, way.

The most sustained deployment of marriage as a metaphor for Christ's relationship to the church across Christian history is in allegorical readings of the Song of Songs,[18] yet even contemporary feminist interpreters note the remarkably unpatriarchal thought-world of the

---

17. See Lucy Peppiatt, *Women and Worship in Corinth* (Eugene, OR: Cascade, 2015) for a helpful outline of the problems and the various proposed readings.

18. Ellen F. Davis claims the Song has been more commented on than any other biblical book save Genesis and Psalms, and notes that over a hundred commentaries were written before 1200 AD. Ellen F. Davis, *Proverbs, Ecclesiastes, and the Song of Songs*, Westminster Bible Companion (Louisville: Westminster John Knox, 2000), 231.

Song.[19] Some recent readers hear two male voices in the Song and see the woman being forced to leave her shepherd-lover to be married, against her will, to King Solomon, but generally it has been heard as a celebration of a perfect relationship between two people. The woman's role in that relationship does not look remotely subservient; she is repeatedly the initiator of events and fully possessed of her own agency. This, in Christian history at least, is the key referent for the "marital metaphor," not the union of "an adult man to a child or teenage girl with little education and fewer legal rights" (DeFranza, p. 89).

DeFranza gives an account of what she describes as "themes which ground a Christian vision of marriage and sexual ethics" (p. 94), which she claims are generally accepted. The first of these is curious, describing singleness as "a rare calling," which is neither a common position in Christian history (at best we may say that most Protestants in the West have recently begun to think like this) nor a plausible reading of the New Testament, as I argued in my own essay. I applaud her account of the ascetic (she terms it "sacramental") vocation of marriage, but I would want to insist on the indissoluble link between marriage and procreation in Scripture and tradition as a common theme as well. (The point DeFranza makes that there is no mention of children in 1 Cor 7 is true, but not particularly convincing: there is no mention of children in the Song of Solomon, a far longer text, yet no one argues that ancient Jewish marriage was divorced from procreation; writers often don't mention things they assume their readers will take for granted.)

DeFranza closes with some pleas for irenicism: "Is it possible for Christians to 'agree to disagree' on same-sex marriage?" I would simply say that I hope so. There is a very regrettable tendency on both sides of this debate for the rhetoric to be inflammatory, with accusations of apostasy or bigotry, and comparisons to nineteenth-century liberalism or to nineteenth-century slave ownership. Of course, there are very poor arguments to be found in public on both sides, some of which might well deserve such censure, but there are also serious and sensitive engagements on both sides, which should be honoured as such. For reasons

---

19. In a survey of recent feminist readings, Robin C. McCall identifies the fact that "the relationship of the lovers in the Song is remarkably equitable" as one of the things that draws feminist interpreters to it. Robin C. McCall, "'Most Beautiful among Women': Feminist/ Womanist Contributions to Reading the Song of Songs," *Review & Expositor* 105 (2008): 417–33, quotation from 421.

I have sketched, I remain unconvinced by Dr. DeFranza's arguments, but I have no difficulty in recognising her essay as faithfully Christian, a serious theological wrestling with the question, transparently based on the authority of Scripture and on Christ's call to holy love. I end as I began: I am grateful to her for it.

REJOINDER

I am grateful to my fellow contributors for their thoughtful and kind responses. They illustrate our ability to engage this conversation charitably, illumine the common ground we share, and put into relief our differing approaches to biblical interpretation and theological ethics which inevitably shape our conclusions.

One difference which has figured prominently is the teaching of Augustine. Both Holmes and Hill receive Augustine as authoritative because of his near universal influence on marital theology but fail to mention that his sway is limited to Western churches. As an evangelical theologian who followed John Wesley into an appreciation for theological insights from the Eastern tradition, I find myself less beholden to the Augustinian legacy. Eastern Orthodoxy has long been critical of Augustine's theological contributions and developed a theology of marriage quite apart from him. Hill and Holmes follow Augustine not only in the *Goods of Marriage* but in the fourth-century bishop's interpretation of Genesis and doctrine of the Trinity. Given the limits of space, I will address the former.[1]

Augustine interpreted Adam and Eve as ideal, mature humans before their sin introduced disaster—virtually destroying the image of God in humanity. Holmes and Hill extend the consequences of the fall to sex and gender. Not knowing how to find a place for intersex persons in the community of faith, both take an Augustinian view by pointing to the fall as that which brought about not only the variations of sex

---

1. Hill reads Adam and Eve through the lenses of Jewish philosopher Martin Buber's categories of I and Thou and Augustine's model of the Trinity which privileges the relationship of Father and Son to the marginalization of the Spirit, setting up an unhealthy vision of marriage which I explain in *Sex Difference in Christian Theology*, 230–38.

development (at times labeled "intersex") but which Holmes suggests has estranged all of us from some [assumed] masculine and feminine ideal. In their estimation, none of us are the men or women we were "meant" to be; the bodies of the intersexed have just fallen a little farther from the models supposedly inscribed in Adam and Eve.[2] I do not think their theological vision is borne out by the rest of the Bible. The prophet Isaiah predicted the inclusion of eunuchs—those who fell short of the masculine ideal—in the eschatological community. They would be welcomed *as eunuchs* and were promised "a memorial and a name better than sons and daughters" (Isa 56:5)—a reward different from that expected by Jewish males. Instead of welcoming eunuchs as eunuchs, our authors teach something the Scriptures never suggest—a restoration of some long-lost masculinity. This proposal may echo the attempts of Augustine to reconcile those in whom "the marks of both sexes appear in such a way that it is uncertain from which they should properly receive their name" with patriarchal masculine ideals. Augustine concedes, "Our established manner of speaking has given them the gender of the better sex, calling them masculine."[3] Once again, Augustine points in the wrong direction.

Hill and Holmes identify ideal gender and ideal marriage in the first two chapters of Genesis. Having lost perfection at the beginning, they look for its recovery in the canonical story, which they locate in Ephesians 5—Christ and church as husband and wife. But here they want to have their cake and eat it too. They want to affirm human marriage as egalitarian—the mutual submission of husband and wife—while grounding this vision in the marriage of church to Christ in Ephesians. I agree with them that we need a "Christ-shaped view of marriage" and a Christologically centered canonical hermeneutic, but I do not believe we can find both in the model of Christ and church in Ephesians 5.[4]

Submit to one another out of reverence for Christ. Wives, submit yourselves to your own husbands as you do to the Lord. For

---

2. Hill, *Spiritual Friendship*, 2; citing Holmes, "Shadows and Broken Images: thinking theologically about maleness and femaleness" August 19, 2015, http://steverholmes.org.uk/blog/?p=7538.

3. Augustine, *The City of God against the Pagans*, trans. Eva Matthews Sandford and William McAllen Green, Loeb Classical Library, vol. 5 (Cambridge: Harvard University Press, 1965), 16.8, 47.

4. Hill, "Response to DeFranza," 111.

the husband is the head of the wife as Christ is the head of the church, his body, of which he is the Savior. Now as the church submits to Christ, so also wives should submit to their husbands in everything. Husbands, love your wives, just as Christ loved the church and gave himself up for her. (vv. 21–25)

Dr. Loader and I agree that the metaphor of Christ and church is built upon an ancient patriarchal pattern of marriage—an unequal relationship between wives and husbands, rooted in ancient assumptions about sex and gender differences which they believed pointed quite naturally to the unequal relationship between the church and Christ. No matter how much Jesus humbled himself, the humiliation of the Messiah was temporary; Christ is not mutually submissive to his bride.

Being found in appearance as a man, he humbled himself by becoming obedient to death—even death on a cross! Therefore God exalted him to the highest place and gave him the name that is above every name, that at the name of Jesus every knee should bow, in heaven and on earth and under the earth, and every tongue acknowledge that Jesus Christ is Lord, to the glory of God the Father. (Phil 2:8–11)

Both Ephesians 5:21–23 and Philippians 2 use the humility of Christ to teach Christians to "in humility value others above yourselves" (Phil 2:3), but in both passages Christ remains "head" and "Lord." Ephesians does not offer us an ideal model of marriage that is also egalitarian.

My theological anthropology is shaped less by Augustine and more by Irenaeus and the Eastern Church, who do not interpret the primordial pair as perfectly human or perfectly male and female. They believe Adam and Eve were created with room to grow.[5] They sinned, they fell,

---

5. Holmes's debt to Augustine seems to follow the Reformed tradition which takes a more negative view of humanity after sin than the Augustinianism of the Roman Church. Augustine's influence shows up in Holmes's argument that all sex/gender is warped "east of Eden" so as to be of little use in understanding the divine intention (Holmes, "Shadows and Broken Images"). He makes a similar case in his response to Dr. Loader, emphasizing the distorted nature of all sexual desire (Holmes, "Response to Loader," 63). In these, he appears to be trying to avoid the accusation that he views same-sex desire as more warped than heterosexuality or that the bodies of the intersexed are more fallen than those who are not intersex. I do not find his attempts convincing. Contrast his distrust of gender and sexual

but not from the height which Augustine assumed nor to the depths he described.[6] The Eastern tradition views Adam and Eve as living at the beginning of the story, not as an eternal ideal to which we must return. I find this theological vision to fit with insights from contemporary biblical scholars such as N. T. Wright and William Webb, who read the canon as an historically conditioned, unfinished drama in which we do not always find God's "ultimate ethic" spelled out with the kind of precision we might prefer.[7] The biblical narrative points not to a return to the garden, but to the future, inaugurated by Christ but not yet consummated.[8] For these reasons, I do not expect to find the ideal model of marriage in Genesis or even in Ephesians.

Taking a Christologically oriented view of Scripture and redemptive history, I see the example and teachings of Jesus as applying to men *and* women *as well as to* intersexed people, gay and lesbian people, and others. The understanding that the call to emulate Jesus is not the privilege or burden of men/husbands, but all of God's children, has radically altered Christian marriage, moving us beyond the softened patriarchy or "biblical marriage" of Ephesians 5 to mutual submission which better reflects Christ's second greatest commandment: "Love your neighbor as yourself" (Matt 22:39). For first-century men to love women "as themselves" would have required granting them honor as equally human, equally made in the image of God, equally empowered to lay down their own lives in imitation of Christ. Equal honor and empowerment have been slow to dawn in Christian marriage, but remain a prerequisite to truly *mutual* submission. The Bible points us toward perfection, but it is

---

desire with that of John Paul II, a Western theologian who nevertheless finds in heterosexual conjugal love an icon of Trinitarian love. John Paul II, *Man and Woman He Created Them: A Theology of the Body*, trans. Michael Waldstein (Boston: Pauline, 2006), 33.

6. Irenaeus, *Against Heresies*, 4.38. Kallistos Ware, *The Orthodox Way*, rev. ed. (Crestwood, NY: St. Vladimir's Seminary Press, 1979, 1999), 50–63.

7. N. T. Wright, "How Can the Bible Be Authoritative," *Vox Evangelica* 21 (1991): 7–32. William J. Webb, *Slaves, Women & Homosexuals: Exploring the Hermeneutics of Cultural Analysis* (Downers Grove, IL: InterVarsity, 2001). Webb unpacks "ultimate ethic" in ch. 2. Although I disagree with Webb's assessment of "homosexuality," I affirm his redemptive-movement hermeneutic and commentary on 1 Cor 7: "Pastoral moderation shapes the apostle's instructions. . . . Paul gently moves them away from the most harmful implications of an ascetic view of sex. However, he does not come close to sketching an ultimate ethic on sexuality. . . . The Spirit of God and the human authors provide pastoral instruction for their flock, which gently moves them along in a good direction." Webb, *Slaves, Women & Homosexuals*, 59.

8. DeFranza, *Sex Difference*, 181–85 and ch. 6.

a perfection found in Christ, not in Adam and Eve nor in first-century models of marriage.

Christian marriage today is not biblical marriage, but it is nevertheless becoming more Christian. Our growing understandings of sex, gender, and sexuality present us with the opportunity and obligation to ask how Christian marriage can be adjusted, yet again, opened up to all God's children.

CHRIST, SCRIPTURE, AND SPIRITUAL FRIENDSHIP

WESLEY HILL

When I was around thirteen years old, I began to realize that what my male friends were feeling toward girls—a vertiginous delight, an emotional and physical longing, commonly referred to as "romantic attraction" or "having a crush" or, more seriously, "falling in love"—I was feeling toward my male friends, toward *men*. I found myself noticing them in a way I never had before—noticing their newly firming muscles, the hue of their skin, and the depth of their voices. I recall sitting outside one summer on a camping trip, struggling mightily to keep from stealing glances at one of my best friends whom I was suddenly, and confusingly, finding *beautiful*. He was wearing shorts, and I realized that I kept surreptitiously looking at his legs the way he would have talked about looking at a girl's legs, my eyes drawn to their curvature, my heart beating faster with pleasure as a result.

But it wasn't just the physical sensations of sexual attraction that confused me. There was something more, something deeper. I wanted to *know* my friend. I wanted to find a way to let him know how much I cared about him, to somehow give him my heart and have his in return. Although I didn't have language for this at the time, I knew I wanted more than what usually passed for "friendship." My longings weren't just about going to bed with a friend but, somehow, exchanging intimate feelings with him—loving him and having him love me back.

At the same time, I also knew that I was a Christian—that I wanted as much as possible to live my life in grateful obedience for God's gift of Jesus Christ, whose life, death, and resurrection had achieved for me the forgiveness of sins and the promise of eternal life. And as I grew older, both of these realities started to seem more central to my developing sense of who I was. I wanted very much to go on being a Christian, to deepen my fidelity to Christ and the life of the church, and I increasingly felt that my sexuality had a kind of fixity or permanence about it. By the time I finished high school, I had a strong sense that the physical and emotional hunger I felt for an intimate relationship with a man was a stable, settled part of my personality, unlikely to be changed easily or at all.

The Catholic writer Andrew Sullivan, himself a gay man, has written movingly about the experience of growing up in the church with a longing to love other men and the unmet hope for some pastoral guidance as to how to go about doing so:

> In my adolescence and young adulthood, the teaching of the Church was merely a silence, an increasingly hollow denial even of the existence of homosexuals, let alone a credible ethical guide as to how they should live their lives. It is still true that in over thirty years of weekly churchgoing, I have never heard a homily that attempted to explain how a gay man should live, or how his sexuality should be expressed. I have heard nothing but a vast and endless and embarrassed silence, an awkward, unexpressed desire for the simple nonexistence of such people, for their absence from the moral and physical universe, for a word or a phrase, like "objective disorder," that could simply abolish the problem they represented and the diverse humanity they symbolized.[1]

My experience in the church tracks closely with Sullivan's. But even more, I am interested in the way he puts his finger on a lack of *positive* (as opposed to merely prohibitive) Christian reflection on the matter of homosexuality. How should a gay man or woman *live*, how should a same-sex-attracted person like me *express* his sexuality, rather than merely repress or try to deny its existence? For surely, like every other Christian, I am to live a life that includes both self-denial *and* an embrace of a positive calling, both "no" and "yes." Surely, as the theologian Oliver O'Donovan has put it, I ought to try to see how my experiences as a gay

---

1. Andrew Sullivan, *Love Undetectable: Notes on Friendship, Sex, and Survival* (New York: Vintage, 1998), 42.

man can "be clothed in an appropriate pattern of life for the service of God and discipleship of Christ."[2]

In what follows, I want to approach these questions largely through attending to Christian Scripture, the canon of Old and New Testaments. First, I want to remark on how I will approach the Bible—what assumptions and paradigms I bring to the task of reading the so-called "problem passages" on homosexuality. Then, second, I will discuss those passages, arguing that they prohibit all forms of same-sex genital intimacy. Third, I will engage a serious, worthy objection to this "traditional" view. And finally, I will return to my opening questions and ask what it might mean for gay Christians like me to live lives that are marked by love and fidelity.

Reading the Bible in Light of Christ

In the days leading up to the Supreme Court of the United States *Obergefell v. Hodges* decision, which ruled that same-sex couples have the right to marry, an image began showing up on posters and T-shirts. Under the heading "Biblical Marriage" was a schematic that included "Man + Woman," "Man + Wives + Concubines," "Man + Brother's Widow," "Man + Woman + Woman + Woman . . . ," "Male Soldier + Prisoner of War," "Male Slave + Female Slave," and so on. The point of the image was clear: There is no such thing as one "biblical" view of marriage, and Christians should not look to the Bible—an ancient collection of texts from foreign and diverse cultures—as if it could provide an answer for how the Supreme Court—a contemporary institution seeking to be responsive to a rapidly changing culture—ought to rule. As a theological document for one major American denomination put it, it is striking "how complex, evolving, and contradictory our Scriptures are on the subject [of marriage], and therefore how tricky it is to speak of 'the biblical view of marriage.'"[3] This popular image (and its more academic counterparts) seems to be an accurate visual representation of how many contemporary Christians approach the Bible and its relationship to the question of same-sex relationships today.

Yet one of the chief convictions of what came to be known as

---

2. Oliver O'Donovan, *Church in Crisis: The Gay Controversy and the Anglican Communion* (Eugene, OR: Cascade, 2008), 117.

3. The Episcopal Church Task Force on the Study of Marriage, "*Report to the 78*th *General Convention*," https://extranet.generalconvention.org/staff/files/download/12485.pdf.

"orthodox" Christian theology is that the Bible has a *center*. The second-century church father Irenaeus of Lyons recognized that the various parts of Scripture were easily susceptible to widely differing interpretations, but he suggested that these parts were best envisioned as pieces of a mosaic which could be properly ordered if one consulted the artist's guidebook. According to Irenaeus, the apostles bequeathed to subsequent readers such a guide, or "rule"—an account of Scripture's overall coherence, a kind of summary of the Christian faith, centered on Jesus Christ—that would enable believers to interpret Scripture as a unified whole.[4] And the main stream of Christian theology followed suit. In the wake of Irenaeus, Christian readers recognized that the properly Christian way to read the Bible was as a two-testament canon whose various parts were not to be played off one another but rather read synthetically with Jesus Christ as their orientating center.[5] It is for this reason that later Christian confessions and theologies would come to speak of the task of reading the Bible as one in which we endeavor not to interpret one passage of Scripture in a way that makes it "repugnant to another."[6]

Given this developing hermeneutical sense, some of the church fathers—St. Augustine of Hippo (354–430 CE) chief among them—came to expound a view of marriage drawn from multiple passages of Scripture and centered on fundamental Christological convictions. Before turning to my own exegesis of the passages dealing with same-sex intercourse, it may be useful to have a sketch of this Augustinian view of marriage in place as a point of departure.

A Scriptural, Augustinian Theology of Marriage

By far the most impressive attempt to synthesize and appropriate biblical teaching on marriage was Augustine's.[7] His easily memorable

---

4. Irenaeus of Lyons, *Against the Heresies*, Eng. trans. ANF 1 (1885; repr. Grand Rapids: Eerdmans, 1987), 1.8.1; 1.9.4. Cf. St. Augustine, *On Christian Teaching*, trans. R. P. H. Green (Oxford: Oxford University Press, 1997), 3.1–2; 3.27.38–3.29.40.

5. Robert W. Jenson, *Canon and Creed* (Louisville: Westminster John Knox, 2010).

6. *The Book of Common Prayer* (New York: Church Pension Fund, 1979), 184. I am drawing here from my own Anglican tradition (see Article 20 of the 39 Articles), but similar statements could be found in other traditions; for instance, in the Westminster Confession of Faith: "The infallible rule of interpretation of Scripture is the Scripture itself: and therefore, when there is a question about the true and full sense of any Scripture (which is not manifold, but one), it must be searched and known by other places that speak more clearly."

7. For accessible translations of the key texts, see Augustine, *Marriage and Virginity* (Hyde Park, NY: New City, 1999); Augustine, *On Genesis* (Hyde Park, NY: New City, 2004). For a

summary of the "goods" of marriage—*proles* (offspring), *fides* (faithfulness), and *sacramentum* (a visible, permanent sign of the love of God in Christ)—belies the sophistication of his achievement. What Augustine bequeathed to the Western church was nothing less than an attempt to chart a trajectory in the canonical Scriptural portrayal of marriage.[8] In what follows, I will attempt to summarize this Augustinian heritage in my own words, relying on critical reading strategies to which Augustine himself had no access and omitting those elements of his vision which I take to be wrong.[9] My summary will be, to those who know the tradition, obviously indebted to Augustine, but it will not be, per se, Augustine's.

First, in terms of their canonical placement and their subsequent prominence in the Gospels (Matt 19:1–6; Mark 10:1–9), the Genesis narratives retain pride of place in any effort to describe a canonical biblical theology of marriage. Whatever else humanity's creation in the image of God as "male and female" might mean in the first creation account, it is clear enough that it is immediately related to the divine blessing of giving birth to offspring (Gen 1:26–28). "Children," writes Robert Song, "do not appear here as an optional extra to the otherwise self-contained nature of marriage. . . . [Rather, procreation] is an inseparable and intrinsic good of marriage, the result of God's blessing and command to be fruitful."[10] The *adam* is differentiated as "male and female" and given the commission to fill the earth and subdue it (1:28).

It is this nexus—between male and female and the offspring their coupling produces—that seems to explain the text's emphasis on sexual difference: "Being created in a relationship of male and female is what

---

useful secondary discussion, see Christopher C. Roberts, *Creation and Covenant: The Significance of Sexual Difference in the Moral Theology of Marriage* (London: T& T Clark, 2007), ch. 2.

8. This perspective is one that I share with the same-sex-marriage-"affirming" author Robert Song; see his *Covenant and Calling: Towards a Theology of Same-Sex Relationships* (London: SCM, 2014), 5–7.

9. In short, I am using Augustine as a foundational source but not, I hope, uncritically. Augustine shared many of the patriarchal assumptions of his culture which Christians today are right to repudiate. On the other hand, it must also be acknowledged that Augustine is the first patristic author to argue, on the basis of the difficult 1 Cor 11:7, that women *also*, alongside men, are created in the image of God. See further, Kari Elisabeth Børresen, "In Defence of Augustine: how femina is homo," in Bernard Bruning, et al. eds., *Collectanea Augustiniana, Mélanges T. J. van Bavel* (Louvain: Institut Historique Augustinien, 1990), 263–80.

10. Song, *Covenant and Calling*, 4–5.

enables humankind to procreate; being able to procreate enables it to fill
the earth and subdue it; being able to rule the earth enables it to fulfil
its role as bearing the image of God."[11]

The second creation account (2:4–25) tells the story differently but
arrives at a similar positioning of man vis-à-vis woman and woman
vis-à-vis man. No one in the animal world is found suitable (Hebrew,
kenegdo) to be a partner for the *adam*, and so God differentiates his
(originally sexless?) earth-formed creature into "man" (*ish*) and "woman"
(*ishshah*) (2:18–23).[12] And on this basis, the man and woman are said to
cling to one another, forming a bond that is described as "one flesh"
and paving the way for the genealogical concerns that shape the rest of
the book of Genesis.[13] Thus the Augustinian tradition's emphasis on
marriage as a created good marked by (1) procreation and (2) fidelity
arises from theological exegesis of Genesis in the first instance.

But, second, that tradition also depends on Jesus' own reading of the
Genesis texts as displayed in the Gospels (Matt 19:1–6; Mark 10:1–9).
In Matthew, the Pharisees confront Jesus about his opinion on divorce:
"Is it lawful for a man to divorce his wife for any cause?" (Matt 19:3
NRSV).[14] In his answer, Jesus fuses together what we call the first and
second creation accounts from Genesis. "Have you not read that the
one who made them at the beginning 'made them male and female,'
[Gen 1:27] and said, 'For this reason a man shall leave his father and
mother and be joined to his wife, and the two shall become one flesh'
[Gen 2:24]? So they are no longer two, but one flesh. Therefore what
God has joined together, let no one separate" (Matt 19:4–6). Jesus, in
other words, reads the sexual difference of humanity in Genesis 1:26–27

---

11. Ibid., 17.

12. According to James Brownson, Genesis is interested primarily in the ontological same-
ness of Adam and Eve and not also in their complementary difference (*Bible, Gender, Sexuality:
Reframing the Church's Debate on Same-Sex Relationships* [Grand Rapids: Eerdmans, 2013],
86–90). But as Ian Paul observes, this is wrong: "The explicit sense of the narrative is that the
animals are not 'suitable' since they are not the *adam*'s equal. But the equally powerful, implicit
sense of the narrative is that it would not be sufficient simply to form another *adam* from the
ground. This 'helper' needed to be equal *but opposite*. . . . The twin themes of similarity and
difference wind their way through the story like a double helix" (*Same-Sex Unions: The Key
Biblical Texts* [Cambridge: Grove, 2014], 8).

13. Ephraim Radner, "The Nuptial Mystery: The Historical Flesh of Procreation,"
in Roy R. Jeal, ed., *Human Sexuality and the Nuptial Mystery* (Eugene, OR: Cascade,
2010), 85–115.

14. Unless otherwise noted, all Scripture quotations are taken from the New Revised
Standard Version (NRSV).

(together with its emphasis on procreation)[15] alongside the affirmation of a bond of faithful union in 2:24. In this way, sexual difference and the meaning of marriage are pulled together and intertwined.

But this is not all. In the third place, the Augustinian tradition is not content to leave marriage defined solely by offspring and fidelity. Reading Scripture in light of Jesus Christ, this tradition points to a further explication of Genesis 2:24 in the New Testament, namely, that found in Ephesians 5. After quoting the conclusion that man and woman will leave their families of origin and cling to one another in fidelity, the author says, "This is a great mystery, and I am applying it to Christ and the church" (Eph 5:32). Already in the Old Testament, God's love for Israel had been compared to the marital bond (Isa 62:5; Jer 2–3; Ezek 16; Hos 1–3), but here that imagery becomes Christologically specific. It is the love of Christ for the church, a love that will culminate in an eschatological wedding feast (Rev 19:7, 9; cf. 21:2), that earthly couples image and in which they participate. The created good of marriage, marked by its openness to children and its faithful union, is taken up into Christian life and made to be an outward and visible sign of the love of God in Christ. In other words, the sacramental sign that marriage already is—for marriage already in the Old Testament is a sign of God's faithful love—is more sharply and definitively rendered in light of God's final self-disclosure in Jesus Christ.

Questions abound about this vision, but its basic outline seems defensible even in light of more recent biblical studies. Many historically minded readers would now want to emphasize a basic distinction between various strands of the Old and New Testaments on the theme of marriage. Whereas marriage and procreation in the Old Testament are easily understandable in terms of Israel's need to survive as an ethnic people, in the New Testament, because of the hope of resurrection from the dead, marriage and procreation are demoted, made optional, rendered—to put it mildly—less than central.[16] The desperate need to

---

15. That Jesus understands marriage to involve procreation is not explicit in Matthew, but is implicit in Luke 20:34–36, since Jesus says there that when the state of resurrection renders death no longer operative in human life, then marriage will no longer feature in human sociality. Why is marriage no longer necessary if death is no more? The most likely answer is that marriage enables procreation, and procreation is the necessary response to the problem of human mortality. Once mortality is dealt with in the eschaton, procreation, and thus marriage, are no longer needed.

16. On this trajectory, see Barry Danylak, *Redeeming Singleness: How the Storyline of Scripture Affirms the Single Life* (Wheaton, IL: Crossway, 2010).

determine one's own lineage is rendered moot in light of the hope that God will raise the dead. One can see this in Jesus' redefinition of family ties in terms of discipleship (Mark 3:31–35; 10:29–31) as well as in Paul's blunt preference for celibacy (1 Cor 7:7–8, 26, 38).

Yet by the time of the later or post-Pauline epistles as well as the so-called "Catholic" and Pastoral Epistles, marriage has received a robust Christological grounding (Eph 5:21–32; Col 3:18–19; 1 Peter 3:1–7; cf. 1 Tim 4:3), being firmly integrated into the life of discipleship, and the place of children in the Christian community is assumed (Eph 6:1–4; Col 3:20–21; cf. 1 Tim 2:15). Marriage, no less than celibacy and the decision to follow Jesus in going without biological offspring, can bear witness to the coming kingdom of God. The New Testament's final, canonical shape is what led to the Augustinian vision and is, in turn, illumined by that tradition: Marriage is a bond of male and female, ordered to procreation,[17] sealed in faithful union, and signifying Christ's love for the church.

Old Testament Homosexuality Texts

In light of this overarching vision of the place of marriage in Christian Scripture, the texts prohibiting same-sex sexual coupling gain their theological coherence. I will briefly discuss the primary ones here.[18]

Leviticus 18:22 and 20:13. These two texts are the most straight-forward prohibitions against same-sex sexual intercourse[19] in the Bible. Embedded in a portion of Leviticus often designated as the "Holiness Code" (chs. 17–26), the first takes the form of a negative command ("You shall not lie with a male as with a woman; it is an abomination"), while the latter underscores its seriousness as well as the penalty for its

---

17. This should not be taken to exclude, for example, infertile couples from marriage, since "the behavioral part of the reproductive process (coitus) remains ordered to procreation even when nonbehavioral factors—like low sperm count—prevent conception" (Sherif Girgis, Ryan T. Anderson, and Robert P. George, *What Is Marriage?: Man and Woman: A Defense* [New York: Encounter, 2012], 75 and the entirety of ch. 5).

18. I have chosen to omit discussion of Gen 19 here, since whatever its interpretation, it does not condemn all forms of same-sex sexual intimacy, which is precisely the ethical question being debated in the church today. For circumspect discussion, see Richard B. Hays, *The Moral Vision of the New Testament* (San Francisco: HarperSanFrancisco, 1996), 381.

19. Contra Saul Olyan, "'And with a Male You Shall Not Lie the Lying Down of a Woman': On the Meaning and Significance of Leviticus 18.22 and 20.13," *Journal of the History of Sexuality* 5/2 (1994): 179–206, the scope of this command would seem to include the actual act of penetration itself without excluding other forms of sexual intimacy.

violation ("If a man lies with a male as with a woman, both of them have committed an abomination; they shall be put to death; their blood is upon them"). In broad terms, the setting for these texts is priestly and covenantal: they describe what Israel's behavior is to be in light of God's initiative on her behalf. In a way that harks back to the first creation account in Genesis 1, Leviticus evinces an overall concern for order and purity.[20] And by stressing God's own holiness, the book ties this priestly concern to Israel's identity as the recipient of divine favor.[21]

Yet the definition of "purity" should be handled carefully here. One way of reading this passage would stress its "casuistic" (or "case law" as opposed to absolute) character, maintaining that the laws here are meant to distinguish Israel in a ritual, rather than a strictly *moral*, way from neighboring nations.[22] Sometimes this strategy is coupled with the claim that what Leviticus 18:22 and 20:13 envision is the specific practice of cultic or sacred prostitution.[23] On this reading, the prohibitions of same-sex relationships are limited in their application: When homosexuality is expressed in forms other than prostitution (for instance, in modern same-sex marriage) and when (for instance) Gentile Christians are freed from the historically specific need to share in Israel's differentiation from the nations, then these Levitical strictures against same-sex sexual coupling may be treated as no longer binding.[24]

But this interpretation overlooks at least two important features of the text. First, the language of Leviticus 18:22 uses the term "male" (*zakar*) together with the more generic term for "woman" (*ishshah*). Woodenly rendered, the passage reads: "And with a male you shall not lie with the lyings [or 'beds'] of a woman; it is an abomination." These words recall the two creation accounts of Genesis 1–2, in which God's creation of "male [*zakar*] and female [*neqevah*]" (who together comprise

---

20. This has been argued most memorably by Mary Douglas. See, e.g., *Purity and Danger: An Analysis of Concepts of Pollution and Taboo* (New York: Routledge, 1966, 2002).

21. Lev 18:2, setting the stage for what follows, implicitly describes the recipients of the commands as those who have already been delivered by God (cf. Ex 20:2).

22. L. William Countryman, *Dirt, Greed, and Sex: Sexual Ethics in the New Testament and Their Implications for Today*, 2nd ed. (Minneapolis: Fortress, 2007), 9–64.

23. Against this claim (found, e.g., in Robert A. J. Gagnon, *The Bible and Homosexual Practice: Texts and Hermeneutics* [Nashville: Abingdon, 2001], 130) is a great dearth of historical evidence, on which see Stephanie Lynn Budin, *The Myth of Sacred Prostitution in Antiquity* (Cambridge: Cambridge University Press, 2009).

24. Brownson, *Bible, Gender, Sexuality*, ch. 9.

adam, or "humankind") in 1:26–27 climaxes with the declaration in 2:24 that "a man [*ish*] leaves his father and his mother and clings to his wife [*ishshah*]." The canonical primacy of the Genesis narratives, coupled with the lack of situational specificity in the prohibition of Leviticus 18:22 (i.e., marital infidelity does not seem to be in view, which in any case has already been proscribed in 18:20), makes it likely that the latter is best heard as an echo of the Genesis creation stories. Put differently, Leviticus 18:22 does not present itself as "case law" that may vary with time and place. And, positively, the text also appears to allude to or echo the foundational narratives of Genesis. This suggests that what Leviticus 18:22 prohibits has wide application and is rooted in the divine act of creation. The text seems to have in view a violation of the creation order of "male and female." It is proscribing *all* same-sex coupling in light of the universal vision of the opening of Genesis, not merely one cultural form of that coupling.

Support for this reading may be found in the immediate context of the passage. After prohibiting a range of behaviors (e.g., adultery, child sacrifice, etc.), Leviticus 18 concludes by stressing that these commands are not limited to Israelites. The sojourner (*ger*) in Israel is addressed in 18:26 as subject to the same regulations of sexual conduct.[25] Not only is Israel expected to act hospitably toward the sojourner (as in 19:33–34), but the sojourner himself is to adhere to the norm of 18:22. As Walter Houston has put it:

> The laws and ethical perceptions in Judaism about sex were rooted in cultural features that were seen . . . to be common to all humankind, and they were therefore held by *gerim* Jews to apply to all human beings, whether *gerim* or not. Even if such perceptions did in fact divide Jews from Greeks, they did so, in the Jewish view, because of pagan corruption, not because the rules in question were designed to make Jews distinctive.[26]

---

25. Christopher R. Seitz, "The Ten Commandments: Positive and Natural Law and the Covenants Old and New—Christian Use of the Decalogue and Moral Law," in Christopher R. Seitz and Carl E. Braaten, eds., *I Am the Lord Your God: Christian Reflections on the Ten Commandments* (Grand Rapids: Eerdmans, 2005), 18–39, at 31.

26. Walter Houston, *Purity and Monotheism: Clean and Unclean Animals in Biblical Law*, JSOT Sup 140 (Sheffield: JSOT, 1993), 270, quoted in Seitz, "The Ten Commandments," 32, n. 19.

The stricture against same-sex sexual intercourse here in Leviticus 18:22 would appear to be rooted in creation, applicable in multiple situations (i.e., it is an absolute prohibition, not an instance of case law) and applicable even to non-Jews (and thus not reducible to a sociological rule for the maintenance of ethnic and theological boundaries). There is no clear reason to believe it does not prohibit any and all forms of same-sex intercourse.

New Testament Homosexuality Texts
Romans 1:26-27

According to the apostle Paul, humanity as a whole is afflicted with a common plight. Downwind of Adam's disobedience, sin and death have spread to all (Rom 5:12–14). Thus, at the beginning of his letter to the Romans, which summarizes much of Paul's message for an audience he had not yet met (1:8–15), after announcing the divine solution to the human plight (1:16–17), Paul includes a lengthy description of that plight (1:18–32 and continuing into ch. 2).

Paul's account falls roughly into two halves, corresponding to his earlier division of humanity into Jews and Greeks (1:16). On the one hand, he indicts characteristic Gentile patterns of idolatry and sinfulness (1:18–32), while he later—in what Richard Hays calls a "homiletical sting operation"[27]—turns the tables on his Jewish hearers who might be tempted to judge others and includes them in the same indictment (2:1–29). What is distinctive about Paul's portrait is not that he traces the origins of the human plight back to creation or that he is especially harsh in his polemics, but rather that he refuses to concede that God's own people Israel are innocent: "All, both Jews and Greeks, are under the power of sin" (3:9). For Paul, "there is no one who is righteous, not even one" (3:10), and only an intervention from beyond the human scene can offer any hope.

The backdrop for Paul's indictment is, however, equally crucial for an understanding of its precise contours. Paul appears to be telling a story rooted in Israel's Scripture and specifically in the Genesis creation narratives. In Romans 1:20 he mentions the creation, and in 1:25 he names God as the Creator. Furthermore, the imagery of

---

27. Hays, *The Moral Vision of the New Testament*, 389.

"birds or four-footed animals or reptiles" in 1:23 would appear to echo the Septuagint rendering of Genesis 1:30. Also in Romans 1:23 are multiple verbal links to Genesis 1:26: in both texts, the same words appear, rendered in English as "images," "resembling," "mortal human being," "birds," "four-footed animals," and "reptiles." And aside from these references, the wider context of Genesis 3 is evoked when Paul speaks of a "lie" (Rom 1:25; cf. Gen 3:5), "shame" (Rom 1:27; cf. Gen 3:1, 8), and the decree of "death" (Rom 1:32; cf. Gen 2:17; 3:4–5, 20, 22–23). In short, the story of God's making the world, God's giving a command to Adam, and Adam's subsequent "fall" form the backdrop for Paul's diagnosis of the human condition in Romans 1.[28]

All this becomes important for discerning what Paul means by "nature" (*phusis*) when he charges human beings with having abandoned "natural" sexual intercourse for "unnatural": "Their women exchanged natural intercourse for unnatural, and in the same way also the men, giving up natural intercourse with women, were consumed with passion for one another" (Rom 1:26–27). The creational and Adamic texture of the narrative fabric Paul is weaving means that "nature" should probably be interpreted in light of Genesis rather than (as some have argued) in terms of an individual's life history. In other words, Paul's canvas is cosmic and historical rather than personal. He is not describing particular persons who, experiencing and expressing desire for the opposite sex, nevertheless voluntarily abandon that knowledge and couple with those of the same sex in defiance of their own innate inclinations.[29] Rather, Paul is telescoping the fate of humanity viewed as a corporate whole in the wake of the fall. Seen as a collective, as those who recapitulate Adam's disobedience, humanity has turned away from how it was originally created to live and worship and has taken up different postures and practices instead. If humanity was created as "male and female"—if in fact that was humanity's "nature" in the beginning—then same-sex

28. Contra Dale Martin, *Sex and the Single Savior: Gender and Sexuality in Biblical Interpretation* (Louisville: Westminster John Knox, 2006), 52–53, the Adamic allusions in Romans 1 are widely recognized; cf. Morna D. Hooker, "Adam in Romans 1," *NTS* 6 (1959–60): 297–306; James D. G. Dunn, *The Theology of Paul the Apostle* (Grand Rapids: Eerdmans, 1997), 91–93. Cf. also Gagnon, *The Bible and Homosexual Practice*, 289–93.

29. Brownson, *Bible, Gender, Sexuality*, 228–29, 231 defends a modified version of John Boswell's position at this point (*Christianity, Social Tolerance, and Homosexuality: Gay People in Western Europe from the Beginning of the Christian Era to the Fourteenth Century* [Chicago: University of Chicago Press, 1980], 110–12).

coupling can only be judged, however common and acceptable it might have been in Paul's day, as theologically "unnatural."[30]

Hence Paul's location of same-sex sexual intercourse in a pattern of "exchange" begins to make theological sense. Paul's diagnosis of humanity is comprised of three interrelated movements. First, in Romans 1:21–23, he describes humanity as having exchanged the glory of God for images. Idolatry being a characteristically Gentile habit, we may be sure that Paul intends to target pagans in this passage. Yet his language also echoes the Greek text of Psalm 106:20, in which Israel's golden calf episode (Ex 32) is described as an "exchange" (using both *allasso* and *homoioma*, both of which appear in Rom 1:23). Thus Israel too is included in the sweep of Paul's narrative, with the implication that "the holy nation is itself deeply complicit in the idolatry and ungodliness that it prefers to ascribe to the Gentiles."[31]

Second, in Romans 1:24–25, the coming eschatological wrath of God (cf. 1 Thess 1:10) is described as *presently* visible, insofar as God gives humanity over to its own devices (cf. Rom 1:18). God's judgment takes the form of a surrender: God yields humanity to its self-inflicted bodily degradations because they have "exchanged" the worship of the Creator for the creature.

Finally, in 1:26–27, God gives humanity up to same-sex sexual coupling—which is itself described as an "exchange" that illustrates or symbolizes the previous two. Paul is giving same-sex intercourse a theological interpretation. Such sexual coupling is not simply transgression of an arbitrary divine norm; it is, rather, a departure from the structures of creation, on a par with what Israel enacted with its worship of a self-made golden idol. As Simon Gathercole has put it, "*Humanity* should be oriented toward *God* but turns in on itself (Rom. 1.25). *Woman* should be oriented toward *man*, but turns in on itself (Rom. 1.26). *Man* should be oriented toward *woman*, but turns in on itself (Rom. 1.27)."[32] What

---

30. As many have noted, Paul's use of *physis* has parallels in Jewish and Greco-Roman literature (e.g., Philo, *Spec. Leg.* 3.37–42; *Abr.* 133–41; Seneca, *Moral Epistles* 122.7; Plutarch, *Dialogue on Love*, 5). In some sense, Paul believes even pagans may share his "moral logic" in condemning same-sex sexual acts (cf. Rom 1:19), but the plain sense of Romans 1 indicates indebtedness to Genesis and its creation narrative and suggests *physis* is best interpreted primarily in that light.

31. Francis Watson, *Paul and the Hermeneutics of Faith*, 2nd ed. (London: Bloomsbury/T&T Clark, 2015), 349.

32. Simon J. Gathercole, "Sin in God's Economy: Agencies in Romans 1 and 7," in John M. G. Barclay and Simon J. Gathercole, eds., *Divine and Human Agency in Paul and His Cultural*

is foregrounded in the plain sense of the text is not a patriarchal commitment to hierarchical gender norms[33] nor a concern with "excessive" heterosexual lust,[34] but rather a departure from what Francis Watson has called the creational "interdependence" of male and female.[35]

The upshot of this threefold pattern of exchange is that Paul intends to condemn same-sex intercourse as a species of a wider theological phenomenon, namely, the "fall" from humanity's original design. In a manner not unlike what we see in Leviticus, Paul's view of same-sex sexuality appears to be stamped by his reading of God's design for human beings as found in the book of Genesis.

1 Corinthians 6:9 and 1 Timothy 1:10

Paul's other references to same-sex coupling may be treated more briefly, inasmuch as they are not as clear as Romans 1 nor as central to the church's longstanding opposition to same-sex intercourse.

First Corinthians 6:9–11 is what is often referred to as a baptismal passage, describing the new identity of the Corinthian believers in contradistinction from their pre-Christian past. They are the "washed," having been transferred into the sphere of Christ's lordship and cleansed by the Spirit (6:11). In context, this is an argument for why the Corinthians should not assimilate to their surrounding pagan society by taking one another to secular courts (6:1–6). If God has wrested the Corinthians out of a pagan past, then they are competent to resolve their own internal disputes (6:2–3). And in order to reinforce their grasp of their own identity as a new people, Paul lists a sampling of the pagan identities that the Corinthians formerly possessed: "Fornicators, idolaters, adulterers, male prostitutes, sodomites, thieves, the greedy,

---

Environment (London: T&T Clark, 2007), 158–72, at 163, 164. For a historical argument that female as well as male homosexuality is in view in Rom 1:26–27, see Bernadette Brooten, *Love Between Women: Early Christian Response to Female Homoeroticism* (Chicago: University of Chicago Press, 1996), 59–60. If Paul is in fact reflecting on Genesis, the relative rarity of female homosexuality in the ancient world matters little to his argument. His bearings are taken from Scripture, not empirical observation as such.

33. As argued in Brooten, *Love Between Women*; Martin, *Sex and the Single Savior*.

34. As argued in David E. Frederickson, "Natural and Unnatural Use in Romans 1:24–27," in David Balch, ed., *Homosexuality, Science, and the "Plain Sense" of Scripture* (Grand Rapids: Eerdmans, 2000), 197–222.

35. Francis Watson, "The Authority of the Voice: A Theological Reading of 1 Cor 11.2–16," *NTS* 46 (2000): 520–36, at 524, n. 8: "In [same-sex] relationships, Paul may have believed, woman attempts to be 'apart from man' and man attempts to be 'apart from woman.'"

drunkards, revilers, robbers—none of these will inherit the kingdom of God" (6:9–10). This warning serves to buttress the Corinthians' confidence in their status as the newly baptized, even as it also functions as an admonition not to fall back into their former way of life and so endanger their eschatological vindication.[36]

The reason this passage is invoked in discussions of homosexuality is because of the two terms that the NRSV renders as "male prostitutes" and "sodomites." This translation is not ideal, as will become clear. On the one hand, the Greek term lying behind "male prostitutes" is *malakoi*, which is a loan word from Latin meaning "soft." It is used elsewhere in the New Testament to refer to clothing (Matt 11:8; Luke 7:25), though here in 1 Corinthians 6:9 it is, as it is in many other extant Greek texts, a substantive. Such a usage was a commonplace in Paul's era; multiple Greek authors attest that *malakos* was a typical way to designate a man who flouted traditional male gender norms and behaved in ways that showed passivity or various shades of "femininity."[37] For this reason, it was a term readily applicable to men who were penetrated in sexual intercourse with other men.[38] On the other hand, the term to which *malakos* is paired, "sodomites"—which other translations have rendered variously as "sexual perverts," "homosexuals," "anyone practicing homosexuality," among other things—is *arsenokoites* in Greek. A compound word (comprised of, literally, "male" and "bed"), it is not attested in any extant Greek texts prior to Paul. It does, however, have a strong verbal connection to the Septuagint renderings of both Leviticus 18:22 and 20:13, where both halves of the compound are used. This has led many scholars to suggest that Paul probably coined the term himself in dependence on the Greek text of Leviticus.[39] And if that is the case, then this text, like Romans 1, points to the deep embeddedness

---

36. Alistair May, *The Body for the Lord: Sex and Identity in 1 Corinthians 5–7*, LNTS (London: T&T Clark, 2004), ch. 5.

37. The term could indicate anything from men who wore feminine garments, accepted castration, or were simply oversexed and lacked self-control from the perspective of the critic (see, e.g., Aristotle, *Nicomachean Ethics* 7.4.2; Plutarch, *On Moral Virtue* 447B).

38. Ovid, *Ars Amatoria* 1.505–24.

39. Robin Scroggs, *The New Testament and Homosexuality: Contextual Background for Contemporary Debate* (Philadelphia: Fortress, 1983), 83, 108. This means, in turn, that Paul chose not to use other commonly accepted terms for same-sex coupling in the form of pederasty. Had he intended to limit his focus to that ancient institution, coining a new word would not have served his purposes.

of Paul's opposition to same-sex sexual acts in Israel's Scripture and, hence, in creation.

Arsenokoites shows up once more in the New Testament, in the epistle of 1 Timothy. Structurally, its context resembles 1 Corinthians 6:9–11: the word appears in a vice list. However, the list of fourteen vices here seems to correspond to the two halves of the Decalogue (Ex 20:1–21). "Lawless and disobedient, . . . godless and sinful, . . . unholy and profane" (1 Tim 1:9) contradict the first table, while "those who kill their father or mother" (fifth commandment), "murderers" (sixth commandment), "fornicators, sodomites [*arsenokoitais*]," (seventh commandment), "slave traders" (eighth commandment), and "liars, perjurers" (ninth commandment) all violate the second table. The author's purpose seems not so much to offer moral directives but to paint a representative portrait (cf. "and whatever else is contrary to the sound teaching" [1 Tim 1:10]) of the kind of societal breakdown that even pagans can recognize as unhealthy. The fact that the author includes *arsenokoites* under the Decalogue's rubric of adultery may point to its scope: Not only are certain unvirtuous or exploitative instances of homosexuality condemned here but any and all of its instances—insofar as *all* sexual immorality is understood to fall under the prohibition of Exodus 20:14 (cf. Lev 18:20; Deut 22:22).

A Christian Theology of Homosexuality

Any effort to construct an orthodox Christian theology in response to contemporary questions must be responsive to the "pressure" exerted by the two-testament canon of Christian Scripture.[40] The question confronting the churches at present is *how* to receive the pressure of the scriptural material just surveyed. On the one hand is the position represented in the *Catechism of the Catholic Church* which states: "Basing itself on Sacred Scripture, which presents homosexual acts as acts of grave depravity, tradition has always declared that 'homosexual acts are intrinsically disordered.'"[41] In this traditional understanding, any and all same-sex sexually intimate behavior, regardless of its intention or

---

40. See C. Kavin Rowe, "Biblical Pressure and Trinitarian Hermeneutics," *Pro Ecclesia* 11 (2002): 295–312.

41. *Catechism of the Catholic Church* 2357, http://www.vatican.va/archive/ccc_css/archive/catechism/p3s2c2a6.htm.

context, is ruled out (just as any and all sexual intimacy *in general*, even between persons of the opposite sex, is also ruled out, save in marriage). On the other hand, many recent Christian discussions of homosexuality stress that *some* forms of same-sex sexual behavior (e.g., exploitative or violent ones) must of course be prohibited, but consensual, faithful forms of same-sex sexuality—such as what we see now in Western countries in the form of same-sex marriages—should be blessed and affirmed in the churches precisely because of (rather than in spite of) certain strands of biblical teaching.

One of the best discussions of this latter view is by the Anglican theological ethicist Robert Song, whom I have already quoted above. Song offers a theologically robust rationale for a revision to the traditional Augustinian view of marriage and sexuality. Here is his thesis in brief:

> According to the Christian narrative of the redemption of the world in Christ the Church has no ultimate stake in the propagation of the species or the indefinite continuation of society outside of Christ . . . Sex BC is not the same as sex AD. . . . Life in the community of the resurrection is life in which the hope of children is no longer intrinsic to the community's identity.[42]

In other words, with the coming of Christ, the axis of history shifted (Mark 1:14–15; 1 Cor 10:11). The need of the believing community to procreate in the face of death is gone, since Christ has defeated death. In the resurrection, when death is abolished, Jesus says that "they neither marry nor are given in marriage" (Matt 22:30). There would be no need for marriage and child-rearing in a world without death. Therefore, since Christians believe that that decisive defeat of death has happened already in the events of Good Friday and Easter Sunday, we are those who can sanction—and indeed celebrate—sexual partnerships that are not oriented to bearing children.

Song's argument is based on dense, rich exegesis of the Genesis creation narratives, Jesus' teaching about marriage (Mark 10; Matt 19, 22), and the apostolic preference for celibacy (1 Cor 7). He seeks to integrate all this material in a theologically coherent synthesis by pointing

---

42. Song, *Covenant and Calling*, x, 18.

to the radical, apocalyptic disjuncture between the norms of creation, in which marriage bears an intrinsic relation to child-bearing and the new eschatological creation, in which celibacy (and marriage?) points to a deathless kingdom in which procreation is no longer necessary in the way it formerly was.

When one couples this kind of theologically coherent account with the recognition that many self-identified gay and lesbian people today experience their sexual orientation as something that enables them to form life-giving bonds with the apposite (but not the opposite) sex,[43] then we can begin to feel the powerful tug of the revisionist case. If certain people are unlikely to be able to love someone of the opposite sex in a way that would make traditional marriage viable for them,[44] and if they *are* likely to be able to love someone of the same sex in a permanent, faithful, stable way,[45] and if the gospel has opened the door to contemplate vocations that do not include bearing children, then it would seem that there is good reason to question the Augustinian consensus and make space in the church for the celebration and solemnization of same-sex partnerships.

In my judgment, however, there is good reason to question Song's way of seeking to receive the pressure of Christian Scripture today. In the first place, his argument would seem to depend on teasing apart the canonical voices on marriage and sexuality. By prioritizing one particular strand of the New Testament, Song loses the linkage between the three Augustinian goods of marriage. His thesis makes very good sense of what Paul says in 1 Corinthians 7 about the goodness—and indeed preferability—of the celibate life. But he has trouble offering a theological account of why marriage would still, even after the advent of Jesus Christ, be a legitimate Christian vocation. Although he claims

---

43. I have often been struck by Eugene Rogers's way of putting this point: "For gay and lesbian people, the right sort of otherness is unlikely to be represented by someone of the opposite sex, because only someone of the apposite, not opposite, sex will get deep enough into the relationship to expose one's vulnerabilities and inspire the trust that healing requires" ("Sanctified Unions: An Argument for Gay Marriage," *The Christian Century* [June 15, 2004]: 26–29, at 28).

44. It is probably too early to say whether this way of putting it will hold up in light of further psychological research. Our knowledge of the malleability of sexual desire and "orientation" is still in its relative infancy. See, e.g., Lisa M. Diamond, *Sexual Fluidity: Understanding Women's Love and Desire* (Cambridge, MA: Harvard University Press, 2009).

45. Jeffrey John, *Permanent, Faithful, Stable: Christian Same-Sex Marriage*, 2nd ed. (London: Dartman, Longman, and Todd, 2013).

that procreative "marriage can still be modeled on the relationship of Christ and the Church," he ultimately concludes that it is "redundant."[46] This would seem to be a symptom of prioritizing the kind of vision we see in 1 Corinthians 7, where celibacy is elevated and marriage relegated to the status of "permissible," at the expense of the remainder of the New Testament canon (e.g., Eph 5–6), in which marriage is seen as a more overt *complement* to celibacy. Putting it differently, Song's thesis proceeds as if the eschaton—in which death is finally and irreversibly defeated—had already arrived in its fullness. But the full breadth of the New Testament canon makes clear that, although Christ's resurrection represents the dawn of the new creation (Rev 1:5), death has not yet been completely eradicated (1 Cor 15:20–28). And this opens the door for later apostolic voices, such as the author of Ephesians, to explore ways in which marriage and child-rearing are forms of discipleship in and of themselves, rather than simply way stations on the road to an imminent end. Simply stated, Song can easily explain why Paul recommends celibacy in 1 Corinthians 7; I don't see that he can so easily explain why Ephesians is so interested in marriage and children as part and parcel of a Christian life.

Beyond those considerations, we may also wonder whether the Bible's construal of marriage and sexuality invites us to question some of our most basic modern assumptions about what constitutes human identity. Song's argument trades on the notion that there is a class of persons—"gay and lesbian people"—whose sexual desires are more or less permanently directed to members of the same sex and who, consequently, experience themselves as called to express that sexual desire by forming traditional marriage-like relationships of fidelity and sexual expression with one another. All of this represents, arguably, the triumph of the movement for gay and lesbian rights in the modern era. Prior to the cultural triumph of that movement, what received ethical attention in the Christian tradition were same-sex sexual acts. Regardless of whether there was any grasp of an inborn inclination toward same-sex sexual acts in premodern cultures,[47] it is clear that there was nothing like

---

46. Song, *Covenant and Calling*, 20, 15, 27.

47. See David Halperin, *One Hundred Years of Homosexuality* (New York: Rutledge, 1990), 3–40; Holt N. Parker, "The Myth of the Heterosexual: Anthropology and Sexuality for Classicists," *Arethusa* 34 (2001): 313–62. Paul, at least, in Rom 1:27 seems to envision some kind of mutuality ("consumed with passion for one another"), but whether he had in

a contemporary understanding of a homosexual person, whose romantic and sexual desires and acts are bound up with a publicly recognizable identity and embedded in a thriving subculture. And, consequently, there was nothing like a condemnation—nor an advocacy for—gay and lesbian people as such. When Thomas Aquinas, for example, treated the question of same-sex sexual acts, he discussed it under the rubric of lust.[48] It would only be later, in the wake of the so-called Sexual Revolution and the pitched battle for the recognition of the existence of such a class of human beings as "gay people," that Western cultures (among others) came to contemplate the possibility that there might be such a thing as a fixed inclination toward same-sex coupling and that it might not be merely a symptom of perversion or illness.[49]

One could easily view this as a cultural and societal advance, insofar as treating those who perform same-sex sexual acts as motivated by love seems vastly preferable to treating them as flagrantly oversexed or simply sick. Yet we must also ask whether something crucial to Christian theology is lost in the process—a question that an argument like Song's does not explore. Once "gay identity" has been established in the way I've described, it becomes difficult, for instance, to comprehend the gospel's demand that all of our assumed identities be relativized in light of the "new name" (cf. Rev 2:17) given to each of us in baptism: "There is no longer Jew or Greek, there is no longer slave or free, there is no longer male and female; for all of you are one in Christ Jesus" (Gal 3:28). Although there is a sense in which Christians go on belonging to the races, social classes, and constructed identities in which they lived prior to baptism (Paul can still distinguish between Jews and Gentiles in the Roman church, for instance [Rom 15:7–13]), there is a more powerful sense in which Christians are no longer tethered to their previous identities: "It is no longer I who live, but it is Christ who lives in me" (Gal 2:20; cf. 1 Cor 12:2: "When you *were* pagans . . ."). How does an argument like Song's encourage gay Christians to *interrogate* their

---

mind anything like contemporary same-sex "unions" or "marriages" is doubtful (see Thomas K. Hubbard, "Peer Homosexuality," in Thomas K. Hubbard, ed., *A Companion to Greek and Roman Sexualities* [Chichester: Blackwell, 2014], 128–49, many of whose examples [e.g., Achilles and Patroclus] may not quite fit the thesis he wishes to advance).

48. *Summa Theologiae* IIae Q.154, arts. 11–12.

49. See David F. Greenberg, *The Construction of Homosexuality* (Chicago: University of Chicago Press, 1990).

experienced, socially constructed identities, to treat those identities as in need of purification and transformation, not just "affirmation" and "expression"? For me, it is difficult to see that it does.[50]

Finally, Song's argument seems to ignore entirely the possibility of permanent, faithful bonds that are not sexual, and it is to that possibility that I wish to turn in the final portion of this essay.

The Calling of Spiritual Friendship

To return to the beginning, what is a gay Christian to *do*, positively, in light of all of this? Whatever else we may say in answer to that question, we must insist that gay Christians are called—like all other believers—to love and be loved. For Christians like Robert Song, the conclusion seems to be that in order to love fully and completely, gay Christians must be able to express that love through acts of same-sex genital sexuality. It would be, one gathers from arguments like Song's, a kind of cruel gnosticism to encourage gay Christians to love with their hearts and minds but to withhold their bodies from one another.

Yet one wonders whether, in the words of Christopher Roberts, "we cannot imagine existing in our culture without the haven of an erotic partnership because our capacity to belong together in more chaste ways is so limited."[51] Is our longing to bless our gay and lesbian friends with marriage a sign that we have located permanent, faithful intimacy more or less exclusively in marriage, in such a way that we can no longer imagine it existing elsewhere?

The scriptural material, while not (mostly) in the form of prohibitions or commandments, would appear to rule out any and all gay sex in the lives of Christian believers. But this is not the same thing as saying

---

50. What Roberts, *Creation and Covenant*, 197, says about Graham Ward's arguments I would also say about Song's: "He assumes where there is [sexual] desire there must be theologically significant difference [between straight and gay people] and does not interrogate same-sex desire at any point, asking if it might be postlapsarian in origin and hence, unlike sexual difference, testifying to sin and not to ontologically significant differences. It is as if Augustine's argument against the Pelagians, to the effect that human desires must be subject to theological judgment and cannot simply be trusted for their goodness, had never been made." I would simply add that if we urge gay and lesbian Christians to interrogate their sexual identities thus (cf. Michael W. Hannon, "Against Heterosexuality," *First Things* [March 2014]: 27–34), we must ask the same of *all* Christians who self-identify as "straight," "bisexual," or whatever. Gay Christians must query their felt identities and experiences precisely because all Christians must, in light of the gospel's relativization of any identity other than "Christ."

51. Roberts, *Creation and Covenant*, 227.

that Scripture prohibits bonds of fidelity and love between members of the same sex. As a recent document published by the Catholic Bishops' Conference of England and Wales has put it, "Insofar as the homosexual orientation can lead to sexual activity which excludes openness to the generation of new human life and the essential sexual complementarity of man and woman, it is, *in this particular and precise sense only*, objectively disordered."[52] What is *not* disordered is the desire on the part of a man to love another man—or a woman, another woman—with depth, faithfulness, and greater devotion than what one often finds in anemic versions of "friendship" on offer in contemporary culture.

The theologian and Episcopal priest Kathryn Greene-McCreight has written:

> The church could indeed go so far as to acknowledge the "goods" which can come from homosexual relationships. The self-giving of two individuals in a committed relationship can, after all, reflect the sacrificial love of Christ. The contribution to the wider community which may come of homosexual relationships can also be acknowledged as a "good," such as the time and talents given in service to the church and the love and care rendered to the adopted children of gay and lesbian couples. The church can recognize as a "good" the pastoral, preaching, and teaching ministries of gays and lesbians which further the church's witness to Christ. To recognize these goods, however, is not to sanction the sexual activity which may (or may not) accompany such relationships.[53]

It is this distinction—between the love of persons of the same sex and the sexual intercourse that they may be inclined towards—that is crucial. The latter is the target of biblical condemnations, while the former is viewed as a good.

But in what form can same-sex love be a good? No doubt there are many possible answers to that question. For myself, I have increasingly

52. Catholic Bishops' Conference of England and Wales, *Cherishing Life* (London: Catholic Truth Society, 2004), 111, emphasis mine.
53. Kathryn Greene-McCreight, "The Logic of the Interpretation of Scripture and the Church's Debate over Sexual Ethics," in David L. Balch, ed., *Homosexuality, Science, and the "Plain Sense" of Scripture* (Grand Rapids: Eerdmans, 1999), 242–60, at 259.

come to understand my calling as a gay Christian to be one of "spiritual friendship." In contrast to relationships of convenience or minimal commitment, in which personal autonomy and the ability to move at whim are prized above all, I am learning to pursue deeper, more permanent sorts of bonds with friends of the same (and opposite) sex, all the while maintaining my commitment to sexual abstinence (or, as I prefer, "celibacy").[54] In this, I believe myself to be standing in a venerable Christian tradition.

Throughout much of Christian history, in both the Christian East and West, friendship was capable of solemnization, celebrated with public recognition, and strengthened by mutual promissory bonds. For instance, the twelfth-century monk Aelred, who served as the abbot of Rievaulx Abbey in the north of England from 1147 to 1167, famously elevated the love of friendship, viewing it as a form of kinship with its own kind of durability and obligations. It is probable that Aelred himself, prior to his entrance into the monastic life, was sexually involved with male partners.[55] He writes in veiled terms about youthful dalliances and losing his virginity. Yet by the time he wrote his famous dialogue *Spiritual Friendship*, he had bound himself to the teachings of the church and foresworn sexual liaisons. The man who could describe a friend as one "to whom you so join and unite yourself that you mix soul with soul" and one whom you could embrace "in the kiss of unity, with the sweetness of the Holy Spirit flowing over you" had apparently given up sex with persons of the same sex.[56] What Aelred called "spiritual friendship" was a form of same-sex intimacy that did not sanction its genital expression of erotic passion but rather—to borrow a later psychological vocabulary—sublimated or transmuted it.

In one of his letters, C. S. Lewis suggests that rather than fixating

---

54. I have written at length about this in *Spiritual Friendship: Finding Love in the Church as a Celibate Gay Christian* (Grand Rapids: Brazos, 2015).

55. On Aelred as "gay," see Boswell, *Christianity, Social Tolerance, and Homosexuality*, 222–23. Compare also, though, the discussion in Brian Patrick McGuire, *Friendship and Community: The Monastic Experience, 350–1250* (Ithaca and London: Cornell University Press, 1988, 2010), 302–304 which critiques Boswell for greater confidence in his interpretation than Aelred's texts warrant. In the end, however, McGuire agrees that Aelred experienced same-sex attraction: "Insofar as Aelred indicated that he had to cope with a sexual desire for other men, Boswell's interpretation captures one aspect of the special quality of the earlier part of the twelfth century," 303.

56. Aelred of Rievaulx, *De speculo caritatis*, as quoted in Boswell, *Christianity, Social Tolerance, and Homosexuality*, 225.

on the psychological roots of same-sex attraction and seeking to pinpoint its origins, modern-day Christians would do well to focus their attention more on what the person experiencing same-sex attraction is capable of offering to the church in which she finds herself:

> Our speculations on the cause of the abnormality are not what matters and we must be content with ignorance. The disciples were not told why (in terms of efficient cause) the man was born blind (Jn. IX 1–3): only the final cause, that the works of God [should] be made manifest in him. This suggests that in homosexuality, as in every other tribulation, those works can be made manifest: i.e. that every disability conceals a vocation, if only we can find it, [which] will "turn the necessity to glorious gain."

Lewis goes on later in the letter to describe "a certain pious [homosexual man who] believed that his necessity *could* be turned to spiritual gain: that there were certain kinds of sympathy and understanding, a certain social role which [only he could play]."[57] To ask that question—about what particular role a celibate gay or lesbian believer can play in the church—is to ask how the special temptation or weakness or fallenness that same-sex attraction is may come to be understood as the site or occasion or circumstance in which a vocation to love is discovered. I suggest that we might follow Lewis's lead today.

---

57. Sheldon Vanauken, *A Severe Mercy* (New York: Harper & Row, 1987), 147.

WILLIAM LOADER

I warm to Wesley's sharing his own experience of being gay. I also fully respect his decisions in the light of it. Everyone's story is different, but the more people share their experiences in this way, the more difficult it becomes to deny that this is how it is for some people. This has been a major shift in discourse about same-sex relations, so that it has become increasingly difficult to dub such orientation a perversion or a pathology.

I also appreciate the way Wesley draws attention to the need to interpret Scripture from its center, namely Christ. Like Stephen, he affirms Augustine's view of marriage and sees it as the result of approaching Scripture from this centering perspective. At the same time he invites us to look beyond Augustine to the strength of his portrayal as a scriptural theology of marriage. In this Genesis 1:26–28, the command to procreate, takes pride of place, but then so does fidelity, which he finds expressed in the second creation account in Genesis 2:4–25. I would argue that it is more than fidelity. Rightly, Wesley notes how Jesus connects the two in his response to the question about the legitimacy of divorce (Matt 19:1–6; Mark 10:1–9). He then follows Augustine in pointing to the use of Genesis 2:24 in Ephesians 5, making marriage an outward and visible sign of God's faithful love in Christ, a sacrament as it now stands in Roman Catholic tradition.

I find myself in broad agreement with Wesley in his interpretation of Leviticus 18:22 and 20:13. He reads them canonically, suggesting they are influenced by the creation stories in Genesis. I am more inclined to see them as belonging to older independent legal material, but certainly they would then have been read in the light of their wider literary context. With Wesley, I am not convinced that they had only limited application. My own research on attitudes towards sexuality in the four centuries leading up to the end of the first Christian century shows that the prohibitions were understand in an absolute way and were also extended to same-sex relations among women.[1] It became one of the markers Jews used to distinguish themselves from cultures around about, as already in Leviticus 18, and then in Jewish literature, right through to Paul's exposition of the world's sin in Romans 1.

On Romans 1, I also find much common ground with Wesley. Clearly Paul has the creation stories in mind, both in his depiction of idolatry and images of animals and when he speaks about same-sex relations. Here I would note in particular the language of "male" and "female" (Rom 1:26–27), which must be alluding to Genesis 1:27. When, however, Wesley writes, "In short, the story of God's making the world, God's giving a command to Adam, and Adam's subsequent 'fall' form the backdrop for Paul's diagnosis of the human condition in Romans 1," I would want to offer some correction or at least qualification. Of course, for Paul all sin traces its origin to the fall, and the sin in Romans 1 is no exception. Paul's argument in Romans 1, however, is not that the particular sin of having a perverted sexual response derives from the fall, but that it derives from having a perverted response to God. One perversion, as he sees it, produces another.

I very much concur with Wesley's understanding of "contrary to nature" in Romans 1:26–27 as alluding to what God created people to be. We miss the point of Paul's argument if we think he is speaking only about what seems to most people not natural or a little odd. For Paul, as for Philo and other Jews of the time, contrary to nature is contrary to God's created order. The allusion is to Genesis 1:27, reflected, I suggest, in the terms used, as noted above. There is more, however, to the passage than Wesley's brief comments bring out. Paul is not just writing about acts or even intent to act, but about what he sees as a twisted orientation which is a manifestation of a twisted response to God. Something has gone wrong with the mind. It is darkened (Rom 1:21) and unfit (1:28). Its orientation, not just its actions, is contrary to God's creation. For on the basis of his reading of Genesis 1:27, Paul, like other Jews of his time, believes that human beings are only male or female—in our terms, heterosexual. Anything other than that is a perversion. This is then the logic of those who, espousing Paul's view, offer redemptive therapy to help gay people be restored to the way God created them to be.

---

1. William Loader, *The New Testament on Sexuality* (Grand Rapids: Eerdmans, 2012) (=*NTS*), 22–33.

My own reading of the two terms which appear in the lists of 1 Corinthians 6:9–11 and 1 Timothy 1:9–10 is close to Wesley's and concludes that on the balance of probability, the words do refer to active and passive partners in male same-sex relations.[2]

In Wesley's discussion of a theology of marriage, I found myself agreeing that one cannot minimise, let alone eliminate, procreation from marriage on grounds that the promise of life beyond death renders it redundant. There do seem to have been some believers at Corinth who believed that we should all live now as we will in the world to come, namely as celibates, since in the age to come sexual relations and marriage cease.[3] Paul counters them in 1 Corinthians 7. Wesley rightly points to the sense of New Testament writers that we have not yet arrived at that state and that we live in the world of God's created order which includes male and female and marriage as the context for sexual relations. In that sense Paul defends marriage as part of God's creation.

A key argument in Wesley's paper is that prior to modern times, the focus of disapproval was on same-sex acts. People did not have the notion of some people having a same-sex orientation as their natural state. I believe that this is incorrect. Plato certainly knew of theories about sexual orientation, such as the one espoused by Aristophanes which offers an explanation of why some women are attracted to women, some men to men, and the rest of us to the opposite sex (Plato *Symposium* 189–193). This was known. Philo cited it (*Contempl.* 57–63) and, like Plato, did not agree, but with more substantial grounds, for it contradicted Genesis. God created only male and female. Paul similarly assumes that all people are male or female and that their natural orientation is towards the opposite sex. This, he argues, was distorted not because of Adam's fall but as a result of a perverted understanding of God, producing in them a perverted orientation towards members of their own sex.

Wesley's final section on spiritual friendship is a welcome contribution to the discussion, already so well enunciated in his book.[4] The sexualization of discussion of male-male and female-female friendship has been most unhelpful. In close, committed, lifelong friendships, there

2. *NTS*, 326–34.
3. *NTS* 453–67.
4. Wesley Hill, *Spiritual Friendship* (Grand Rapids: Brazos, 2015).

is inevitably a sexual component—in touch, in embrace, for instance, as he acknowledges. This is healthy and wholesome. To embrace this option will mean for some that they draw a boundary: the expression of sexual feelings must stop at some point, usually at least at the point of genital sex, but often also at other passionate expressions such as the kiss or bodily fondling. This can become a little complex when following the lead of Jesus that we turn our focus not just to acts but also to attitudes, such as in his saying about adultery (Matt 5:28) and on inner attitudes (Mark 7:21–23). Christian ethics has always directed us to the inner and not just the outer. Sex is not the center of such friendships, and its implicitness and presence are usually manageable.

Wesley's discussion does, however, raise the issue of boundaries. Most believers today uphold marriage as lifelong commitment to love and fidelity and as a context appropriate for the bearing and the bringing up of children. Roman Catholics deem it a sacrament, following Augustine, but even without that category, it is a relationship which can be seen to share in, reveal, and affirm God's love for us in Christ. Marriage matters also because by it, people declare to society that they are a unit and ask for respect and support, and this comes in both informal and formal legislative ways. All of this is true also of people who marry but have no prospect of bearing and bringing up children for various reasons or who, for an extended period, sometimes years, will not do so. I submit that we should not see their marriages as any less of a marriage for that reason. Nor should we, in the logic of Augustine's model and formal Roman Catholic rulings, require that they not use contraception, that is, that they remain effectively celibate in marriage. And certainly it seems absurd to go to the extreme of limiting sexual union to fertile days, banning it from the rest of the menstrual cycle and during pregnancy.

Our understandings of marriage have indeed changed, and I believe these changes are not contrary to biblical principles. They are, of course, in many ways different from the understanding of marriage of biblical times, when fathers arranged marriages, premarital dating was minimal, there was no effective contraception, adultery mandated divorce, and men married women close to half their age and were deemed the head and superior (making marriage a suitable image for Christ's headship over the church in Ephesians). Notwithstanding these significant differences, however, the divine love which redeems and sustains us continues to provide the model for the love which is to characterize the marriage relationship and is also its inspiration. Out of such love, life and love, in turn, are born, whether in procreation or in other creative ways.

The question which Wesley's sharing and reflections raise acutely is: If, contrary to the anthropology of Paul and Jews of his day, we believe that same-sex orientation is natural for some and not itself a manifestation of a perverted state of mind, are there grounds for excluding such people from forming lifelong, committed relationships of the kind described above as constituting marriage? The sticking point has less to do with marriage itself than with a prior question: Is it a sin in such contexts to give full sexual expression to one's love in intimate closeness? If we determine that it is not a sin for heterosexual people to do so who are infertile or choosing not to procreate, why would it be so for people with a same-gender orientation?

Ultimately the ground for saying no is the prohibition in Leviticus. People have rightly revisited other prohibitions, including Jesus' prohibition of divorce and remarriage, and chosen alternative paths based on insights and understandings drawn from the center of Scripture and from contemporary reflection. The early church found itself having to do so very early on circumcision, food, and purity laws. I see no substantial grounds for upholding the Leviticus prohibitions in our day, but in saying that I do so with respect for why they are there and for the assumptions they reflect about the heterosexuality of all human beings. Changing that assumption (that all human beings are heterosexual) has, to my mind, to have implications for how we read both Leviticus and Paul. Scripture deserves our humility and respect even when we find ourselves, as Jesus did, needing to override some of its provisions with others at its heart which are more weighty. That generated heat and controversy then, and the current discussion is no different.

It has been a privilege to have teamed up with my fellow contributors in this volume and experienced a genuine sense of fellowship amid difference and a mutual respect for each other's positions.

MEGAN K. DEFRANZA

It is an honor to respond to such thoughtful and godly men in this book project, Dr. Wesley Hill being no exception. He has done the conservative Christian community great service in his willingness to share his own journey here, in his books, and on his blog. It is men and women such as Wes who are changing the nature of this conversation—people who choose costly discipleship and still have not experienced a change in orientation from gay to straight.

Dr. Hill articulates a needed corrective to the assumption that "same-sex attraction" (SSA) is about sex. To be gay is to desire to know and be known in the biblical sense but also in the broader sense of romantic relational love. Of course, gay and straight people alike can shrink love to faceless, self-centered sex. Still, we dishonor the humanity of our gay friends and family members when we caricature their love as lust.

We need Wesley Hill, as we need all of God's children—each of whom has gifts for the building up of the body of Christ. Hill is honest about the pain of growing up gay in church, where the pain of prohibition can be compounded by the deafening silence of churches that would rather deny the existence of some of their members than offer welcome, pastoral care, and the invitation to serve.

Standing in this gap, Hill is working for change. In this he has my deep respect and admiration, but this does not mean that we see eye to eye on the ways to respond to the current crisis. Hill recommends recovering aspects of the tradition of religious celibacy, encouraging gay men and women to see the benefit in their same-sex attraction, the good that exists in a desire to love another human being regardless of their sex or gender. Following the example of Jesus and Paul, Hill believes he is called to celibacy. But where Jesus admitted, "Not everyone can accept this word, but only those to whom it has been given" (Matt 19:11), and Paul conceded that not all have the same gift (1 Cor 7:7), Hill teaches that those who cannot enter into heterosexual marriages are *de facto* "called" to a life of celibacy.

As my own contribution to this volume details the ways in which I read the biblical canon and specific texts differently, I will limit my response to a few ideas upon which much seems to depend: the centrality of Adam and Eve, the authority of Augustine, and spiritual friendship in place of marriage.

Adam, Eve, and Augustine

Hill's interpretation of Adam and Eve influences all that follows:

> First, in terms of their canonical placement and their subsequent prominence in the Gospels (Matt 19:1–6; Mark 10:1–9), the Genesis narratives retain pride of place in any effort to describe a canonical biblical theology of marriage. Whatever else humanity's creation in the image of God as "male and female" might mean in the first creation account, it is clear enough that it is immediately related to the divine blessing of giving birth to offspring. (p. 128)

As I have argued in this volume and at length elsewhere, Adam and Eve (male and female) can just as easily be read as the human majority rather than the moral model for all people. Genesis 1 describes creation in broad brush strokes, omitting a number of God's good works—particularly those which blend general categories (amphibians who bridge land and sea, dawn/dusk which blend morning and day/evening and night, intersex people who combine male and female). We do not consider the former to be products of the fall. What then is the logic for interpreting the latter as other than God's plan? Even in the gospel passage which Dr. Hill cites above, Jesus acknowledged that God made them "male and female" and then went on to speak of those who did not fit those categories—naturally born eunuchs—people whose bodies are not exclusively male or female (Matt 19:12). Rather than explain their existence as the result of sin, Jesus raises them up as an icon of radical discipleship.[5] As the majority of humans are clearly male or female,

---

5. For the longer version of this argument, see my *Sex Difference in Christian Theology: Male, Female, and Intersex in the Image of God* (Grand Rapids: Eerdmans, 2015), especially chs. 1, 2, 4.

so the majority of humans are heterosexual and fertile. If the earliest people were not heterosexual and fertile, they would not have been able to fulfill the command to "fill the earth and subdue it" (Gen 1:28). Procreation played an essential role in this early part of God's story. But, as Augustine himself argued, at the coming of Christ, the command to fill the earth was completed, making procreation optional or, in the Bishop's opinion, the lesser good.[6]

I appreciate Dr. Hill's reminder of the importance of tradition as an interpretive lens for careful Bible reading—indeed, I teach that the ecumenical creeds provide the big picture of the Christian story—but Augustine's *On the Goods of Marriage* is not on the same plane. As I explain in my response to Dr. Holmes in this volume, Augustine goes outside of Scripture when he asserts that children are the primary purpose of marriage. No biblical author teaches that marriage is for children. But because Hill views Adam and Eve as paradigmatic, he believes all married humans are to be fruitful as they were fruitful.

His reading of Adam and Eve influences his interpretation of other texts. Because Leviticus uses the terms "male" and "woman," Hill argues that the first two chapters of Genesis provide the backdrop, directing the reader toward a universal principle rather than a particular prohibition (p. 129). (One might ask what other terms are available to communicate the proscription.) Similarly, Hill reads Romans 1 as referring to the creation story despite the fact that Adam is not mentioned nor is sin said to result from a single source as the apostle teaches in chapter 5. "As many other scholars have noted, the scenario Paul sketches in Romans 1 has to do with the invention of idolatry and its consequences, not the fall of Adam. . . . We have no evidence that Paul considered Adam an idolater."[7] Dale Martin believes that the analysis of his colleague Richard Hays, who contrasts the sins of the Gentiles in chapter 1 with those of the Jews in chapter 2, also points in the direction of reading the first chapter as the origins of idolatry and its consequences.[8] Furthermore,

---

6. Augustine, *De bono coniugali, De sancta uirginitate*, ed. P. G. Walsh (Oxford: Clarendon, 2001), XVII, 37; VI, 15.

7. Dale B. Martin, *Sex and the Single Savior: Gender and Sexuality in Biblical Interpretation* (Lexington, KY: Westminster John Knox, 2006), 52. In rabbinic sources, idolatry is traced to Kenan, the generation of Enosh, or the influence of the Watchers. Martin, *Sex and the Single Savior*, 53.

8. Ibid., 54.

Paul's own logic assumes a mythological structure unknown to most modern persons, Christians included. Most of us do not believe that all of humanity was once upon a time monotheistic, only later, at a particular historical point, to turn to polytheism and idolatry; nor are we likely to believe that homosexuality did not exist until a sudden invention of polytheism. . . . If we were to follow Paul's logic, we would have to assume that once idolatry and polytheism were forsaken, homosexuality would cease to exist, which is probably what Paul believed; after all, he never even hints that any Jew or Christian engages in homosexuality.[9]

Paul was writing to a particular Jewish and Roman context—using arguments from Jewish mythology and first-century Roman conceptions of "nature."[10] We must respect the distance between his arguments and our current concerns.

Augustine saw vestiges of the Trinity wherever he looked. We should be careful not to posit Adam and Eve wherever male/female or woman/man appear in a biblical text.

Spiritual Friendship in Place of Same-Sex Marriage?

In the latter half of his chapter, Hill suggests that instead of intimacy in marriage, same-sex-attracted Christians should channel their love into nonsexual friendships with others—relationships of "depth, faithfulness, and greater devotion than what one often finds in anemic versions of 'friendship' on offer in contemporary culture" (p. 145). He is certainly right to lament the difficulty many men experience in developing rich relationships with other men out of fear that intimacy will bleed into homoerotic love. Too many people are in desperate need of intimate friendships uncomplicated by sexual desire. Still, it is fair to ask whether directing erotic love into friendship will solve the current confusion or add to it.

Furthermore, I worry that Hill is building a theological case on the withered stereotype of contemporary Western masculine friendships.

---

9. Ibid., 55.
10. See my comments on Romans 1 in my chapter in this volume, pp. 134–37.

Women, who tend to have more intimate friendships, including an openness to chaste physical closeness—hand-holding, hugging, cuddling on the couch, even sharing a bed—may be in a better position to discern the difference between close companionship, spiritual friendship, and the kind of love that points people to marriage. Just as many straight women experience intimate companionship with other women and still long to be married (irrespective of a desire for children), I worry that gay and lesbian persons will find that spiritual friendships will not satisfy their relational needs because friendship, while an indispensable component of a healthy marriage, is not the reciprocal desire of lover and beloved. Even in other eras when Western men defended male friendship as the epitome of all loves, they continued to differentiate it from *eros*.[11]

As I have written elsewhere, spousal love is so much more than the *eros* of joyful, reciprocal desire, and reducing spousal love to the sexual distorts and endangers marriages.[12] Still, *eros* remains one of the drivers which moves friends beyond friendship, a desire which, when not mutual, can cause friendships to fail in frustration. As C. S. Lewis warned,

> Friendship on one side may be mistaken for Eros on the other, with painful and embarrassing results. Or what begins as Friendship in both may become also Eros. But to say that something can be mistaken for, or turn into, something else is not to deny the difference between them. Rather it implies it.[13]

Lewis was speaking of friendship "turning into" *eros*, but one can apply the logic in the other direction—channeling sexual desire into friendship may make for a deep friendship, but it is unlikely to satisfy *eros*.

Of course, marriage does not exist to "satisfy" *eros*. Many couples learn rather quickly that satisfaction is beyond them as they discover differences in sexual drives, lack of fit, illness, or circumstances that render arousal difficult or impossible. At these times marriages, while

---

11. C. S. Lewis, *The Four Loves* (New York: Harcourt Brace, 1960, 1988), 57–58. See also DeFranza, *Sex Difference*, ch. 5.

12. DeFranza, *Sex Difference*, 213–38.

13. Lewis, *Four Loves*, 73.

challenging, can become particularly beautiful icons of divine love. As spouses continue to choose one another, insisting that against these odds, "You are my delight. I still desire you; not only your companionship but your bodily presence," they cultivate the sexual and noncoital intimacy which communicate desire, choice, a deeper satisfaction. Lewis admitted the instability of *eros*, describing it as a love born of need, maintaining that *eros* requires the self-giving divine love *agape*. But in his account, *agape* does not eliminate *eros*; it enables *eros* to become what it should be—a human love capable of becoming a revelation of the love of God.[14] As Rowan Williams described it so eloquently, this is the body's grace—a grace distinct from that which is communicated in friendship.[15]

I suppose more formal "vowed" friendships, modeled after monastic pledges, could offer many of the gifts typically associated with marriage—public accountability, exclusivity, permanence—and some people may find this an alternative to which they are called. Still, the history of sexual scandals in churches and monastic communities warrants weighing the dangers of forcing the yoke of celibacy on those without the attendant gift.

As we consider reimagining religious celibacy by extending monasticism to spiritual friendships, we would do well to reconsider marriage, expanding it to include our lesbian, gay, and bisexual siblings-in-Christ who desire companionship, fidelity, and permanence as well as the blessing and task of reflecting God's self-giving love in Christian marriage.

---

14. Ibid., 133–34.
15. Rowan Williams, "The Body's Grace," in *Theology and Sexuality: Classic and Contemporary Readings*, ed. Eugene F. Rodgers Jr. (London: Blackwell, 2002), 309–21.

STEPHEN R. HOLMES

Dr. Hill's essay is beautifully written and carefully argued, as we have come to expect from his work; I am grateful for it. His opening sections describe with clarity and power his experience of his own sexuality, which is a necessary contribution to the discussion we are having in this book. His biblical analysis is convincing at every turn, and his closing comments are pastorally important.

After the opening comments, Hill offers careful biblical engagement. His comments on how to distinguish between the many imperfect examples of marriage reported in the Scriptures and a stable biblical vision are extremely helpful. He locates the broadly Augustinian understanding of the Christian tradition that we share within the scope of biblical theology in ways that I simply applaud. He works carefully and seriously with the famous texts about same-sex intercourse, proposing that some of them can be shown to have deep connections to the Genesis account and so can and should be read as strong affirmations of the basic male-female nature of marriage. He engages seriously with Robert Song and offers a concluding vision of what a positive Christian ethic might look like for lesbian and gay Christians. There is essentially nothing of substance that I disagree with here.

My comments in what follows go in three directions. Some are merely supportive, indicating additional reasons for agreeing with Hill's arguments; others identify points of connection between his essay and mine, showing how our arguments complement each other; still others are points of development, reflecting on themes suggested but not explored by his essay.

Hill's opening reflections on how a proper theological understanding of the Bible cuts through the various popular, but ignorant, accounts of the varieties of "biblical marriage" are well-argued and important. His sketch of the exegetical basis for an Augustinian account is quite excellent, and I am very grateful to him for it. It does work that I did not have space to do in my own essay, and does it far better than I could have done. His use of this account to read the standard "homosexuality" texts in Leviticus and Paul is convincing; I was particularly struck by the point that the Leviticus 18 texts are explicitly directed to the whole of humanity, not just to the people of Israel.

The implications of the concept of "nature" in Romans 1:26–27 is clearly the major point of exegetical dispute in this volume, even if its importance is somewhat relativised in Hill's argument, as it is in mine, by locating it within a broader theology of marriage. Hill provides extensive textual evidence for seeing a direct background in Genesis 1 here, a position Loader noticed but rejected. As a nonspecialist, I look forward to seeing Loader's response to Hill's evidence in order to evaluate the argument, but if Hill is correct, a conscious appeal to the fall narrative in Romans 1 certainly illuminates some otherwise dark aspects of the passage, particularly the appeal to "nature." Hill's analysis of same-sex intercourse being singled out and condemned here not as a discrete reality but as a species of a much wider category of fallen human life seems to me both convincing and helpful.

Hill borrows Kevin Rowe's concept of biblical "pressure" to describe how the texts should inform our theology; this seems to me to be a helpful metaphor. Using it, he critiques Song's proposal in much the same way as I have done in my own essay, for separating the different Augustinian goods of marriage. He locates the cultural pressure that drives Song's arguments in the modern Western discovery of sexual orientation and asks how "an argument like Song's [might] encourage gay Christians to *interrogate* their experienced, socially constructed identities" (pp. 143–49).

I have two comments to make here by way of extension of Hill's argument. One is to recall a line of cultural analysis I offered in my own essay, concerning our perceived necessity of sexual activity for human flourishing; Hill closes his criticisms of Song with the comment that there is no mention of the possibility of faithful relationships that do not involve sexual activity, which suggests that Song's argument depends on an unstated assumption about sexual activity being normal or necessary for (virtually?) every human person. This assumption, I suggest, is culturally normal in the late-modern West, and so it is not a surprise to find

Song making it without stating it or defending it, but identifying it helps to highlight the necessity Hill finds for "interrogating" our "socially constructed identities."

My second point is to open up Hill's invited interrogation. As a gay Christian himself, he can legitimately focus in on the "interrogation," "purification," and "transformation" of the "socially constructed identities" of gay Christians, but for me to merely echo this point would be inappropriate. I pointed out in my own essay that the concept of "heterosexual" was coined simultaneously with "homosexual" and that straight identity is just as culturally local as gay identity. This suggests that we straight Christians need to submit our socially constructed identities to interrogation, purification, and transformation, just as much as our LGBT+ sisters and brothers do. I said a significant amount about this in my own essay, and Hill notes it in a footnote, but the point perhaps bears repeating here as a supplement to Hill's arguments.

Hill closes his essay with some reflections on a positive vocation for the gay Christian and on the historical practice of vowed friendship. Both of these are important areas for reflection. The idea of vowed friendship has been criticised, but it offers one way for celibate Christians (straight or gay) to find the deep relationships—intimacy—within the church that we all need. As such, the rediscovery of the practice is itself a criticism of the narrow patterns of church life that we have created, which assume that a sexual relationship is necessary to human life and that all adult church members will marry. I suggest here, as I have done in my own essay, that a renewal of the vocation of celibacy for straight people is a necessary part of a good response to questions of sexuality.

However, many of us live fairly peripatetic lives in late modernity, and each time we relocate we take families, but not church communities, with us. This suggests that even the perfect local church could not adequately answer the need for intimacy for the single Christian. Reflections like this suggest that the recovery of intentional relationships such as those Hill describes will be necessary in any renewal of the vocation of celibacy: there must be some form of relationship that transcends locality and survives relocation.

Many of the examples of vowed friendship in Christian history come from the religious orders. Of course, there was much wrong (as well as many humble and heroic examples of holiness) in the history of those orders, as their continual renewal movements testify. They do represent, however, a lasting and serious attempt to provide contexts for discipleship, relationship, and human flourishing for celibate people (straight or gay), the sort of attempt it is very difficult to locate in the contemporary Protestant churches.

Vowed spiritual friendship is one practice we might recover from this rich tradition; there are others. Eve Tushnet explores several in the closing chapters of her book *Gay and Catholic*,[16] including practices of service that (to borrow Hill's language) sublimate and transmute sexual desire into a different pattern of love. It seems to me that in such recoveries we might find the rich resources to suggest different forms of positive vocation for celibate people.

This is not yet, however, a positive vocation for LGBT+ people; here too I agree with Hill, and the idea he finds in C. S. Lewis, that being gay is an aspect of personal identity which is therefore—like every other aspect of our personal identity—open to transformation in this life and glorification in the next. Once again I do not want to differentiate fundamentally between being gay and being straight or, indeed, being British (say). Each is an aspect of personal identity, not chosen, which may be embraced or struggled with, but which will remain inescapable. Each shapes our desires, reactions, and personalities in deep ways which we probably cannot identify ourselves. Each creates in us particular weaknesses; each exposes us to particular temptations; and each opens us to particular forms of holiness. Each is capable, by the grace of God, of transformation into something beautiful.

---

16. Eve Tushnet, *Gay and Catholic: Accepting My Sexuality, Finding Community, Living My Faith* (Notre Dame, IN: Ave Maria Press, 2014).

WESLEY HILL

Is the "traditional" view of homosexuality—that Christian marriage is "male and female," and that all believers, including same-sex-attracted ones, who are not married are called to sexual abstinence—still viable today? Megan DeFranza and William Loader have offered some weighty reasons for answering "no." In this final portion of my part in this volume, I would like to respond to what I take to be three of the strongest of those objections.

First, DeFranza suggests, both in her main essay and her follow-up rejoinder, that the canonical prioritization of "male and female" in marriage (Gen 1:26–27; 2:24; Matt 19:4–6) is *representative*, not *normative*.[1] In other words, although the majority of people may fall into those categories, there are others—"eunuchs," for example (Matt 19:12)—who do not fit easily into this binary division. And "rather than explain their existence as the result of sin," DeFranza writes, "Jesus raises them up as an icon of radical discipleship." I have already offered reasons for thinking that "male and female" is paradigmatic and normative rather than simply representative, but what about DeFranza's claim that Jesus valorizes eunuchs and does not explain their existence as the result of sin? Certainly I would want to resist the notion that any particular individual instance of fallenness—such as being born with sexual organs that prevent one from using those organs for their intended purpose—is the direct result of that individual's (or another's) sin (cf. John 9:3). It is not that an individual "eunuch" (or intersex person) sins and is thereby made a eunuch. But I would equally resist the claim that I think DeFranza's statement implies, namely, that the condition of being born a eunuch

---

1. Compare her fuller argument in her *Sex Difference in Christian Theology: Male, Female, and Intersex in the Image of God* (Grand Rapids: Eerdmans, 2015), 177.

(or, for that matter, a "normal" male or female) bears no relation to sin. Reading Scripture as a coherent narrative rather seems to me to invite reflection on how *all* present human conditions, those of being "male" or "female" included, are in some radical and profound way "not the way they're supposed to be."[2] Persons living in broken conditions (which includes every last believer) are, as DeFranza rightly points out, called to radical discipleship, but such discipleship should not be confused with a divine endorsement of those conditions themselves.

Second, both DeFranza and Loader seek to decenter procreation from a Christian account of marriage and sexuality. DeFranza argues eschatologically; since the coming of Christ, "the command to fill the earth was completed, making procreation optional or, in [Augustine's] opinion, the lesser good." Loader, for his part, highlights the problem of infertility and voluntary heterosexual contraception as instances of Christian sexual expression that do not have procreation in view. Why then "would it be [sinful] for people with a same-gender orientation?" Since I take it that Stephen Holmes's essay has effectively answered the latter objection (i.e., infertile opposite-sex couples remain what we might call structurally open to procreation, and all-or-nothing contraception seems biblically and theologically problematic), I will focus (briefly!) on DeFranza's. I agree that procreation is decentered—in a sense. What is actually decentered is *marriage*. Unlike the Old Testament, in which singleness was not a good, the New Testament—or, more properly, the coming of Christ—opens up, for the first time in redemptive history, the possibility of viewing marriage completely as a *freely chosen* vocation. It is not necessary in the way that it once was, and singleness is now an equally (or more!) honorable calling. But, crucially, this does not alter the definition of marriage. Marriage remains what it always has been: when Ephesians 5 contemplates it from the perspective of the advent of Christ, it reaches back to Genesis to describe its "male and female" structure, and the following verses imply that procreation has not disappeared from it (Eph 6:1–4). What is now available, in Christ, is the option of *not* marrying. This is different from DeFranza's claim that what is now available is the option of marrying *in a different way* (i.e., non-procreatively).

2. Cornelius Plantinga Jr., *Not the Way It's Supposed to Be: A Breviary of Sin* (Grand Rapids: Eerdmans, 1996).

Third, and perhaps weightiest of all, is DeFranza's objection that "channeling sexual desire into friendship may make for a deep friendship, but it is unlikely to satisfy *eros*." As I indicated in my essay, I feel the force of this objection especially keenly, at a visceral level. As a celibate same-sex-attracted person who desires deep intimacy with my male friends, I know all too well the feeling of dissatisfied eros. Yet two responses to this objection seem especially crucial. First, we do well to remember that even married heterosexual Christians are asked to embrace "dissatisfied eros." All couples have to live without sexual "fulfillment" in some sense. Normally, marriage involves periods of sexual abstinence,[3] and sometimes, through circumstances beyond the couple's control, it may even involve lifelong sexual abstinence (or ongoing sexual dissatisfaction). I think, for instance, of the Princeton theologian B. B. Warfield, whose wife was struck by lightning on their honeymoon and paralyzed.[4] They lived, I presume, the rest of their lives without sex. It's no wonder Russian Orthodox theologians compare the marriage vows to monastic vows![5] But, second, I would admit that traditional Christianity *is* asking gay and lesbian people to make a hard choice. Much like the believers whom Paul describes as "groan[ing]" and "wait[ing] eagerly for … the redemption of [their] bodies" (Rom 8:23), we gay Christians are called to a challenging, often painful and frustrating obedience, and I trust that God's grace is there to sustain us and catch us when we fall.

---

3. A point made recently and powerfully by Sarah Coakley, *The New Asceticism: Sexuality, Gender, and the Quest for God* (London: Bloomsbury/Continuum, 2015).

4. John Piper, "Warfield's Supernatural Patience," *Desiring God*, June 11, 2008, accessed April 12, 2016, http://www.desiringgod.org/articles/warfields-supernatural-patience.

5. Eugene F. Rogers Jr., "Same-Sex Complementarity," *The Christian Century*, May 11, 2011, accessed April 12, 2016, http://www.christiancentury.org/article/2011–04/same-sex-complementarity.

LISTENING TO THE PAST AND REFLECTING ON THE PRESENT

STEPHEN R. HOLMES

On Theology and Theological Disputes: An Introduction

The primary task of theology is the patient listening to, and repeating of, the scriptural witness, together with the conceptual work of proposing ways of understanding the world that allow the breadth of biblical teaching to be held without qualification or evasion. In this work the witness of the tradition is a valuable aid, offering an accumulation of others' attempts to hear and repeat the same witness. These attempts have often been made in very different cultural and intellectual climates to our own and have been extensively explored and tested, so they can offer us guides which are weighty, if not finally authoritative, as to how to do the work.

Coupled with this, however, is a secondary task of understanding our own cultural and intellectual context well enough that we are able to identify those aspects of the biblical witness which our particular church community will need to reexamine. At times that work of reexamination will lead us to re-present or (I write as a Protestant) revise our understandings of what the Bible says. At other times it will require us to give clearer and more patient explanation of the biblical witness, together with sufficient cultural analysis, to help our particular church communities "understand the times" and so see that a particular local revisionary pressure is in fact wrong.

That such "reexamination" is a "work" implies a process of proposing answers and testing proposed answers; in such a process there always has been, and inevitably will be, dispute over the extent to which revision or reassertion is the correct way forward. Such disputes should be serious, for serious matters are at stake; such disputes should also be sharp, at least in the sense of being intellectually precise; such disputes may, sadly, contribute to the scandalous fragmentation of the church when one side or another decides that eucharistic fellowship can no longer be maintained. All that said, such disputes are necessary and can, with effort, be carried forward in a spirit, no doubt imperfect, of Christian charity.

Western Christians are presently involved in such a process of reexamination, and in such disputes over the right result, on the question of the ethical status of committed, exclusive, lifelong same-sex sexual relationships.[1] This work is especially difficult and painful because it focuses on the lives and identities of our gay and lesbian Christian sisters and brothers. The law of love must control any adequately Christian treatment of the question. The law of love, however, does not remove the duty to engage in the work—and there is a duty of love also towards those non-Western sisters and brothers who are horrified at the thought of any change in position on this issue (a duty of love that remains even if they are badly wrong).

My task here is to propose an argument that will suggest that despite the present cultural pressure, there is no need to change historic Christian ethical positions in this area—although there is certainly a need to restate them more carefully. The editor has chosen to separate "biblical" from "theological" approaches, so my essay cannot be narrowly exegetical. Instead, my task is to explore the broad concept of Christian marriage found in the Scriptures. To summarise the following argument, I accept without question that the churches of the West have discriminated in demanding a far higher standard of sexual ethics from LGBT people than from straight people. When set against a historic Christian theology of sexuality, however, I argue that the right response to this is not (primarily) to become more lax in our pastoral dealings with LGBT people, but to become more rigorous in our pastoral dealings with straight people. We need, that is, to recover a Christian understanding of

---

1. I am conscious that "same-sex sexual relationship" is a clumsy phrase; I do not wish to use "homosexual" as it is considered offensive by some, at least in the UK, where I live and work. I will use gay and lesbian to refer to contemporary Western patterns of relationship, but not all sexual activity between two men or two women fits these contemporary patterns, and so a broader term is necessary.

human sexuality as primarily oriented towards procreation, not towards pleasure, and to restate an ethic that takes this orientation seriously.

To argue this I will first outline the historic position—which, I will suggest, is remarkably unified. From this I will propose three possible ways in which the historic understanding of marriage might be opened to same-sex couples. I will then examine the cultural context which leads to pressure for revision and show that, understood well, the same three possible revisionist moves are suggested by cultural analysis. I will then consider each of the possible moves, rejecting two but allowing a certain limited space for the third. All of this will inevitably be done rather quickly, given the space available, but I hope the sketch of an argument will prove of some interest or worth.

An Outline of a Christian Sexual Ethic
Sexuality and Marriage

A Christian sexual ethic is inevitably going to be fairly centrally concerned with marriage. As we shall see, the question of the moral status of lesbian and gay relationships in the church cannot be reduced to the question of the licitness of same-sex marriages, but the question will be of great significance. Let me start, then, with some biblical reflection on the appropriateness of marriage.

If we ask who should marry, then at least one plausible answer from the New Testament texts is that no one should. Paul says this straightforwardly and repeatedly in 1 Corinthians 7 (see variously vv. 8, 26–27, 38, 40). When Jesus sketches the moral conditions of the married life, and his disciples respond by saying his account is so rigorous that it would be better not to marry, his cool response is to speak of those who were born unable to marry, those rendered unable to marry, and those who choose not to marry because of the kingdom (Matt 19:10–12). Jesus is not demanding that they should not marry, but he is at least rather unconcerned if this is what they conclude, and then he turns to play with some children (Matt 19:13–15). (As we shall see, this enacted reaffirmation of the value of children is very significant to the question of the appropriateness of marriage.) He points out elsewhere that marriage is something passing, a reality of this age that will not last into the age to come (Matt 22:30), again, seemingly devaluing marriage.

There are two specialists in the biblical material writing in this volume, and so I will not presume to judge whether this reading of the NT is the best. I will, however, assert that it has been common and important in Christian history: rightly or wrongly, this is often how we have heard the Bible. For the first four centuries of the life of the church, most writers took this position and justified it from Scripture. Virginity was valued; marriage was acceptable but definitely second best.

Modern readers tend to hear such strictures as coming from some hatred of, or disgust at, sexual acts, and/or from some "platonic" distrust of the physical world of bodies. The second of these positions, at least, is demonstrably wrong: these early Christians knew all about distrust of the physical; it was repeatedly urged upon them by those movements we now tend to describe as "gnostic"; they resisted it with energy and passion. Irenaeus of Lyons, amongst the earliest and greatest of these writers, made the central points with care and emphasis: God became incarnate in Jesus of Nazareth; the centre of our practice of worship is eating bread and drinking wine; bodies are good, good enough for God to have one; bodily functions such as eating are holy, properly used—in the specific case of the Eucharist more holy than anything else we can possibly do. To denigrate the physical is to be fundamentally unchristian. The church Fathers knew that well.

For these same reasons, the extreme gnostic rejection of all forms of sexual intimacy as evil was generally resisted by early Christian writers. If they thought celibacy was better, marriage remained good. So why did they distrust marriage? There is a pithy phrase that echoes repeatedly through the writings on sexual ethics we have from those centuries, which identifies the real core of their belief: "Where there is death, there is marriage."[2] Marriage, they believed, was intimately connected to the fact of death. All human beings are destined to die; because of this, without the arrival of children, the human race will end in a generation. Marriage is the context in which children are conceived, born, and nurtured, and so we marry to escape the fact of death.

---

2. Robert Song has recently drawn attention to this theme in *Covenant and Calling*, citing John Chrysostom. The idea is held very generally, however, the phrase going back at least to Tertullian, and the point being made by (at least) Basil of Caesarea, Gregory of Nazianzus, Gregory of Nyssa, Athanasius, Jerome, and Ambrose (see Josiah Trenham, *Marriage and Virginity according to St John Chrysostom* (Durham theses), Durham University, available at Durham E-Theses Online, http://etheses.dur.ac.uk/1259/) p.89, n. 102). It is striking that the post-Marxist sociologist Zygmunt Bauman rediscovers this link in his meditations on mortality, *Mortality, Immortality, and Other Life Strategies* (Cambridge: Polity, 1992); see especially 29.

But Christians believe in the resurrection. Death is already defeated, and so we do not need to marry to escape its power. The early Christian struggle to make sense of the goodness of marriage was not about any distrust of the physical world or disgust at the sexual act, but was about belief in the resurrection. As such, we should, as fellow believers in the resurrection, take their struggle with seriousness: their inherited account of sex focused on procreation as a response to death. No longer fearing death, or needing to procreate, they needed a new way to talk about sex that was not so exclusively focused on the need to procreate.

They looked to the Scriptures for help, of course. Paul is interesting here: in 1 Corinthians 7 he seems to say straightforwardly that celibacy is better than marriage, although allowing that "it is no sin" to marry (7:36 NRSV) and indeed that those who struggle with sexual continence should marry (7:9). In Ephesians 5, however, marriage has become something apparently usual and assumed (5:33), with the Genesis mandate reaffirmed (5:31), and has become an image of Christ's love for the church (5:32).

We could, of course, read this as reflecting a decline of eschatological expectation in the decades following the ascension of Jesus. If we assume a degree of consistency in Paul's theology, however, we will need an alternative explanation. The problem the Fathers faced is already there in the Pauline corpus: how is marriage both something to be refrained from, if possible, and something that can image Christ's love for the church?

Augustine and the Goodness of Marriage

Augustine, supremely, offered the young church ways to make sense of this dual reality. Some of his ideas have become so universal in Christian reflection on marriage that we cannot make much sense of our inherited theology and liturgy without listening to him. Marriage becomes usual, if never normal, because of the reality of human sinfulness. First Corinthians 7 allows those who struggle with sexual continence to marry. Augustine suggested that we all struggle with continence in every area of our lives, including our sexual desires, and so we should expect marriage to be commonplace amongst Christians. In view of our theme, it is worth stressing that at the heart of a Christian sexual ethic, and a Christian theology of marriage, is a confession that the erotic desires of every fallen human person are misdirected, warped, and broken. This is true indifferently of straight, gay, lesbian, bisexual—and indeed asexual—desires.

This is still pastoral accommodation, however, not an account of the goodness of marriage. Augustine did that work too: marriage is a good thing intended by God, even for Christians who believe in the resurrection, and not merely an inferior mode of life to virginity. There are, he famously argued, three goods of marriage: children, faithfulness, and sacrament.

Augustine arrives at his conviction that procreation is the fundamental good of marriage not by denying the connection of marriage and death, but by looking behind it to the creational command to "fill the earth" (Gen 1:28). God intends there to be human beings on the earth. Human beings are necessarily social and properly exist in community, so the continuation of the race until Christ returns is a good in itself, a good that can only be realised by the continuation of marriage. This was true before the entrance of death into the world, and remains true now that death has been done to death by the resurrection of Christ.

This focus on procreation as the primary good of marriage means that marriage must involve man and woman. Gender complementarity is a creational reality that is ordered towards reproduction. Heterosexual sex is the only proper mode of sexual expression for human beings because it is directed towards the begetting of children.

"Faithfulness" refers to the exclusivity of the marriage union. Wife and husband commit themselves to each other without reserve and irrevocably, and refuse to countenance ever forming a similar relationship with anyone else. "Sacrament" refers, for Augustine, primarily to the permanence of marriage, which he believes is a result of a particular divine grace given in marriage. Taking seriously the horror of the disciples at the high ethical demands of indissoluble marriage in Matthew 19:10, Augustine suggests not a weakening of the demand, nor a criticism of the disciples' judgment, but an account of divine help in achieving that which humanly would indeed be intolerable and impossible. We might say that, on Augustine's account, Christian marriage is quite literally a miracle—an achievement of impossible levels of self-forgetfulness, self-sacrifice, and self-surrender by the infusion of power from God. (To preempt my argument, a church that has made marriage possible or even easy in its own pastoral guidance is teaching a different theology than Augustine's.)

This account of the "miraculous" nature of Christian marriage leads us to the final element of the Augustinian account: marriage is a school in which our desires are reordered. Augustine understood our present fallen estate primarily in terms of misdirected desire: we lust after that which will kill us and are unmoved or repulsed by the one thing that in fact brings life. There is a popular misconception that Augustine held sexual desire to be particularly evil. This is not true (pride is the root sin in his theology), but he certainly did not exempt our sexual desires. We are all as broken in this area as in every other (to emphasise again, straight people just as much as LGBT people).

Much of his analysis of marriage reflects this. Following 1 Corinthians 7:1–9, he teaches that marriage contains lust. Whilst the only good reason to copulate is out of a desire to beget children, nonetheless intercourse to satisfy sexual desire is pardonable within the marriage relationship (so long as nothing is done to prevent the possibility of conception, which excludes both contraceptive devices and sex acts that are not in principle able to result in fertilisation). Further, Augustine suggests that in the mutual submission and self-surrender of marriage, and in the openness of the marriage relationship to children, with the demands of self-sacrificial love that the arrival of children bring, there is a discipling process. Our desires are reordered as we live out the marriage relationship (just as they are when we live out a celibate life) so that we are rendered fit for the kingdom—and marriage and celibacy alike are ways of life, thick clusters of practices, that tend to this reordering of our desires when lived seriously. In this sense marriage is properly named an "ascetic" practice.

With all this in place, Augustine is able to take seriously the teaching of Ephesians 5:31–32: the exclusivity and permanence of marriage make it a fitting image of the bond between Christ and the church. Here a love that is foreign to the present fallen world is lived out in endless mutual submission and self-surrender.[3]

---

3. This account may be maintained regardless of the position one takes on the presently contentious issue of the extent to which Eph 5 and other texts demand a gendered specifying of this mutual self-giving with language of "submission" and "headship." I take the symmetrical mutuality of 1 Cor 7 to be normative and do not find it hard to read Eph 5 in those terms.

Receiving Augustine: Modern Theologies of Marriage

I have spent so long on Augustine's account of marriage because it became normative for the church and remains embedded in our thought and practice. To offer only one example, marriage liturgies, even amongst us Baptists (who are not generally beholden to Christian tradition), virtually always assume and assert these three Augustinian goods of marriage. When we Western Christians think and pray about marriage today, we still instinctively think and pray in Augustinian ways. This might need to change, and I will consider this at the end of my essay, but it is presently true. Because of this, we need to hear Augustine and take him very seriously.

This does not mean we accept everything Augustine ever said about marriage—but the central logic which I have sketched above has become normal for us. We might compare the question of how God's grace relates to human free will in salvation where, similarly, the heart of Augustine's logic has become just normal, accepted by Catholics, Arminians, Calvinists, and everyone else. We have put aside some of his related ideas as just wrong—there, his account of how original sin was passed from parent to child; here, his patriarchal understandings of gender relations—but in both instances Augustine's basic logic remains and is just assumed in all our statements and discussions.

There are two changes to the Augustinian heritage that deserve some attention. Many Protestant denominations have accepted the licitness of contraception within marriage and have made pastoral accommodation for remarriage after divorce; properly understood, I suggest, these are both modifications, and fairly minor ones, to the basic Augustinian understanding, not rejections of it.

The argument over contraception took place in the first half of the twentieth century. With only one exception that I can discover (the 1930 Lambeth Conference of the Anglican Communion), the assumption that procreation is the primary purpose, and primary good, of marriage was not rejected—indeed it was barely even questioned. In the context of Malthusian worries about overpopulation, and of massively decreased infant mortality, the change made was that openness to procreation was the primary good of every particular sexual relationship, not of every particular sexual act. This is unquestionably a change to the Augustinian understanding, and perhaps it is an illegitimate one, but it is hardly a fundamental reversal.

Similarly, the gradual growth of openness to remarriage after divorce in Protestant traditions is not a denial of the belief in the permanence of marriage—a single glance at liturgical material for marriage demonstrates this—but a pastoral response to the reality of failure. We might compare the more ancient Orthodox tradition of second marriages (whether after divorce or bereavement), which is deliberately penitential and witnesses both to the brokenness of divorce and to the Orthodox belief that death does not fundamentally dissolve the marriage bond. These various pastoral responses may be wrong—certainly a willingness to consider remarriage needs policing because exceptions can easily drift into norms—but they are in no way departures from the basic Augustinian understanding. Instead, they are pastoral accommodations, ways of making space in the life of the church for the messiness of human realities.

In summary, then, marriage is the proper place for the bearing and raising of children. The exclusive, indissoluble bond of love between husband and wife, different yet united, is also a powerful image of God's love for Israel, and of Christ's love for the church. Marriage is a place where desires are contained and reordered, where we grow in holiness and continence. Sexual activity is ethical—indeed, positively good, within the context of marriage so defined, and not otherwise. The otherness of the two spouses and the possibility of procreation are intrinsic to marriage on this understanding. Outside of marriage, sexual activity cannot be licit, and so celibacy is the only ethical option.

As I have indicated, there has been virtually no deviation from this broad position in the history of Christian ethical reflection, once the key question about the goodness of marriage had been settled. Certainly there have been widely differing legal arrangements and social expectations around marriage, and at times (notably in the case of polygamous converts in various mission situations) extensive pastoral accommodations have been developed, but this core ethical position has remained unchanged. Sexual activity belongs within marriage, and sexual relationships are properly directed to procreation. Marriage is a school in which, by God's grace, our desires are reordered to make us more Christlike.

To aid the argument that follows, one negative point needs to be explicit here. The traditional Christian position, despite certain currently popular American evangelical presentations, is emphatically not that any and all forms of sexual activity within marriage are permissible and even praiseworthy. Augustine is clear that any sexual act that is not open to the possibility of procreation is in fact sinful even within marriage, if only venially so.[4] Marriage is a place where our wayward sexual desires are reordered (and, again, all of our sexual desires are wayward), not a place where we are permitted to indulge such wayward desires.

To turn, finally, to the theme of the book, on this basis it would seem that the inclusion of sexually active lesbian and gay people in the church can happen only in one of three ways:

> This Christian understanding of marriage might be developed in a way that opens it to same-sex couples.
> We might create a wholly new way of life that sits alongside marriage and celibacy, that offers an ethically acceptable sexually active mode of life for same-sex couples.
> We might accept the wrongness of same-sex sexual activity but make pastoral accommodation for some people to live that way (as many Protestant churches have done with divorce).

Let me note that my argument so far has made no reference at all to the famous handful of biblical texts that speak directly about same-sex relations. If we understand sexual ethics the way the church, almost universally, has done for the past fifteen hundred years, then these texts are just not very significant for the ethical debate. Their proper place is in a footnote, indicating that they offer a welcome, but small, degree of confirmation that a position reached for other, much weightier, exegetical and theological reasons is indeed correct. If these texts had never been in Scripture, the church would still face the same struggle with same-sex marriage, because our understanding of marriage is built on procreation and otherness. To the reader who is familiar with only very recent writings on the subject, this will be surprising, but it remains true. Consider even Karl Barth, who wrote at very great length on marriage and whose theology is famously saturated with Scripture. In noting that

---

4. Roman Catholic theology traditionally divides sins into "venial" and "mortal," the former being less serious than the latter.

a Christian doctrine of marriage has no place for same-sex marriage (a point he describes as "almost too obvious to need stating"[5]), he makes no mention at all of Leviticus 18 and only one passing reference to Romans 1:26–27. These texts are just not important for the argument, which turns rather on procreation and complementarity.

I will explore each of my three options listed above, to test their adequacy. Before doing that, however, I will ask obvious, but too often ignored, questions: Why now, and why here? Why has this issue become pressing for early twenty-first-century Christians in the West, when it was essentially unasked before our day, and when our asking of it is almost offensive to some of our sisters and brothers across the world? To answer these questions, we need to turn to cultural analysis.

The Signs of the Times: Understanding the Present Cultural Pressure
Marriage in Christian History

The entire second part of Thomas Aquinas's great *Summa Theologica* is devoted to ethics. With nearly three hundred questions treated, what we would call sexual ethics is dealt with in four of those questions, as a minor theme under the virtue of temperance (ethical questions around eating and drinking, dealt with immediately before, are given five questions). One of those questions, on the species of lust, is divided into twelve articles, of which one relates to same-sex sexual activity (or "the vice against nature," as Thomas calls it). Most of his discussion concerns whether same-sex desire is properly considered lust or not. That it is wrong is evident already on the basis of the natural fittingness of male and female together and the proper end of sexual activity in procreation.

Thomas may be right or wrong in this, but what is interesting is the rapidity with which he can deal with the question. The issue was neither difficult nor controversial for him. The same could be said of any Christian ethicist prior to about 1900, although we do need to notice three different cultural contexts in that broad claim: minority Christianity in the Roman Empire, Christendom, and missionary Christianity in the majority world.

Thomas Aquinas will serve as our example for Christendom. From about the fifth century on, the predominant culture of Europe was

---

5. Karl Bath, *Church Dogmatics* III.4 (Edinburgh: T&T Clark, 1961), 166.

unreflectively Christian (as were the predominant cultures of those European [ex-]colonies which became predominantly white European in culture by whatever process: North America except Mexico, Australia, New Zealand, etc.). Same-sex sexual activity was certainly not unknown—we may surmise that Thomas, living in all-male communities, was well aware of it, at least as a possibility to be avoided. It was classed, however, with a range of other licentious behaviour that was culturally marginalised and comprehensively rejected. In English law, for example, the (capital) crime of "sodomy" long referred not specifically to anal intercourse, or to male same-sex sexual activity, but to any act terminating in ejaculation which was not directed towards procreation, including the use of contraception in marriage.[6]

It is well known that ancient Rome—and ancient Greece before it—had a developed culture of same-sex sexual activity. The details are somewhat disputed. Certainly in Attic Greece the norm was for a man (of the ruling class) to be sexually active both with his wife and with one or more pubescent male apprentices. There is little dispute that in Rome sexual penetration was perceived as a mark of true masculinity, and so as a way of establishing or reiterating power over the one penetrated. A slave owner might routinely engage in anal intercourse with his male slaves to demonstrate his ownership.[7] More recent research has proposed that there is evidence that the Roman Empire knew also more equal same-sex relationships, although they would appear to have been rather rarer.[8] In these contexts the young church was implacably opposed to every form of same-sex sexual relationship of which it was aware.

Clement of Alexandria's *Instructor* (*Paedogogos*; c. AD 200) offers an illustrative example: he inveighs against same-sex sexuality twice, in 2:10 and 3:3. In 2:10 he treats "the procreation of children" and discusses sexuality directly (sufficiently directly that the nineteenth-century translators blushed at it and translated the Greek into Latin rather than English!). Clement unsurprisingly understands the purpose of sex to be procreation and bluntly criticises those who seek sexual pleasure with people of the same

6. Nikki Sullivan, *A Critical Introduction to Queer Theory* (New York: New York University Press, 2003), 2–4.

7. See Craig A. Williams, *Roman Homosexuality* (Oxford: OUP, 2010) for extensive evidence.

8. Williams, *Roman Homosexuality*, 279–86 surveys some of the evidence.

sex. The subject of 3:3 is luxury, which Clement sees as a temptation to all sorts of immorality. Perhaps following the example of Paul in Romans 1, he returns to same-sex sexual practice as the height of unnatural indulgence.

The question of the possible goodness of a same-sex sexual relationship does not even occur to Clement, as it did not to Thomas. The moral wrongness of same-sex sexual activity is self-evident to him, a point to be argued from (to demonstrate the danger of a love of luxury for instance) rather than a point to be argued for. We might suggest that he had no knowledge of the minority tradition of equal same-sex relationships, so his assumed condemnation had to do with the collision of sex, slavery, and power. We cannot prove this, however, and his rhetoric seems to point in another direction. For Clement, sexual complementarity points to the naturalness of male-female marriage. Further, the purpose of marriage is procreation, so a proper sexual ethic restricts sexual activity to male-female marriage relationships.

Mission churches in the majority world inevitably had to negotiate those practices of sexual behaviour which were locally culturally acceptable. This certainly routinely involved same-sex sexual relations. We must not, however, as some recent writers have done,[9] read back contemporary Western understandings into precolonial cultures. The evidence we have suggests that equal, exclusive, lifelong same-sex sexual relationships are extraordinarily rare across human history.

In a survey of anthropological work on sexuality, Jenell Williams Paris proposes that there are four broad traditions of same-sex sexual activity visible across the variety of human cultures. "Age-structured" relationships, like those familiar from classical Greece, require an age difference between partners, typically an adult inducting an adolescent into adult ways. "Gender-structured" relationships are based around complex, non-binary, cultural gender patterns. "Profession-based" relationships are those in which generally nonstandard patterns of sexual behaviour are legitimated for prostitutes or people in certain religious roles. Finally, "egalitarian" relationships are between equals.[10]

Crucially, almost every cultural instance of "egalitarian" relationships

---

9. See, e.g., Alan Wilson, *More Perfect Union: Understanding Same-Sex Marriage* (London: DLT, 2014), ch. 8.

10. Jenell Williams Paris, *The End of Sexual Identity: Why Sex Is Too Important to Define Who We Are* (Downers Grove, IL: IVP, 2011), 62–69. Stephen O. Murray's classic *Homosexualities* (Chicago: University of Chicago Press, 2000) uses three of the four same categories to

outside of the modern West is temporary and occurs before or alongside a heterosexual marriage.[11] Lifelong, exclusive, equal same-sex partnerships are virtually unknown to human history and anthropology outside the contemporary West. Same-sex sexual activity is common, but it almost never takes this cultural form. Realising this is very important for understanding contemporary ecclesial debates over sexuality.

At the heart of at least some of the implacable opposition of sub-Saharan African churches to any openness to gay and lesbian relationships in the church, for example, is a remembered narrative in which male same-sex sexual activity was a ritualised form of asserting dominance and ownership (as it had been in ancient Rome) and in which the refusal of early Christian converts to submit to this led to their martyrdom.[12] Now, the ethical argument here is clearly flawed: sexual violence is wrong because it is violence. That a particular example of sexual violence involved same-sex activity does not imply anything at all about the moral status of consensual, loving same-sex sexual activity. The point, however, is that if, culturally, the only form of same-sex sexual activity known or imaginable is violent, then there will be a general assumption against any form of same-sex sexual activity.

That said, I have no doubt at all that the leaders and theologians of the young churches of the majority world would be deeply offended at the thought that their opposition to gay and lesbian relationships was merely cultural. Rather, they would claim to be faithful to the plain teaching of Scripture. They would challenge those of us in Western churches with the fact that our willingness to consider the idea of the moral licitness of gay and lesbian relationships is historically and culturally unique, and so would suggest that any cultural blinkers are ours, not theirs.[13]

---

structure his extensive data (Murray regards "profession-based" relationships as a subset of "gender-structured" ones).

11. See Murray's chapter on "Premodern Egalitarian Homosexualities," in *Homosexualities*, 359–81, for extensive examples.

12. The recently retired Anglican archbishop of Uganda, Henry Orombi, described a narrative like this as part of the reason he cannot imagine giving any space to gay and lesbian relationships. Male same-sex intercourse, he suggests, was historically a mode of imposing and demonstrating control of social inferiors. When in June 1886 a number of page boys of the king of Buganda refused to submit to his sexual advances because of their new-found Christian faith, they were killed. (See, e.g., Orombi's influential essay "What Is Anglicanism?" *First Things*, Aug/Sept 2007, http://www.firstthings.com/article/2007/07/001-what-is-anglicanism-50.)

13. Consider, for example, two popular Singaporean books: Li-Ann Thio is a lawyer who has served in the Singaporean parliament and holds degrees from Oxford, Cambridge, and

The Uniqueness of the Contemporary West: Marriage in Our Culture

This brings us back to my controlling questions for this section: Why here, and why now? What is it about our culture that makes the issue of the moral status of same-sex relationships urgent for us, when it is not for other churches across the world and has not been for other churches through history? There is a simple answer to this, which, however, requires some examination. We have discovered that some people are gay/lesbian—that is, exclusively erotically attracted to people of the same sex—and so it is a matter of justice that gay and lesbian relationships should be permitted, indeed celebrated, in the church. A subsidiary argument would point to the virtues instantiated in and developed through gay and lesbian relationships. There is simply much here to celebrate, even if justice did not demand the celebration.

Let me identify some of the premises at play here and examine each one:

1. The "orientation" premise: people are in fact straight or gay or lesbian.

2. The "right to marry" premise: it is a matter of justice that people (consenting adults lacking impediments) should be permitted to marry if they so desire.

3. The "demonstrable virtue" premise: there are in fact many obvious virtues exhibited in gay and lesbian relationships.

4. The "makes licit" premise: the existence of demonstrable virtues within many/most/all examples of a particular sort of human practice renders that practice morally acceptable.

Let me deal with the "demonstrable virtue" premise immediately: I cannot imagine it being seriously questioned by anyone living in the West. One would need to be possessed of a tiny and unrepresentative social circle, or blinded to the obvious by bigotry, to doubt this point. The others deserve a little more examination.

The "orientation" premise—that people simply are gay or lesbian or straight—needs careful handling. This is unquestionable in mainstream Western political discourse, although it is now routinely rejected

---

Harvard. Nonetheless, her *Prophecy, Pansexuality, and Pandemonium: The Political Arm of the Spirit of Lawlessness in the Acharit-Hayamim* (Singapore: Genesis, 2013) is every bit as extreme to a Western reader as the title suggests. The National Council of Churches' *A Christian Response to Homosexuality* (Singapore: Genesis, 2004) is more measured in tone, but still regards "Should a homosexual be baptised?" (p. 93) as a valid question to ask.

by academics working on sexuality and human culture. The reasons for denying this account of orientation are not hard to trace: the more we study the variety of human sexual norms across history and across cultures, the more we realise that it is normal everywhere except the modern West to be sexually attracted to, and probably sexually active with, both men and women. The contemporary Western assumption that it is normal to be attracted only to men or only to women is, culturally speaking, very unusual. Of course, it may be that we are right and every other human culture has been wrong, but we might reflect that we would need some exceptionally strong evidence for that assumption not to appear simply racist and imperialistic.

If most people are sexually attracted to and sexually active with both men and women, however, this fact makes being straight unnatural just as much as it makes being gay or lesbian unnatural. These categories—"gay" and "straight"—in fact share a history, famously invented (then as "heterosexual" and "homosexual") around 1869 in Germany.[14] They are modern Western constructs.

They are enormously powerful constructs for us Westerners, however. The recent academic development of queer theory[15] suggests (following Foucault and Butler[16]) that every society proposes/imposes certain recognisable sexual norms to which members of the society are conformed by socialisation.[17] Queer theory decries such socialisation, but it is of course inescapable. I cannot choose to be unsocialised from the various identities that I am conformed to—nor in many cases would I want to be. Recognising that these identities are not perfect, they nonetheless give me contexts and narratives and histories and community to make sense of the maelstrom of my experience. As I listen to gay and lesbian people, I hear the owning of these identities in this sort of way—even if they are cultural constructs, they are both inescapable and genuinely life-giving.

---

14. Hanne Blank, *Straight: The Surprisingly Short History of Heterosexuality* (Boston: Beacon, 2012), 15–21.

15. "Queer theory" is a recent academic approach to the study of sexuality which denies the existence of any norms. See Sullivan, *Critical Introduction.*

16. Michel Foucault, *The History of Sexuality: The Care of the Self,* vol. 3 (trans. ed., New York: Random House, 1986), and Judith Butler, *Gender Trouble: Feminism and the Subversion of Identity* (New York: Routledge, 1990).

17. See Sullivan, *Critical Introduction, passim.*

I propose, therefore, that we should accept the "orientation" premise as at least currently locally true. Contemporary Westerners in general are straight or gay or lesbian. (I say "at least" because, although I am convinced by the queer critique of accounts of universal innate sexual orientation, my argument does not depend on rejecting it.)

The "right to marry" premise is more difficult. It needs careful statement if it is not to lapse into nonsense. Clearly, no individual person has a "right to marry" (any pastor will have loved and supported people desperate to marry but unable to find a partner willing to marry them). That said, the careful statement is not very hard: two people who may marry should not be prevented from marrying if they so desire. Notice, however, that the phrase "who may marry" here already conceals a number of ethical judgments. To take examples that are live in the Christian tradition: What degree of consanguinity prevents marriage? Does previous divorce (assuming a surviving ex-spouse)? It is not hard to find historic or contemporary cultures where it would be assumed that interracial marriage, or marriage across certain class or caste boundaries, or marriage below a certain age, would be unacceptable.

Now, my point here is not to support or decry these judgments. I assume all readers of this book will think that the prohibiting of interracial marriage is just as abhorrent as the permitting of child marriage, and I would of course concur. But in speaking of a "right to marry," we have already made a set of assumptions about what constitutes a valid marriage. We can only support same-sex marriage from a general "right to marry" if we have already assumed that same-sex marriage is acceptable. There is no argument here, only a hidden assertion.

This raises a problem, however: this "right to marry" argument has enormous contemporary cultural traction in the West, which requires explanation if it is indeed obviously worthless. I suspect that the felt force lies in another contemporary Western cultural assumption, that it is necessary to be sexually active to be a fulfilled, or even a properly adult, human being. We could no doubt trace the root of this assumption to Freud, but I trust it is evident once named, displayed repeatedly in our popular music, in the Hollywood assumption that the existence of a "40-Year-Old Virgin" is self-evidently hilarious, in our newspaper advice columns that prioritise sexual satisfaction as a personal need, and in countless other ways.[18] The (Protestant) churches have visibly surrendered to this cultural assumption, making marriage an inevitable part of Christian maturity for much of the twentieth century. We looked askance at ministerial candidates who were not married and constructed church programmes on the basis that the only single people around were young adults preparing for marriage or widows.

The collision of the inescapable reality of fixed sexual orientations in our culture and this deep set of assumptions about the necessity of active sexual life for human flourishing makes the pressure to extend marriage to gay and lesbian people enormous—and perhaps unavoidable (I will return to this). To refuse to find some account of how gay and lesbian people can actively express their sexuality appears to be unspeakably cruel, denying the possibility of true human flourishing of any sort of fulfilled life or indeed of adulthood, to a significant number of people.

There is a trite theological answer to this: to prove that sexual activity is not necessary to a well-lived human life, we need to say only one word, "Jesus." We cannot stop there, however, because of the reality of cultural pressure on human life, which is different in different cultures. Jesus lived in a world where marriage was normal, certainly, but there the necessity came from an ethical duty to marry and the need for an insurance policy for old age, not a basic human need. For Jesus to refuse to marry was eccentric, certainly, and probably disreputable, but in his culture it did not exclude him from any possibility of human flourishing. Jesus' singleness does not, then, give us an easy answer to our own cultural pressures. Even if we want to insist theologically that an active sex life is not a basic human need—as we should—we cannot pretend that we or those we pastor can simply escape our cultural conditioning here. There is a huge, and theologically appropriate, pressure to find a way of making space for same-sex marriage in the Western church at present.

At the same time, reflecting on this cultural reality might cause us to realise how far we have, within our churches in the West, surrendered to it in our accounts of opposite-sex marriage. It is not hard to find "Christian" teaching arguing that all forms of sexual activity are not just permissible but even praiseworthy within marriage. This is a surrender

---

18. Given the space constraints of these essays, I am merely gesturing at areas of evidence here, trusting that the point will be fairly self-evident once made. For a fuller argument, see Foucault, *History*, vol. 1, 155–57.

to a contemporary idolatry, and if we are going to surrender, clearly we should do so for lesbian and gay people in just the same way that we do for straight people. Of course, the better way is to refuse the idolatry in all our accounts of marriage. Our sexual desires are not in pressing need of being fulfilled; they are in pressing need of being mastered and reordered so that we may grow into Christlikeness. Marriage is a discipline for the latter, not a permission for the former. If we were faithful in teaching this to straight couples, we might find that the cultural pressure to allow gay/lesbian people sexual fulfillment would be much less compelling.

My final premise above is about how we argue for ethical positions. People in same-sex relationships exhibit virtue; does this not prove the goodness of those relationships? There is a weak form of this which is fairly easy to dismiss: that someone engaged in a particular practice happens also to display virtue in some area of his/her life is no argument for the ethical status of that practice (consider the stereotype of the gangster who is devoted to caring for his mother, for example). The more interesting form of the argument follows the suggestion of much recent Christian ethical writing that practices in fact inculcate virtues.[19] On this basis, many writers have proposed that lived sexual relationships can be shown to generate certain virtues and so must be ethical. A lesbian couple have visibly grown in maturity, selflessness, and love precisely through their commitment to each other; surely, therefore, that commitment must be good?

Abstracted from the particular example, the claim here is that any human practice which leads to growth in virtue must be something good. However, I can show that this claim is false. Note that the argument that follows is entirely negative: I am trying to show that one particular form of argument often offered to prove the goodness of gay/lesbian relationships in fact does not work. This does not mean that such relationships are not good, only that this form of argument cannot determine that question.

The claim above will be shown to be false if we can propose examples of human practices that we must accept lead to growth in virtue but that

---

19. The most accessible sustained argument for this proposition is now J. K. A. Smith, *Desiring the Kingdom: Worship, Worldview, and Cultural Formation* (Grand Rapids: Baker, 2009), but it is also the point that almost all of Hauerwas's writings make one way or another.

we must also regard as unethical. Let me suggest two such examples, one from the area of sexuality and one from inter-religious dialogue.

For the first, consider contemporary polyamorous relationships,[20] in particular the common "Poly-Z" relationship in which two people, A and B, have a sexual relationship, whilst A also has a relationship with C, and B also has a relationship with D (drawn as a diagram, it looks like a capital Z, hence the name). Such relationships work only when there is an exceptional level of honesty, humility, love, and self-surrender. The relationship depends on each participant putting the needs/desires of the others before any sense of possessiveness and jealousy on his/her own part. People living in such relationships almost inevitably display remarkable levels of unselfishness and self-awareness, virtues which arise out of the hard practice of making the complex relationship work.

For the second example, consider a lived practice of prayer, sacrifice, and devotion to a number of deities of the Hindu pantheon, which over the years generates in the heart of the worshiper a detachment from worldly appetites and a serenity in the face of the troubles of life.

I suggest that in both these cases, it is demonstrable that a practice—polyamory or idolatry—that is very difficult to reconcile with any traditional form of Christian ethics can nonetheless be shown to produce real virtues in the lives of those who engage in it. Of course, praiseworthy practices—say, daily reception of the Eucharist—do the same thing, so my point is not to claim that gay/lesbian relationships are like polyamory or idolatry—or that they are like Eucharistic devotion—but to insist that the fact that my "demonstrable virtue" premise above cannot be questioned is not sufficient, in itself, to establish the moral status of same-sex marriage in Christian reflection. Partners in a same-sex marriage may grow in holiness, but that does not make the marriage holy; some other argument is needed.

We should also note that in our culture, same-sex marriage has until very recently been of questionable status even, perhaps particularly, amongst activists for LBGT rights. In the UK, the most significant pressure group, Stonewall, only began campaigning for equal marriage

---

20. To forestall a common criticism, I am not here comparing gay relationships to polyamorous relationships. I am testing an argument used to justify gay relationships by inserting an entirely different reality—polyamory—into the argument to see where it leads. I could do the same thing with gun owning, prayer, or baseball-card collecting, except that these examples would not yield useful data (as far as I can see).

in late 2010, sometime after mainstream political figures had declared their support. Stonewall's campaign on the issue was careful to reaffirm the "special and unique status" of civil partnerships for gay and lesbian people. The context here is a suspicion, arising out of the historical entanglement of LGBT rights with feminism and the sexual revolution of the 1960s, that marriage was the problem, not the solution. Many theorists had argued that marriage was an inherently patriarchal and homophobic institution that needed to be overcome, not colonised, and so the existence of uniquely queer legal relationships (in the UK "civil partnerships") was politically important.

Arguments for Same-Sex Marriage

This gets us back to the three possible ways for including sexually active gay and lesbian people in the church that I noted at the end of the previous section: extending Christian marriage, finding a new form of sexual vocation (here, "civil partnership"), or making pastoral accommodation because the cultural pressure is so huge. I turn to these themes.

Is Our Definition of Marriage Extensible?

Eugene Rogers's *Sexuality and the Christian Body* remains, to my mind, the best book by some distance arguing for a revisionist/affirming position in this debate.[21] This is because Rogers, almost uniquely[22] as far as I can see, argues from the theology of marriage with which I began and tries to make sense of same-sex marriage in properly theological terms. Marriage, he insists, is an ascetic practice just as monasticism is; both are modes of community oriented towards the slow transformation of self into Christlikeness. His ethical challenge then becomes powerful: Why should the gay Christian be denied this path to holiness?[23] Rogers engages at length with Thomas Aquinas on natural law and with Karl Barth on divine command, arguing that neither ethical tradition, properly read, excludes same-sex marriage.

---

21. Eugene F. Rogers, *Sexuality and the Christian Body: Their Way into the Triune God* (Oxford: Blackwell, 1999).

22. Robert Song, whom I will consider in the following section, is the only other example that comes to mind, at least among book-length treatments.

23. "The trouble with most conservative accounts is not that in denying same-sex couples the rite of marriage they would deny them true self-satisfaction . . . [but] that they would deny them true self-denial." Rogers, *Sexuality*, 70.

If we are to argue for an extension of Christian marriage to same-sex couples, Rogers shows the way it should be done. Let me return, however, to my sketch of the—remarkably uniform—traditional Christian theology of marriage above, and the central claim there that the primary purpose of marriage is procreation. If my arguments there were correct, this seems an intractable problem for the extension of marriage to same-sex couples.

Of course, this point is hardly new in the debate, but with a clear view of a theology of marriage in place, it is striking how many of the attempted rejoinders fail very quickly. The claim is sometimes made that marrying elderly couples (couples including post-menopausal women being the relevant issue) demonstrates that the churches do not really believe that procreation is essential to marriage. When we take seriously the utterly central place of procreation in the theology of marriage, however, this argument can only fail. If a successful analogy between post-menopausal marriage and same-sex marriage can be drawn, then we should not conclude that same-sex marriage is therefore allowable, but rather that the churches have erred in celebrating post-menopausal marriages. At most, that is, this argument is a suggestion that we should stop allowing elderly women to marry. There is no possible argument to defend same-sex marriage in this area. (I happen to think that the defences of the practice of allowing elderly/infertile couples to marry are robust enough to avoid this conclusion, but that is not the point here.)

A second response to the insistence on procreation in marriage is to suggest the world is overpopulated, so we should not insist on procreation. Even if we accept the premise, however, this argument cannot support same-sex marriage. The Christian response to overpopulation would, rather straightforwardly, be a renewal of the vocation of celibacy, not an evisceration of the vocation of marriage. That said, the fact of death remains decisive: if we all stopped procreating tomorrow, in not much over a century the world would be unpopulated, not overpopulated. Christian ethics suggests that some should be celibate and others should marry and reproduce; concerns over population levels might lead to a discussion of the proper balance of those two ways of life in the church, but cannot be a reason for a change to either pattern.

The most interesting responses to this question are those that suggest that same-sex marriages can be made good by including some form of surrogate procreation. This at least takes a Christian theology of marriage seriously. It needs careful specification, however: whilst it is true that opening a bond of love to care for children is an intrinsic part of the self-sacrifice of marriage (as I argued above), what is intrinsic to marriage is the *generation* of children, not merely their *care*. Adoption, caring for the orphan, is a profoundly Christian act, but it is not something that answers the procreative nature of marriage. (The care of orphans—alongside widows and refugees—is a duty enjoined on society in the Torah and on the community of the church in the Epistles; it is nowhere linked to marriage.) We need, therefore, to reach for various forms of surrogacy and/or assisted conception to try to make sense of a same-sex marriage.

That said, when the distinction is drawn as I have drawn it above, surrogacy and (at least most forms of) assisted conception as currently practiced are more nearly forms of adoption than forms of procreation. A child is conceived and born and then taken into the household. That the conception and birth of this child were planned in order that s/he might then be adopted by a particular couple certainly raises some interesting ethical questions, but it does not change the fact that what has happened is a species of adoption.

Let me, however, propose a limit case: an in vitro fertilisation of an egg of one partner in a lesbian marriage using genetic material derived from her wife's own eggs. I do not know if this is scientifically possible; even if not, it offers an interesting thought-experiment. This looks more like an unusual form of procreation than a form of adoption, certainly. If intended by the couple when they marry, would it be enough to render the marriage appropriately procreative, and so properly Christian? This is finally a question worth debating. We would need to reflect on the criticisms of separating conception from the sexual act which have been explored in discussions of the ethical appropriateness of IVF. We would also need to return to the question of the complementarity of male and female in marriage which I have not explored extensively in this essay for reasons of space, but which is also part of the tradition.[24]

---

24. The best book exploring this area remains Christopher Roberts, *Creation and Covenant: The Significance of Sexual Difference in the Moral Theology of Marriage* (New York: Continuum, 1997). See also Beth Felker Jones, *Marks of His Wounds: Gender, Politics, and Bodily Resurrection* (Oxford: OUP, 2007).

In Christian belief and practice, procreation is the proper end of marriage. A relationship that is not ordered towards procreation may be good and right and holy, but it is not a marriage. Discussions of the marriage of elderly people or of overpopulation do not change this at all. Whilst it is possible to invent an imagined case which would bear further reflection, the basic reality is that the centrality of procreation for marriage makes same-sex marriage very difficult to imagine in Christian terms.

Is There Space for a Third Calling alongside Marriage and Celibacy?

Given this, we might ask whether there is space for a new discipline, a same-sex relationship that is not trying to be a marriage, but is trying to conform to Christian standards of holiness. Robert Song has explored this possibility in his recent *Covenant and Calling*,[25] which offers an argument that is richly theological and serious. He traces the connection of marriage, procreation, and death I have noted above and the consequent Christian openness to celibacy. Song argues that this embracing of celibacy reorders marriage within the church away from a focus on procreation and opens up the possibility of imagining an eschatological space, a third calling (Song calls it "covenant partnership") that can sit alongside marriage and celibacy as a way of being authentically Christian. Such covenant partnerships will be marked by faithfulness, permanence, and a commitment to non-procreative fruitfulness. These "covenant partnerships" are not marriages because they are not ordered to procreation; they are a new way of life that Song suggests can be properly Christian. They can also, Song believes, be sexual, because in Scripture sex can be about faithfulness and permanence without mention of children (as it is in 1 Cor 7).

This is an argument from silence with which I am uncomfortable. Song's broader argument places considerable weight on the decision of the 1930 Lambeth Conference to permit deliberately childless marriage, a decision which is very eccentric in the Christian tradition, and which was not taken for the best of reasons.[26] Song attempts to separate sexual

---

25. Robert Song, *Covenant and Calling: Towards a Theology of Same-Sex Relationships* (London: SCM, 2014).

26. For both these points, see Anna Poulson, *An Examination of the Ethics of Contraception with Reference to Recent Protestant and Roman Catholic Thought,* PhD thesis, King's College London, 2006, https://kclpure.kcl.ac.uk/portal/en/theses/an-examination-of-the

activity from its traditional linkage with marriage and procreation. I am simply unconvinced that his arguments are adequate to this task.

That said, his insistence on the need for fruitful, covenantal, same-sex relationships in the church seems to me to be important: as I indicated earlier, our Western Protestant capitulation to the idea that sexual activity, and so marriage, is essential to human maturity has led us to neglect any space for the flourishing or service of the unmarried in our churches. Traditionally this need was met by religious communities which were not intended to be places of sexual activity, but places of vowed commitment between people of the same sex in which and from which they could grow to maturity and love and serve the world. Song says nothing about this—rather significant—strand of the Christian tradition, unfortunately, so does not explain how his proposals relate to it.

Song highlights helpfully, however, that any ethical construction of a "third calling" in this area is going to need to find a way of separating sexual activity from both marriage and procreation. Given the strong way in which these three themes are interwoven in the theology I sketched above, it is difficult to see how this might be done.

What Space Is There for Pastoral Accommodation in This Area?

If the Christian theology of marriage is not extensible to same-sex couples, and if there is no space for a new discipline of "covenanted partnership" that includes sexual activity, what are we left with? The answer, it seems to me, is pastoral accommodation. Churches that believe same-sex partnerships to be wrong might nonetheless find space within their life for people living in such partnerships out of pastoral concern.

As I have noted above, both Protestant and Orthodox churches have made space like this for divorced people. In neither case has the theology or liturgy of marriage been modified to make theological space for divorce, but within pastoral practice there has been a willingness to find space for (some) divorced people to remarry and to remain in good standing in the church. A similar accommodation may be seen in some African churches with regard to polygamy, particularly in the context of mission. The earliest response, often insisted upon by Western missionaries, was a demand that converts in polygamous marriages dissolve their family, putting aside all

-ethics-of-contraception-with-reference-to-recent-protestant-and-roman-catholic-thought
%28f20ad0c1-2706-416f-bf6f-b95f901e888c%29.html.

wives but the first married. This of course rendered women and children destitute, and so was soon recognised to be extremely cruel. As a result, space was made in various ways in various churches for the continuation of polygamous marriages that had been entered into before conversion. There was—is—no acceptance of polygamy, but a pastoral accommodation to the cultural and missional reality of that particular context.

A sharp distinction needs to be made between this sort of pastoral accommodation and a genuinely affirming theology; they are different, and seriously so. I have suggested so far in this essay that the various arguments recently presented for an affirming theology of same-sex marriage have little traction. I have also suggested that the pressure in the contemporary West to find space for same-sex marriage in the life of the churches is both huge and theologically appropriate. This seems strong reason for supposing that some form of pastoral accommodation might be appropriate, particularly given the demand for a basically loving orientation that must control all Christian theology and practice.

Now, to love adequately certainly means to teach the full counsel of God. Pastoral accommodation does not mean pretending ethical standards do not exist. As with divorce in the West and polygamy in parts of the global South, however, pastoral accommodation might mean making space for imperfect patterns of life whilst maintaining a clear witness to perfection. In these terms, should there be space for pastoral accommodation within Western churches?

We might imagine a particular congregation or denomination that was assiduous in resisting temptations to conform its teaching about opposite-sex marriage to the present cultural standards of the world. It might reach back into Scripture and history to challenge straight single people with a call to celibacy as the Christian norm, and to challenge married couples with the idea that their sexual activity should be directed to procreation far more than to pleasure, and that periods of abstinence might be appropriate (1 Cor 7:5). Such a Christian community could with good conscience refuse any pastoral accommodation to lesbian and gay people. Every church and denomination I know well, however, could not claim to be so clear in its general sexual ethics, and so might struggle to justify a refusal to find some sort of space for sexually active lesbian and gay people. If we are allowing straight people to conform to the sexual norms of the culture, when we know those norms differ from classical Christian ethics, we must at least ask ourselves how we can refuse to give the same permission to gay people.

The right response to this should at least be a renewed focus on ethics within our churches for straight people. At the same time, however, we must consider appropriate pastoral responses to lesbian and gay people. I do not want to propose particular pastoral actions except in very broad terms. The essence of responsible pastoral work is taking the particularities of each person's life seriously, and so general rules or guidelines are almost always unhappy. Let me, however, highlight some of the particularities that might be relevant.

The first context we might consider is evangelistic and catechetical. Suppose a gay couple with children profess faith as a result of the outreach of the church. Is the breaking up of the family unit a prerequisite for taking their profession of faith seriously? For baptism? For membership? (Here the experience of the African churches that had to face up to polygamous converts seems to me to be very relevant.) The next is pastoral and discipling work: What spaces are there in our churches for celibate gay, lesbian, or straight adults to find community and intimacy? If we have allowed converts to join the church whilst still in sexually active relationships (same-sex or opposite-sex) that are not marriage, will there be limits on the areas of service we invite them into? How will we relate to gay and lesbian church members who come out later in life; what space will there be for them to be honest and open within the fellowship about their sexuality, and how will we support both them (and their spouses if they are married) in deepening their discipleship? What support is in place, and what strictures will surround, young people who come out, or who remain closeted, who are part of our fellowship? Not every answer to these questions will require us to alter our ethical convictions, but each of them invites us to consider whether we should in particular cases.

I do not think proposing generic answers to such questions is helpful, beyond the platitudinous ("be loving and gracious," "the gospel call is always to repentance"). Pastoral questions are properly answered at the level of individual lives, not at the level of generic themes. When I talk about issues of human sexuality to churches, I always place a number of empty chairs with me on the stage, each representing an LGBT person I know with a different story, which I have permission to share. Some are people who have embraced traditional Christian ethics and are flourishing. Some are people who have found a home in an affirming church. Some are people who have left the church, driven away because they felt unloved because of their sexuality. I challenge people (not always successfully) to imagine that these friends are overhearing as they speak in the sessions, and I encourage them to think about real people and their experiences in thinking through the issues.

Admitting I Might Be Wrong: A Conclusion

The argument sketched above relies on two pillars: (1) an account of a Christian theology of marriage, which leads me to a non-affirming position; and (2) an account of present cultural realities, which leads me to critique sexual ethics applied to straight people in Western churches and to propose that some measure of pastoral accommodation is probably necessary in this area at present.

I admit fairly readily that my cultural critique could be flawed. I find queer theory generally persuasive, but recognise that this is a minority position at present, and I acknowledge that this is not my area of specialty. If I am wrong here, then my rejection of same-sex marriage still stands, but there is less reason for pastoral flexibility. By contrast, I am fairly confident both that my account of the theology of marriage is accurate and that the claims I make on its basis are solid. That said, there is a weakness in my argument here as well. What if an Augustinian theology of marriage is just wrong? If it is, all my arguments here are irrelevant. I was invited to write a theological essay to sit parallel to a biblical essay, so I have not attempted to justify this position by extensive exegesis; that is someone else's territory.

I have, however, given reasons for supposing that the core of the Augustinian account is remarkably stable and normative in the Christian tradition, which I take as significant confirmation that it is correct.[27] This is not incontrovertible, of course. To overthrow an Augustinian theology of marriage, though, will require a new theology, equally carefully developed and equally biblically plausible, to be offered in its place. I cannot claim to have read everything ever written, but in what I have read, I do not see anywhere where this task has even begun to be recognised, let alone attempted.

---

27. I made this argument in general terms, not focusing on marriage, in my *Listening to the Past: The Place of Tradition in Theology* (Carlisle: Paternoster, 2003), particularly chs. 1, 2, 10.

WILLIAM LOADER

The candid humility and clarity of Stephen's contribution makes it a pleasure to read and to engage. He poses the question in conclusion: "What if an Augustinian theology of marriage is just wrong? If it is, all my arguments here are irrelevant." I would not go so far as deeming the arguments irrelevant, but I do suggest that a revision of Augustine's theology of marriage is indeed called for. But first let me underscore the implications of taking Augustine's view of marriage as our foundation. Stephen's paper sets this out clearly.

The task of theology is "patient listening" to "the scriptural witness" and to do so "without qualification or evasion." At the same time we face "a secondary task of understanding our own cultural and intellectual context well enough that we are able to identify those aspects of the biblical witness which our particular church community will need to reexamine." That includes dealing with the "local revisionary pressure" which may lead to wrong conclusions. These principles are brought to bear on the current issue of "the ethical status of committed, exclusive, lifelong same-sex sexual relationships." Stephen's argument is that "we need . . . to recover a Christian understanding of human sexuality as primarily oriented towards procreation, not towards pleasure, and to restate an ethic that takes this orientation seriously."

Stephen notes that this focus and, indeed, the de-emphasis of marriage both in 1 Corinthians 7 and in similar terms in Matthew 19:12 reflect not distaste for the body as in second-century Gnosticism, but a preference for celibacy over marriage, both good, but the first better than the latter. He cites the explanation that marriage reflects concern with death, whereas celibacy reflects confidence in life beyond death. I can add from my own research that where celibacy appears in early Judaism, it is mostly concerned with holy space and time and the assumption that nakedness and sexual activity have no place in the holy sphere. We see this also in Paul's recommendation that couples refrain from intercourse for a time for the sake of prayer, but it also plays a significant role in early Christian expectations that the age to come will be holy space. In such holy space, which Paul and others believed they would soon enter, they neither marry nor are given in marriage; life like the angels in holy space leaves no room for sex. Paul must then defend marriage against those who apparently wanted to insist that all should live now as they would then. For marriage is not something evil but part of God's order of creation in this age,[1]

I am not a specialist in Augustine, but am sufficiently familiar with the issues to recognise the accuracy and potency of the argument which Stephen mounts, that Augustine laid the foundation of current Christian understandings of marriage. Augustine was not, of course, infallible, but on marriage his assumptions remain. His focus is on "procreation as the primary good of marriage." With that prior understanding, same-sex marriage is a contradiction in terms. It cannot fulfill that aim, which requires the male-female complementarity of penis and vagina. Accordingly, even when accepting sexual intercourse to satisfy desire, there must be the proviso: "so long as nothing is done to prevent the possibility of conception, which excludes both contraceptive devices and sex acts that are not in principle able to result in fertilization." Stephen notes two changes which have taken place in Protestant understandings of marriage: the acceptance of contraception and the possibility of divorce and then remarriage as sometimes pastorally appropriate. Both modifications Stephen sees as "fairly minor ones, to the basic Augustinian understanding, not rejections of it." In addition he points out that the logic of Augustine's position excludes all sex acts, including within marriage, which are not procreative, as sin.

A prior question in relation to discussion of same-sex marriage is the legitimacy of same-sex relations at all. Stephen rehearses the way in which such relations have often been pederastic, abusive, violent, and related to prostitution and exploitative. At most one might consider egalitarian relationships, but evidence for these in history as permanent, he argues, is thin. This raises for Stephen the legitimate question: Why has it become an issue in contemporary Western societies? Here he raises

---

1. On celibacy, see the discussion in William Loader, *The New Testament on Sexuality* (Grand Rapids: Eerdmans, 2012) (=*NTS*), 430–90.

objections to arguments that virtues displayed by gay people somehow legitimize their lifestyle or give them a right to marry. He also calls into question the popular assumptions about being necessarily born one way or the other, whereas this may vary. Nevertheless he is prepared to accept "the 'orientation' premise." As he rightly points out, however, "We can only support same-sex marriage from a general 'right to marry' if we have already assumed that same-sex marriage is acceptable." I would suggest that much of the opposition to gay marriage is rooted, in fact, not in understanding of marriage but in prior assumptions about the sinfulness of same-sex intercourse.

In the end both his starting point and his analysis of attempts to counter it, such as with civil unions or arguments about overpopulation or surrogacy, lead Stephen to reassert Augustine's theology of marriage: "In Christian belief and practice, procreation is the proper end of marriage. A relationship that is not ordered towards procreation may be good and right and holy, but it is not a marriage."

I found the argument compelling if one shares his starting point. He rightly acknowledges that its implications are far reaching and might not sit well with those for whom sex in marriage is much more than procreative. That acknowledgment also brings him to discuss marriage where procreation is not possible. One implication could be that infertile couples and post-menopausal women should not marry or indeed should abstain from sexual intercourse. In my view, Stephen underplays the significance of these exceptions. As noted in my response to Megan, Plato proposes a strict regime for propagation of the best citizens involving fertile women and insists that sexual intercourse must be for procreation, but then concedes that to demand that infertile older couples abstain would be unjust. Philo argues similarly, despite sharing Plato's insistence and that of many philosophers of his day whose teaching strongly influenced church fathers, that sexual intercourse must be for procreation, the sole rationale for marriage. If one took such strictures to the extreme, one would also need to argue that sexual intercourse during menstruation (forbidden on purity grounds in Lev 18) and also during pregnancy should be forbidden. Indeed, our more accurate knowledge of the menstrual cycle should imply that sexual intercourse take place only on those days when fertilization is possible.

The reality then and now is that sexual engagement cannot be restricted to attempts to procreate and entails much more (or one might say much less) than acts which produce orgasm of one partner or the other or seminal emission. Love and intimacy find physical, emotional expression in a variety of ways which can enrich and enhance a relationship. People knew that then, in biblical times, but also in Augustine's time, even though marriage then was usually of a male roughly twice the age of his wife and arranged by worried and/or wise fathers for the sake of the household and the extended family. Megan's contribution underlines how we have moved beyond the patriarchal model which made a good metaphor for Christ as head of the church in Ephesians. There is also arguably some recognition in the etiology of marriage in the two Genesis creation stories that procreation is not the only role for sexual union. The first has a clear focus on male and female receiving the mandate to multiply in Genesis 1. Genesis 2, however, has God declare that it is not good for the man to be alone and makes him a companion like himself. This then becomes an etiology of sexual attraction as the two come together again. Leaving one's parents' house to begin a new one will surely include the sense of offspring, but it is not the primary focus of the passage.

The same may be said of the accounts of Jesus' combination of male and female from Genesis 1:27 and becoming one flesh in Genesis 2:24. The focus is the new relationship of one flesh created by the union. Procreation is to be assumed but it is not the center of attention. It is interesting that Paul too does not focus on procreation in his discussions of sexual relations and marriage. It was, however, virtually impossible to separate lovemaking as a tender expression of intimacy from procreative intercourse. Faced with the prospect of impending eschatological fulfillment (and an age to come without sex and marriage), the need to propagate did not loom large for Paul. Nor should we reduce his statements to seeing marriage as merely a bulwark to control sexual drive, because he also speaks in 1 Corinthians of love and affection (7:3–5, 32–34).[2] Reducing the alternatives to seeking to procreate or seeking pleasure, as in Stephen's words, "a Christian understanding of human sexuality as primarily oriented towards procreation, not towards pleasure," denies the affirmation of human intimacy and love.

---

2. *NTS* 182–222.

What they already affirmed, and inextricably bound up together, we now acknowledge as belonging to the core of our understandings of marriage. The love and mutuality, already suggested by Paul, plus cultural and theological reappraisal of older attitudes towards women as inappropriate have produced an understanding of marriage where the biblical value of intimate partnership plays a far greater role. In addition the very recent advent of contraception has enabled people to differentiate procreative sex from sex as an expression of intimacy. The advent of effective contraception is not to be treated as compromising true marriage, but as enriching married partnerships with new opportunities, a richness measured in the currency of the love and compassion which also enabled the church, or at least some churches, to see that gospel values may point on occasion to divorce and remarriage as a more redemptive option.

Augustine's model needs updating in the light of the abandonment of patriarchal marriage, of arranged marriages, of the absolute prohibition of divorce and of remarriage, of the inseparability of sex for procreation and sex as an expression of intimate oneness, and of the prohibition of contraception. While one might want to mount the argument that at each point of abandonment we abandon key values in the interests of laxity and self-indulgence, this will simply not do.

Once one allows that Augustine's model is no longer adequate, then this at least opens the possibility that a marriage between two people who are not able to be procreative need not be deemed not a marriage on that account. This applies to infertile couples and, indeed, for significant periods to most modern marriages. Why might it not apply to two people of the same gender? The objection that they cannot procreate is rather lame—contradicted by so much of the way marriage operates today. Of course in some jurisdictions, they can adopt, and parenting by same-gender couples may be equally as effective as that by heterosexual couples provided such parenting in both contexts exposes children to a wider range of adults.

Some people choose celibacy, including many whose orientation is toward their own gender, sadly sometimes for fear of the prejudice and suffering they may be faced with in intolerant societies. But it is an option, and for some their life of faith enables them to adapt to see this as their calling—like Jesus and Paul. Both firmly resisted generalizing this to all (Matt 19:12; 1 Cor 7:7). Generalizing it to all with same-gender orientation seems also on the same grounds to be inappropriate. The compassion in Paul which affirms that for those for whom celibacy is not an option, entering marriage is acceptable and not a sin (1 Cor 7:8–9, 28) might apply to those whose orientation is towards their own, a state which Paul could only deem the result of perversion. Once we acknowledge that for some it is not, we find ourselves asking what is the most caring and healthy form through which such people might express their relationship. Sex will often not be the centre, as it is often not for heterosexual marriage, but simply an aspect of a lifelong commitment to partnership which they want wider society to recognize and bless and respect.

MEGAN K. DEFRANZA

We are indebted to Dr. Steve Holmes for modeling the work of theology as it relates to biblical interpretation: "patient listening" to Scripture with the help of those who have lived in times vastly different from our own, whose perspectives can help us avoid the all-too-easy mistake of reading into the Bible our own cultural prejudices. Holmes also reminds us that we must listen charitably to our queer siblings in Christ as well as to the church global. All of these assist us in listening for the voice of the Spirit, who can lead us in the Way of Jesus.

Dr. Holmes has carefully outlined the essentials of the traditionalist approach—essentials we identify in each of our chapters as procreation and complementarity. In fact, there is much we agree upon: the timeliness and theological appropriateness of this conversation, the urgency to end discrimination in the church where LGBT Christians are held to higher standards than straight members, and concerns over the ways in which secular culture has infiltrated Christian teaching on sexuality (pp. 180, 167, 185). "Our sexual desires are not in pressing need of being fulfilled; they are in pressing need of being mastered and reordered so that we may grow in Christlikeness" (p. 184). We both view marriage and celibacy as ascetic practices developed by the church historic to guide and assist the sanctifying process, but differ in pastoral particulars. Holmes is willing to consider ecclesial accommodation for same-sex couples modeled along the lines of pastoral responses to less than ideal circumstances (such as divorce in the West and polygyny in Africa). I believe the tradition of Christian marriage can be opened up to those for whom procreation is not possible—same-sex partners, infertile heterosexual couples—as well as fertile spouses who pursue goods other than childbearing.

Of course, the idea that marriage is for having children is rooted in the long tradition of the church. Early Christians viewed marriage (with its connection to childbearing) as a remedy for death—children carried the name of the family forward even after death. But Christ's victory defeated death, ushering in the celibate ideal. With literal marriage delivered of its primary purpose, its value remained as a way for Christians to manage their passions (1 Cor 7). Meanwhile, marriage morphed into theological metaphor, becoming "an image of Christ's love for the church" (Eph 5) (p. 170).

The notion that matrimony existed for children was not unique to early Christians. Secular sources confirm this cultural assumption, but with a caveat: Marriage was a privilege of the free, established to secure not simply children but *legitimate* children. Slaves were not granted the right to marry, and marriage between classes was discouraged (as Augustine's personal history illustrates). These Roman ideals appear enshrined in the language itself. "Matrimony" comes from the Latin for mother (*mater*); "one could say that a basic function of Roman marriage was to make a *mater, pater* [father], and *liberi* [freeborn children], the mother serving the function of creating the legitimate offspring to whom the property of the father could be handed down."[3]

For the early desert monastics, it was this connection between family and financial resources, more than any aversion to sex, which led them to see celibacy as the way to live free of worldly entanglements.[4] It was to this culture—which saw marriage tying one to the economy of this world—that Augustine wrote to defend marriage as having intrinsic goods, even if these goods were not the "better" of the celibate religious life. Holmes helpfully outlines Augustine's three goods of marriage: procreation, fidelity, and sacrament. "'Sacrament' refers, for Augustine, primarily to the permanence of marriage, which he believes is a result of a particular divine grace given in marriage" (p. 171). Given that same-sex couples are able to live faithfully and uphold the permanence of marriage, it is on the basis of the first "good" which Holmes finds them to be incompatible with Christian marriage. He takes Augustine's goods to be authoritative, given their longstanding "stable" use, a stability which he takes "as significant confirmation that it is correct" (p. 193).

---

3. Craig Williams, *Roman Homosexuality*, 2nd ed. (Oxford: University Press, 2010), appendix 2, 280–81.
4. Peter Brown, *The Body and Society: Men, Women, and Sexual Renunciation in Early Christianity* (New York: Columbia University Press, 1988), 220.

This is where my own perspective parts ways with Holmes. While I would agree that we must pay attention to the wisdom of the past, I remain suspicious of tradition, even when it has been stable. As a female theologian, I do not find the stability and majority of the tradition to be sufficient warrants for its authority. Recognizing how long it has taken churches to recognize the full humanity of women and our gifts for service in the church, I am particularly attentive to the ways in which traditional theologies of marriage are related to ancient assumptions about sex and gender.

As Holmes admits, his argument is built on two presuppositions: (1) procreation as the primary end of marriage, and (2) the complementarity of the sexes. The former supplies the majority of his chapter, whilst the latter he does not address due to the very real space limitations of this project. Still, I believe it is essential that we unpack both premises.

If I read Dr. Holmes correctly, he views sex/gender complementarity as something beyond reproductive complementarity since the latter forms the basis of his first premise. But what is gender complementarity? I value complementarity more generally—indeed, I experience complementarity in my own marriage to my husband of nineteen years—but as I have written elsewhere, if we are to get beyond stereotyping and sexism, we must define our terms carefully and submit them to scrutiny.[5] I would wager that in every marriage, complementarity looks and feels different, so much so that the idea of finding a complementary spouse of the same sex is not beyond imagination.

We need to know what Holmes means by gender complementarity because it is essential to his argument. For if the primary purpose of marriage is procreation, then we must ask why Christians appear untroubled when infertile couples and those beyond the age of childbearing tie the knot. Astute theologian that he is, Holmes is ready for this rebuttal.

> A relationship that is not ordered towards procreation may be good and right and holy, but it is not a marriage. Discussions of the marriage of elderly people or of overpopulation do not change this at all. (p. 189)

---

5. See my *Sex Difference in Christian Theology: Male, Female, and Intersex in the Image of God* (Grand Rapids: Eerdmans, 2015), especially ch. 5.

This is a strong assertion but, unfortunately, one Holmes does not defend. He provides no explanation why our willingness to marry those who cannot conceive does not relate to discussions of same-sex marriages which are ruled outside of the tradition for precisely this reason—the non-procreative nature of their union. I believe the key to his assumption lies two sentences prior: "the question of the complementarity of male and female in marriage which I have not explored for reasons of space but which is also part of the tradition" (p. 188). I am quite sympathetic to the need for more space to explore these matters, having penned several hundred pages in my own attempt to unpack the ways in which the tradition has construed sex difference and our urgent need to reconsider it in light of our growing understanding of sex and gender differences.[6] Still, some attempt to address this half of his argument is needed.

Given that Dr. Holmes concedes the culturally conditioned nature of sexual orientation, I am surprised that he does not also concede the culturally conditioned nature of gender—the ways in which societies invest the bodies of men, women, intersex, and others with meaning and socialize them accordingly (p. 181). Attempts to find essential psychological and behavioral gender differences continue to flounder on the shoals of cultural and individual diversity. As behavioral neuroscientist Melissa Hines has explained, "Although most of us appear to be either clearly male or clearly female, we are each complex mosaics of [so-called] male and female characteristics."[7]

I believe our modern willingness to make exceptions for the elderly and infertile illustrates that we have already moved past Augustine's evaluation of procreation as the preeminent marital good. I say this because the church has not always been willing to make such accommodations. When Roman law was wed to Christian theology, those known to be infertile (such as castrated males—the second type of eunuch mentioned by Jesus in Matt 19:12) were forbidden to marry. Such restrictions remained on the books through centuries of European law.[8]

Interestingly, while castrated eunuchs were forbidden to marry

---

6. DeFranza, *Sex Difference*, especially chs. 3 and 4.

7. Melissa Hines, *Brain Gender* (Oxford: University Press, 2004), 18–19. See also Mary E. Frandsen, *"Eunuchi conjugium"*: The Marriage of a Castrato in Early Modern Germany," *Early Music History* 24 (2005): 53–124.

8. Anne Fausto-Sterling, *Sexing the Body: Gender Politics and the Construction of Sexuality* (New York: Basic, 2000), 36.

because of the assurance of infertility, naturally born eunuchs (those born with physical differences which would have included some kinds of intersex) as well as hermaphrodites or androgynes were not typically banned from marriage. Although the bodies of some of these individuals called into question neat and clean notions of "opposite sex" marriage, they were nevertheless permitted on the possibility of procreation.[9] Similar instructions can be found in early rabbinic literature.[10] It appears that for the majority of the tradition, those known to be infertile were not allowed to marry, while those whose bodies undermined sex/gender complementarity could.

Christians have already moved past Augustine's assessment of procreation as the justification of marriage, and for good reasons— procreation is never presented in the Bible as an essential component of marriage. Certainly the first parents were called to "fill the earth" (Gen 1:28), and offspring are viewed as a blessing and heritage (Ps 127), but there are no passages which present children as the goal of marriage. They are conspicuously absent from the Song of Songs and Paul's extensive instructions on the reasons for or against marriage found in 1 Corinthians 7. Long before concerns about overpopulation, Augustine argued that humans fulfilled the command to "fill the earth" at the birth of the Messiah.[11]

Holmes worries that without procreation, we will not be able to justify marriage theologically, but I do not share his worry. The Roman Catholic revision of Augustinian priorities—a revision which places the union of the spouses on par with procreation—has been well received. Pope John Paul II's *Theology of the Body* painted spousal love as the primary image of the love found in the Trinity made visible in Christ's self-sacrificial love for the church.[12] Catholic theologian David Matzko

---

9. Mark Brustman, "The Ancient Roman and Talmudic Definition of Natural Eunuchs," a paper presented at a conference on *"Eunuchs in Antiquity and Beyond,"* Cardiff University, July 27, 1999, http://www.well.com/user/aquarius/cardiff.htm.

10. See Alfred Cohen, "Tumtum and Androgynous," *Journal of Halacha and Contemporary Society* 38 (1999): 62–85. John Hare, "Hermaphrodites, Eunuchs, and Intersex People: The Witness of Medical Science in Biblical Times and Today," in *Intersex, Theology, and the Bible: Troubling Bodies in Church, Text, and Society,* Susannah Cornwall, ed. (New York: Palgrave MacMillan, 2015), 86.

11. Augustine, *De bono coniugali, De sancta uirginitate,* ed. P. G. Walsh (Oxford: Clarendon Press, 2001), XVII; 37.

12. John Paul II, *Man and Woman He Create Them: A Theology of the Body,* trans. and ed. Michael Waldstein (Boston: Pauline Books and Media, 2006), 163, homily 9:3, 427, 77:2. See

McCarthy explains that Catholic theologians are working to correct older theologies of marriage which taught that "marriage is not a good in itself but produces only external goods like children and social stability."[13] The pope's vision of spousal love as the gift of the whole self has been echoed among Protestants, most of whom do not share the Vatican's concerns about contraception within marriage.[14] Certainly the metaphor of marriage for the church's relationship to Christ is one that excludes the idea of children. Since the children of God become the bride of Christ, most would view these images as mutually exclusive. Marriage can continue to serve as an icon of the self-giving love of God even when couples are not able to conceive.

The ancients married for many reasons—"duty . . . and the need for an insurance policy for old age"—reasons Holmes admits are different from our own (p. 183). Marriage and children render little status in contemporary Western society. The few perks (e.g., tax breaks for couples with children) are hardly sufficient incentives to lure the growing number of those choosing to remain single if rarely celibate. Still, those who don't marry for children still wed for very biblical reasons; many feel deeply the assessment of God in Genesis 2:18: "It is not good that the [human] should be alone." We desire "a helper as [our] partner" (NRSV), a "suitable" (NIV) "companion" (Complete Jewish Bible), one who will help us in life's challenges, share in life's joys, and whose faithful love makes visible, even tangible, the self-giving love of God. This companionate vision of marriage can be traced back at least to Protestant Reformers who added companionship and pleasure to Augustine's marital goods.[15] For most, this partner will be a person whose sex differs from their own, with the majority of these having procreative potential. But there remains a minority for whom there is no "opposite sex" and

also John Paul II, "Commitment to Promoting Women's Dignity," (general audience, Nov. 24, 1999), in *The Trinity's Embrace: God's Saving Plan, a Catechesis on Salvation History* (Boston: Pauline Books and Media, 2002), 289.

13. David Matzko McCarthy, *Sex and Love in the Home: A Theology of the Household,* 2nd. ed. (London: SCM, 2004), 4–5. Despite these improvements, McCarthy worries that the personalist account of conjugal love goes too far when using this lens as the primary pattern of divine and Christian love. For my analysis of these developments in Roman Catholic and evangelical theology, see especially DeFranza, *Sex Difference,* ch. 4.

14. Stanley J. Grenz, *Sexual Ethics: An Evangelical Perspective* (Louisville: Westminster John Knox Press, 1990), 87–89.

15. Ibid., 149.

another subset who find that someone of the same sex is most suitable, given their orientation.

Protestants have long sifted Augustine's theological contributions—holding on to insights they find useful and disregarding those incompatible with their interpretations of the Bible and their experience. The Reformers rejected Augustine's construal of marriage as a sacrament, reducing the number of sacraments to two or three; at the same time they added pleasure and companionship to their theologies of marriage. I would think that these are changes Holmes would approve, given his identity as a Baptist theologian.

It may require some innovative thinking to outline the already shifting priorities of marriage which we are seeing among a number of contemporary followers of Jesus, but this is the task of theology. As we attend to voices long left out of the tradition—the voices of women, sex, gender, and sexual minorities, as well as those of non-European descent, etc.—we may begin to hear the voice of the Spirit in the Scriptures leading us in fresh and still altogether faithful ways.

RESPONSE TO STEPHEN R. HOLMES

WESLEY HILL

Stephen Holmes and I wrote our essays for this volume independently of each other, so I was gratified and emboldened when I saw that we had arrived at what I think are similar, compatible conclusions. Holmes and I agree that Christian marriage is the faithful bond of male and female which is open to the new life of children and bears witness to Christ's love for the church. He therefore argues that if we are to speak of the full inclusion of LGBT people in the church, we must either come to a new understanding of marriage that does not depend on sexual difference, or come to a new understanding of the possibility of faithful sexual coupling being sanctioned outside the marital relationship, or attempt some kind of "pastoral accommodation" for those living in same-sex sexually expressive relationships. Holmes judges the first two of these three options to be untenable, and he finishes his essay by advocating a certain form of the third. In my response, I want to make a few comments about the exegetical basis of the "Augustinian" theology of marriage Holmes has offered, and I want also to try to tease out more of the implications of Holmes's suggestions for pastoral accommodation.

One of the key claims of Holmes's essay is that Augustine bequeathed to the church an understanding that "marriage is a good intended by God, even for Christians who believe in the resurrection, and not merely an inferior mode of life to virginity." I think Holmes—and Augustine—are right in making this claim, but I feel the force of what Holmes later asks himself toward the end of his essay: "What if an Augustinian theology of marriage is just wrong?" Holmes admits he has not attempted the exegetical heavy lifting that would be needed to undergird his Augustinian claims, and I would like to point to some of the ways he might have done so.

My essay suggested that Augustine's view has proved so resilient throughout church history because of its ability to synthesize a broad range of canonical material in a way that unveils a trajectory or coherence in that material. As my coauthors and I put it in a recent essay on same-sex marriage in the Episcopal Church, "Augustine came to his threefold account of the goods of marriage by way of strenuous wrestling with the first three chapters of Genesis, the affirmation by Jesus of marriage's created goodness in Matthew 19, and the claim of Ephesians 5 that marriage is a figure of Christ and the Church."[16] What this means is that the persuasive plausibility of Augustine's view depends on our being able to follow the way he interweaves Genesis, Jesus' affirmation of the Genesis stories, and the later Pauline view that marriage not only fulfills the Genesis affirmations (Eph 5:31) but also gains its ultimate coherence when seen as an image or icon of Christ's love for the church (5:32; cf. Rev 19:7; 21:2, 9). For many of us who are trained to read historically, this will involve us in tracing out the historical unfolding of the canon and giving priority to its final shaping.[17] It is unlikely that we would arrive at Augustine's view if we only had 1 Corinthians 7 to go on. Rather, it is only when we attend to the final form of the Pauline letter collection, in which we find Ephesians' robust affirmation of marriage and the expectation of a growing Christian household that includes children, that we are able to take Augustine's view seriously as a fulsome Christian position.[18]

Would we, as Holmes suggests, still find this view opposed to same-sex marriage and same-sex genital intimacy if we lacked the infamous biblical passages that address same-sex relations explicitly (for instance, Rom 1)? I think so, though I hope my essay provided the exegetical "footnote" on Leviticus 18, Romans 1, and 1 Corinthians 6 that Holmes mentioned as being desirable, thereby "offer[ing] a welcome, but small,

---

16. John Bauerschmidt, Zachary Guiliano, Wesley Hill, and Jordan Hylden, "Marriage in Creation and Covenant: A Response to the Task Force on the Study of Marriage," *Anglican Theological Review*, accessed March 9, 2016, http://www.anglicantheologicalreview.org/static/pdf/conversations/MarriageInCreationAndCovenant.pdf.

17. I acknowledge my indebtedness to Brevard Childs, among other so-called "canonical critics," at this point.

18. What I am suggesting is that it is actually the historical development within the canon that leads to Augustine's theology of marriage. Most likely Ephesians itself intends to supplement or adapt the views expressed in 1 Cor for a slightly later moment in early Christian history. On this, compare John M. G. Barclay, "Ordinary But Different: Colossians and Hidden Moral Identity," in *Pauline Churches and Diaspora Jews*, WUNT 275 (Tübingen: Mohr Siebeck, 2011), 237–55. What the later Pauline letters intend is "to interpret household relations within the framework of allegiance to the Lord" (p. 247).

degree of confirmation that a position reached for other, much weightier, exegetical and theological reasons is indeed correct."

But if this Augustinian view is correct and those of us who are lesbian or gay are therefore obliged to refrain from the kind of sex we feel most "hardwired" to experience, what are we to do? How shall we go about living our lives? Holmes rightly pinpoints this as the crucial question facing those churches who wish to maintain the "traditional" view of marriage and sexuality today: "What spaces are there in our churches for celibate gay, lesbian, or straight adults to find community and intimacy?"

I would like to press him—and, by implication, the wider Christian community—on just this point. If, as it seems, the best psychological and anecdotal evidence suggests that people not only need a wide network of acquaintances and friendly supporters but also more intimate attachments and kinship relations in order to flourish, where does that leave celibate lesbian and gay Christians? I have been involved for the past several years in promoting the vocation of "spiritual friendship" in the church, urging pastors and counselors and families and single believers alike to esteem friendship more highly than they have done hitherto and view it as a bond capable of permanence and public honor.[19] But I am all too aware that I am swimming upstream. Even the very strongest and closest friendships that I know of can be quickly downplayed or even jettisoned if one decides, say, to make a cross-country move. In our Western culture, friendship just isn't a very "thick" bond, and many lesbian and gay believers have told me that it seems like a cheap consolation prize when placed alongside the former more venerable "til death do us part" commitment of marriage. As one lesbian bluntly put it, "The suggestion that friendships are all any LGBT person needs or deserves is cruelty masquerading as kindness."[20] The sentiment here, I think, is not merely one of self-indulgence ("I need my friends to meet all my intimacy needs"); it is much more powerfully a desire for self-sacrifice ("I need to be able to offer love and care to someone"). In the face of these sorts of heartfelt yearnings, is it enough for Holmes and me to

---

19. Wesley Hill, *Spiritual Friendship: Finding Love in the Church as a Celibate Gay Christian* (Grand Rapids: Brazos, 2015).

20. Casey Pick, "Friends Without Benefits," accessed March 9, 2016, http://www.believe outloud.com/latest/friends-without-benefits.

trumpet "community" and "hospitality" in the church while at the same time recommending that lesbian and gay believers refrain from entering into a sexually intimate relationship with a life partner? I don't think so.

A gay Christian friend of mine wrote the following in a letter to me:

> It was a great relief to me to realize that if God is, in fact, calling me to a vocation of celibacy it does not mean I am called to "singleness." God does not call anyone to singleness [as we conceive it in contemporary Western societies]. We are all created by God to live within kinship networks wherein we share daily life in permanent relationships. . . . It is often said that singleness can be a blessing because it gives a person more options. . . . The Church has [bought] into the lie that "singleness" allows a person "freedom" to serve the Lord. This sounds very spiritual and noble. But what does that even mean? That we are to go off like the Lone Ranger to save the world by ourselves? No, if we have been called to a celibate, non-marital state in order to better serve, we must do that within the context of kinship— covenanted brothers, sisters, mothers, and fathers with whom we share daily mutual support.[21]

This seems exactly right to me. But it puts an uncomfortable question mark over our current ways of life in the church. What would have to change in order for us to become the sorts of communities that could provide thick, covenanted kinship networks for nonheterosexual celibate believers? Adapting the words of Peter Maurin, of the Catholic Worker Movement, what must we do in our churches to make it easier for lesbian and gay Christians to be virtuous?

Holmes's essay gestures toward an answer in very broad terms, as he admits. He rightly criticizes general rules as being typically inattentive to the particularities of individual human experience. But I want to make a couple of concrete proposals, using my own experience as a sort of test case, to stimulate the ecclesial imagination. For starters, I want to propose that churches embracing a traditional Christian, "Augustinian" sexual ethic consider looking for ways to publicly honor

---

21. Personal correspondence, August 25, 2013. Used with correspondent's permission.

and celebrate nonmarital forms of belonging and kinship. Practices such as godparenthood are ripe for fresh attention in this connection (I speak as an Episcopalian for whom the practice of infant baptism is assumed). Churches could counsel young parents to choose godparents for their children whom they wish to draw more deeply into the circle of their family. After my friend Jono called me and asked me to be a godfather to his and his wife Megan's daughter Callie, I wrote an email to him in which I said, "I take comfort from this—that, in Jesus' economy, leaving the prospect of being a husband and father myself does not mean being without a family."

Beyond this, I think churches should consider promoting communal living among their members. As a friend of mine who relocated with his wife and children to an impoverished inner-city neighborhood has written,

> More families—yes, even families with small children—should open their homes to single adults. My friends and I may represent only a small sample, but I'm happy to say that we've had four housemates in five years of marriage and all involved have judged the experience as positive. Our other friends in the neighborhood—some single, some married—have reported similar blessings from this sort of fellowship. Much of this, I think, is because we all worship together and share the same commitments to loving one another. This has been particularly powerful when people in great need have taken up residence with us. While a lease is a far cry from a vowed friendship, it might be enough of a commitment to get us started.[22]

I don't want to imply that we can find an easy panacea for the pain of celibacy in our culture. In a time when romantic love and sexual "fulfillment" are idolized, it is probably inevitable that celibate persons, even those with the richest and most durable kinship networks, will feel the sting of loneliness. Nor do I wish to give the impression that finding oneself embedded in intentional communities will mean a newly problem-free celibate life. But I do know that the problems of

---

22. Matthew Loftus, "Material Dimensions of Spiritual Friendship," accessed March 9, 2016, http://mereorthodoxy.com/material-dimensions-spiritual-friendship/.

community are vastly superior to the problems of isolation.[23] I want to see our "traditionalist" churches spending more energy caring for their gay members who are bonded and vowed to specific households and therein facing profound challenges rather than shepherding those members through the avoidable and far more tragic heartache of unattachment.

---

23. I owe this way of putting things to Eve Tushnet, who has stressed this point in many contexts over the years. See her *Gay and Catholic: Accepting My Sexuality, Finding Community, Living My Faith* (Notre Dame, IN: Ave Maria, 2014), 168–69.

REJOINDER

STEPHEN R. HOLMES

I am very grateful to my three colleagues for their generous and careful readings of my essay. In response, I wish to address two particular points, make a general comment about the shape of the argument found in the book, and then reflect a little on how we should now order church life.

Let me first pick up Dr. Hill's closing point about community, friendship, and celibacy, and simply agree with him. I said, I think, some of the same things in my response to his essay. I accept that I have talked about these issues in very general terms, whereas he has discussed specific practices. I accept also that my reflection in these areas needs to become more specific. Unless I am missing something, however, I do not think he is pressing me on any point that I do not already support.

Second, I turn to Dr. DeFranza's challenge about gender complementarity. It seems to me exegetically necessary that our account of God's good purposes in creation includes some sort of gender complementarity—Jesus' reaffirmation of Genesis is only the most obvious piece of evidence for this. I also think the reality of our fallenness affects this area of our existence as much as every other. Maleness and femaleness are unattainable ideals for us at this point in our existence (just as humanness is), but these creational norms still order our existence in our brokenness.

I believe that an account like this is capacious enough to cope with the reality of intersex, although I cannot claim to have anything like DeFranza's expert knowledge of that area of human biology. I also suggest on this basis that attempts to find well-defined gender roles out of creational norms are necessarily doomed to failure; we cannot proceed as if we lived still in Eden. Instead, Scripture proposes to us a degree of missional conformity to the accepted gender norms of the culture we happen to find ourselves in, tempered by an absolute insistence on the full dignity and humanity of all people and a conviction that the Spirit is poured out on daughters and sons indifferently, bringing gifts to be used for the edification of the church.

This basic theological orientation of confessing our fallenness is crucial in the debates we are having. Arguments from the fall have sometimes been used very badly. Any suggestion that to be gay (or intersex) is to be somehow "more fallen" than being straight (or male or female) must be resisted strenuously—not just because it is oppressive but because it is bad theology; the category of "fallen" does not admit qualifiers by degree. The response, however, is not to imbue all our desires and existences with prelapsarian perfection, but to confess the indifferent brokenness of every human person.

Once we do this, we can recognise that the point of our theology of marriage is not to determine which desires are wholesome and which less so. In our present condition, none of our desires are wholesome; all spring from what Yeats memorably termed "the foul rag and bone shop of the heart."[1] Marriage or celibacy reorders our desires to teach us to desire rightly. This does not, of course, determine the question of same-sex marriage, but it does orient it.

This leads me to my reflection on the shape of our argument. Too often recent Christian reflection in this area has assumed the perfection of heterosexual desire and addressed a small cluster of texts that have been taken to question the perfection of homosexual desire. I have proposed—and from their responses, I take it that my colleagues have accepted—that this is not a good way to construct the argument. Instead, we need to focus on a wider biblical account of the nature and purpose of human sexuality.

Both Dr. Hill and I turned to Augustine for the contours of this, arguing that Augustine's account has been normative for virtually all Christian reflection in this area. We both acknowledge that there are aspects of Augustine's doctrine that needed to be, and have been, discarded, but also that there is a stable core that is biblically defensible and still determinative for Christian theologies of marriage today.

---

1. From Yeats, "The Circus Animals' Desertion."

Serious argument in this area, I suggest, should focus here if it is to advance the present debate: To what extent is an Augustinian theology of marriage first defensible and second extensible to include same-sex relationships? If it is not defensible, what are we going to put in its place as an account of how our sexual behaviour is ordered to discipline our wayward desires? If it is not extensible, is there any other way in which we might find space for same-sex relationships? These are the important questions, and too often they are left unaddressed by writers or speakers.

I began my essay with an indication that theological disagreement was always a process which thus took time; unsurprisingly, we have not reached agreement at the end of this volume. I have learnt things and had my thinking sharpened by the interactions here, and I am grateful to my three colleagues for that, but the slow development of academic debate cannot be where we end. We can all recall horrific stories of people profoundly damaged, driven out of the church, driven to suicide even, because of their sexuality. In the face of continued academic disagreement, the question is urgent, more urgent than our debates can manage: How then do we live?

At heart, the answer is simple: any church practice that is not fundamentally loving in orientation, and loving not only of imagined perfect people who exist outside of cultural pressures but of real fallen people in all their locatedness, is sub-Christian. At the same time, any church practice that is not centred on the call to (countercultural) repentance and holiness is sub-Christian.

Of course, on either side of the argument, this can be taken as decisive: "I cannot imagine a conservative church practice that is adequately loving to LGBT+ people"; "I cannot imagine an affirming church practice that takes the call to holiness adequately seriously." The response to such exclamations is straightforward: the limits of my (or anyone else's) imagination are not interesting theological data. We are called to go beyond our imaginations, to be led by God's Spirit into church practices that are as welcoming of outcasts as Jesus was during his earthly ministry and as implacable in the face of sin as Jesus was then. Conservative or affirming, this is the challenge we must always put before ourselves.

HOMOSEXUALITY, THE BIBLE, AND THE CHURCH

PRESTON M. SPRINKLE

Our authors set out to articulate a biblical and theological case for their view and to interact with their fellow essayists with convicted civility. From my vantage point, all the authors have succeeded in this regard. They have constructed compelling arguments for their positions in a clear and kind manner. In their responses, the tone was direct yet cordial, clear and compassionate, and still filled with academic rigor and depth. I was most of all impressed that each of the essayists gave much honor to their dialogue partners, even in disagreement. I felt like I was listening in on a gathering of friends in a living room pushing back on each other, yet still able to hit the pub together afterward.

My role as the editor is not to offer yet another critique or to speak *ex-cathedra* about the veracity of each essay. If I can be honest, I found myself agreeing and disagreeing with several points in each of the presentations. To round off the discussion, then, I would like to highlight some salient points that will require further reflection, and then offer some suggestions for future dialogue.

The Prohibition Texts

I was fascinated to find two very different interpretations of the so-called prohibition texts in the essays by Loader and DeFranza—both who argue for an affirming position. DeFranza argues that the biblical prohibitions against same-sex sexual behavior are probably focused on specific types of same-sex relations that were common in the ancient world (pederasty, rape, sex with slaves, prostitution, etc.). She does not believe that the Bible clearly prohibits same-sex relations fundamentally and absolutely. Bill Loader, however, disagrees. Loader argues that the biblical prohibitions do indeed condemn all forms of same-sex relations. He goes on to argue that since the biblical authors didn't have all the knowledge that we have about genuine gay people who are born with a same-sex orientation, we should therefore supplement biblical prohibitions with modern knowledge. And Loader is not alone. There are several biblical and historical scholars who affirm same-sex relations who also agree that the Bible does indeed prohibit all types of same-sex relations absolutely.[1]

The different approaches by Loader and DeFranza raise the question about how the affirming view understands the prohibition passages. Is it necessary to show that the prohibition passages do not apply to contemporary, adult-consenting, marital relations (as DeFranza argues)? Or are questions related to hermeneutics and ethics—whether the Bible's ancient views on human sexuality can inform and dictate a modern ethic—sufficient enough to set aside, or relativize, the prohibition passages? DeFranza's argument seems to rest largely, though not solely, on interpreting the prohibition passages more narrowly, understanding them as *not* applying to adult, consensual, monogamous relations. Does this mean that if Loader is right, DeFranza is wrong? How important is a particular reading of the prohibition passages for the affirming view?

Interestingly, Holmes believes that the prohibitions passages are not crucial to the debate. He argues that a sound Christian theology of marriage by itself excludes same-sex relations. But Holmes very humbly admits: "What if an Augustinian theology of marriage is just wrong? If it is, all my arguments here are irrelevant." If DeFranza is right, that Augustine's theology of marriage is wrong—or at least fallible and incomplete—then perhaps her reading of the prohibition passages will not make or break her argument for the affirming view, since a *Christian theology of marriage itself* is sufficient.

In sum, how significant are the prohibition passages for the debate? In particular, how necessary is a particular reading of the prohibition passages for the affirming view?

---

1. Most notably, Louis Crompton (*Homosexuality and Civilization* [Cambridge, MA: Harvard University Press, 2006]) and Bernadette Brooten (*Love Between Women: Early Christian Responses to Female Homoeroticism* [Chicago: Chicago University Press, 1998]).

Regardless of how we interpret the prohibition passages, both DeFranza and Loader raise questions about the very nature of biblical ethics that will require further discussion. The question is not *whether* the Bible is authoritative, but *how* it is authoritative. DeFranza in particular makes the provocative point that marriages today are not—or should not be considered—"biblical" marriages. When the Bible talks about marriage, it inevitably uses patriarchal categories familiar to its time which do not celebrate the full equality of women. The Bible is moving in the right direction; we see tensions even within the letters of Paul regarding his view of women in marriage and in the church. The faithful reader of Scripture should therefore continue this trajectory beyond the Bible toward the full inclusion of women. And this raises several questions. If we can see an incomplete trajectory within the Bible regarding the full inclusion of women as equal image bearers in marriage and in the church, can the same be done for the full inclusion of same-sex couples? Does the Bible express a similar trajectory or tension regarding same-sex relations? How important is a particular reading of the prohibition passages for this trajectory hermeneutic? And what is the role of modern science in reconsidering the Bible's statements about sexual ethics?

I know that many scholars and writers who have engaged the discussion of faith and sexuality are worn out by endless debates about the "clobber" (i.e., prohibition) passages. I understand the exhaustion, but more work needs to be done not only on the *interpretation* of the prohibition passages but on the *methodology* of their ethical role in the debate as a whole.

The Role of Procreation

Both Hill and Holmes argued that marital sex should be "ordered toward procreation." Holmes clarifies that it's the sexual *relationship* and not every sexual *act* which should be oriented toward procreation. Holmes goes so far as to say that the prohibition texts "are just not very significant for the ethical debate" once we understand and embrace an Augustinian theology of marriage, which includes the "good" of procreation. According to Holmes,

> Procreation as the primary good of marriage means that marriage must involve man and woman. Gender complementarity

is a creational reality that is ordered towards reproduction. Heterosexual sex is the only proper mode of sexual expression for human beings because it is directed towards the begetting of children. (p. 171)

I think every reader should wrestle with the validity of this argument. Evangelical Protestants are generally quite cavalier in how they think about the role of procreation in sex, and yet procreation has been considered one of the primary goods of marriage for the last 2,000 years of church history. I often hear non-affirming advocates point out that same-sex relations have been condemned by the church for the last 2,000 years as well. I wonder if non-affirming Christians who downplay the role of procreation are being consistent when they rely on church tradition for their views on same-sex relations but not on sex for procreation. I therefore applaud Holmes and Hill for (re)introducing us to what has been one of the primary goods of marriage for the last 2,000 years of church history: procreation.

This raises the question, though, of how intrinsic procreation is to the entire scope of the biblical narrative. The New Testament does not seem to replicate the same emphasis on procreation that we see in the Old Testament. It is striking that Paul can develop a theology of marriage in Ephesians 5 with no mention of procreation.[2] Jesus can talk about marriage and divorce in Matthew 19 with no mention of procreation. Paul can talk about celibacy, lust, sex, marriage, and divorce in 1 Corinthians 7 with no mention of procreation.

I've sometimes heard people say that procreation was so self-evident within Judaism that Christianity didn't need to repeat the point. It was already assumed and accepted. However, most early Jewish writers who talked about sex and marriage often made the case for procreation. We see this especially in Josephus and Philo, and elsewhere among Jewish writings. If procreation was the assumed good of marriage, then why are Jewish writers still arguing for it in the first century? What's striking is that some Jewish writings, such as *Joseph and Aseneth*, *Jubilees* (e.g., ch. 3),

---

2. Paul mentions children in Eph 6:1–4, of course, but this doesn't in itself mean that such children intrinsically validate the sexual relationship between the husband and wife in 5:22–33 any more than slaves (6:5–9) justify a legitimate household. In Paul's discussion, household codes are organized the way they are probably to reflect the typical way they were discussed in Greco-Roman society and not to make, or assume, an argument for procreation.

and *Pseudo-Philo* (50:1–5) seem to downplay the role of procreation in marriage. Not every Jew (or Christian) simply assumed that sex should be ordered toward procreation.[3]

The point is: when Jewish thinkers maintained the strict "sex for procreation" motif found in the Old Testament, they argued for it. The New Testament, however, doesn't argue for procreation the same way that the Old Testament or some early Jewish writers do. Also, the New Testament's most thorough statements about marriage were written to a Greco-Roman audience (e.g., Eph 5; Col 3), and unlike Judaism (most branches, anyway), the Greco-Roman culture didn't prioritize procreation. They were much closer to twenty-first-century Westerners than the patriarchs of the Middle Bronze era. If Paul wanted to school his audience in God's intended goal for marriage and sex (namely, procreation), we would expect to see him do it much more explicitly. But again—he doesn't.

The question remains: Are all sexual relations validated by being oriented toward procreation? Is there a generally unified witness in Scripture (both Old and New Testaments), or is there a trajectory moving away from procreation as an intrinsic good of all sexual relations? Did the church fathers get it right, or were they maintaining a cultural perspective (i.e., sex is for procreation) more than a biblical-theological one? Many of the fathers seem to reflect the patriarchy—indeed, the misogyny—of the Greco-Roman and Jewish world, which makes me wonder whether they should serve as reliable guides for a contemporary sexual ethic. Diodore, Chrysostom, and Theodoret questioned whether women possessed the full image of God; perhaps they were an "image of the image," since women reflect the image of man, who in turn reflects the image of God.[4] Cyril of Alexandria believed that "the female sex is ever weak in mind and body"; Chrysostom said that women were in a way twice as fallen as men.[5] Even Augustine seemed to believe that women did not possess the image of God until they were united to their husband in marriage,[6] and that man is superior to woman not only in body but also in mind, which is why women should submit to their husbands (*Sermon on the*

---

3. See Loader, *Sexuality*, 37–41.
4. DeFranza, *Sex Difference*, 119.
5. Ibid, 120–21.
6. On the Trinity, 7.7.10–12.

Mount, 1.15–40–41). According to Megan DeFranza, too many ancient theologians were influenced by Aristotle's declaration that women are "'misbegotten males' with defective souls." Women were believed to be lesser humans; thus "lesser images of God."[7] I would suggest that more discussions are needed not to decide *whether* the fathers should inform our sexual ethic, but *in what way* and *to what extent*.

Even if we assume that most sexual relations are between a fertile man and woman, I still wonder about the so-called "exception" argument. Most sexual relations are orientated toward procreation, but could there be exceptions (non-procreative sexual relations) to what is typical (procreative sexual relations)? Both Holmes and Hill make space for infertile couples or sexual relations among the elderly, and they do so compellingly and consistently (e.g., the sex difference necessary for procreation is still observed in these non-procreative sexual relations). But what if, say, a missionary couple in South Sudan desires to adopt ten kids instead of having their own. Is their sexual relationship invalid because it's not oriented toward procreation, or is this a virtuous exception? And if it's virtuous —what if the missionary couple were two gay men?

I believe that our essayists started a very important dialogue—one which is in no way over. And I hope that future discussions about faith and sexuality will continue to explore questions related to the role of procreation in sexual relations.

Gender Complementarity

Both Holmes and (especially) Hill argued that gender complementarity is a necessary criterion for sexual relations. Valid sexual relations are between a man and a woman. Hill argues for this based on the creation narrative in Genesis 1–2 and Jesus' reference to Genesis 1:27 and 2:24 in Matthew 19:3–4. Such complementarity is rooted in Christianity's theological tradition, as documented by Christopher Roberts in his important book *Creation and Covenant*.[8]

But DeFranza raised a good question in her response to Holmes: "What is gender complementarity? . . . I would wager that in every marriage, complementarity looks and feels different, so much so that the

---

7. DeFranza, *Sex Difference*, 125.
8. Christopher Roberts, *Creation and Covenant: The Significance of Sexual Difference in the Moral Theology of Marriage* (New York: Continuum, 1997).

idea of finding a complementary spouse of the same sex is not beyond imagination." If we assume that some degree of complementarity is necessary for marriage and sex, then does it have to be limited to sex difference? If we argue that sex difference—male and female—is necessary for marriage and sexual relations, then what about intersex persons who aren't clearly male or female?[9] I've heard people say that we shouldn't build an ethic based on exceptions to the norm. But this misses the point. If I read DeFranza (and Loader) correctly, they are not basing an ethic on a minority, but trying to make space *for* the (sexual) minority.

Both Hill and Holmes addressed DeFranza's concern in their rejoinders, and I would commend the reader to revisit their responses to see if you find them compelling. I think Hill's clarification about what he means by "fallenness" and sin as it relates to gender complementarity was particularly important; namely, that "*all* present human conditions, those of being 'male' or 'female' included, are in some radical and profound way 'not the way they're supposed to be.'" While "the fall" can sometimes be thrown down as a quick and easy solution to all the mysteries in creation, any observer of creation—and of the Bible—can easily conclude that on some level, things are "not the way they're supposed to be." Put differently, are sexual minorities and intersex persons a reflection of divinely manufactured *differences* in creation, or are they experiencing—as all humans are—the *fallenness* of creation?

As I reflect on the scintillating dialogue about gender complementarity in this book, it seems clear that there is much more to be said. Is sex and gender difference always and everywhere necessary for legitimate sexual relations? And do the exceptions—intersex persons or people who experience gender dysphoria—challenge the typical binary? As the discussion continues, both sides of the debate should revisit and continue to explore the way in which fallenness and complementarity relate.

Pastoral Accommodation

One of the aspects of this book that challenged me the most was seeing the essayists color outside the lines, as it were—arguing for their conclusions in unpredictable ways. We already mentioned Bill Loader

---

9. It seems to me, however, that when Jesus brings up the eunuch in Matt 19, he does so *not* to expand the definition of marriage, but argues that some people are called to radical discipleship *outside* of marriage. The eunuch, according to Jesus, doesn't marry.

arguing that the Bible condemns all forms of same-sex relations, yet still affirming the sanctity of same-sex relations. Wesley Hill, a gay man with the most skin in the game, argues that he can fully flourish as a human apart from sexual relations. Megan DeFranza embraced a non-affirming position most of her life, yet reconsiders sexual binaries through her work on intersex and sex difference, and now argues for the full inclusion of same-sex couples in the life of the church.

One of the most unpredictable moments in this book was the final few pages of Holmes's essay. Holmes spills a lot of ink arguing that a Christian theology of sex and marriage rules out the sanctity of same-sex unions, but then explores a possible way in which gay couples could be included in the life of the church. He writes, "Churches that believe same-sex partnerships to be wrong might nonetheless find space within their life for people living in such partnerships out of pastoral concern." He argues that the church has done this with divorced couples: "Within pastoral practice, there has been a willingness to find space for (some) divorced people to re-marry and to remain in good standing in the church." Why can't it do the same for same-sex couples?

I think that every pastor and theologian should consider the parallel and wrestle with Holmes's suggestion. I also think it is terribly hypocritical for non-affirming Christians to make a big fuss about same-sex relations while the church is entrenched in greed, materialism, heterosexual immorality, syncretistic patriotism, and an untamed zeal to kill our enemies rather than love them. And yes, we've been terribly lax on divorce and remarriage.

Holmes's proposal raises several questions that non-affirming readers should consider. In what areas has the church made accommodations for people living less-than-ideal lives, and can similar accommodations be made for gay couples? If no, then why not? If yes, then what other "less than ideal" lifestyles should be accommodated to? If a church is unwilling to allow gay couples to become members, should the same church allow a couple who has been divorced and remarried to become members? What about the wealthy CEO who has no concern for the poor? Does she get a free pass? Does a consistent sexual ethic demand that church leaders make pastoral accommodations for everyone living less than ideal Christian lives?

I would suggest, however, that for Holmes's "pastoral accommodation" to be worth its salt, it must reflect the direction and logic of New Testament ethics. Put simply, we should make a distinction between the so-called "is" and the "ought." It's certainly true *that* churches and pastors make accommodation. The ethical question is: *Should* they? Can we make a sound and consistent scriptural argument that when churches are somewhat lenient on some aspects of new covenant obedience that they should therefore accommodate to other aspects?[10]

Even if one thinks that the Bible clearly prohibits same-sex relations, most pastors know that practical questions about ministry are less black and white. I remember talking to a group of pastors about what the Bible says about same-sex relations, and I left the last hour of my talk open for questions. One (non-affirming) pastor said, "A lesbian couple came to church for the first time last Sunday, and they both came forward, hand-in-hand, to accept Jesus. Now what do I do?"

Some might quote Romans 1 at them and send them on their way. But even the most conservative pastors I know recognize that this isn't the best approach and that there may be multiple approaches that are faithful to a traditional sexual ethic. My own response to the pastor above was, "Begin by spending a good deal of time just getting to know the couple, and then pray with your fellow leaders, and the couple, about how to shepherd them in their newfound relationship with Jesus." This doesn't solve the ultimate question: Is there a place for this lesbian couple, as a couple, in the church? But genuine relationships are always the best place to start as we seek to integrate our ethical views in the daily life of ministry.

The Future of the Discussion

As we look back on the discussion in this book and look forward to future discussions on faith and sexuality, here are four suggestions for reflection:

First, I hope that the tone of the conversation in this book serves as a model for future dialogues. Conversations about homosexuality are so often dominated by anger and misrepresentation, confusion and

---

10. Some people argue that the early church's revision of old covenant dietary and circumcision laws (e.g., Acts 15) shows that accommodation is necessary and, indeed, biblical. However, these first-century discussions had to do with the place of old covenant law in the life of the new covenant believer. The question facing the church today is about the teaching of the New Testament itself and not about whether certain laws given to Israel are for the church.

castigation. I hope that the reader has found the arguments in this book to be laced with clarity, kindness, and cordiality. Kindness, of course, doesn't mean we set aside all conviction; rather, we should follow Richard Mouw's advice of dialoguing with "convicted civility." We should argue with conviction but in a civil manner, respecting the humanness of the person you're arguing against.

Second, I found all the essays to be thoughtful and intellectually challenging, and I hope this catches on with a broader audience. Academic discussions are by nature more thoughtful, but I would love to see such thoughtfulness trickle down to the pew. Conservatives should move beyond "Adam and Eve not Adam and Steve" type arguments, and progressives can't rely on a thin definition of love to trump everything the Bible says about holiness and sexual immorality. We need more depth, more precision, and much more time listening to what the other person is actually saying.

Third, as stated in my introduction and demonstrated in all the essays, we need to move beyond what the Bible *says* and seek to understand what it *means*. We also need to ask *how* (not *whether*) the Bible applies to the twenty-first-century church. We cannot leap too quickly from *meaning* to *application*. I hope that future conversations give more attention to ethics and theology, and not just exegesis—though the latter will also be necessary.

Lastly, we simply cannot think about questions related to homosexuality at arm's length from sexual minorities. And this is why I'm so thankful that all of our essayists have worked out their views in the context of real people. Straight people who want to know more about same-sex relations should get to know gay and lesbian people. Experience should not dictate our ethics, but it should shape the way we integrate our ethical views into real life.

Rigorous, thoughtful, intellectual discussions and debates about faith and sexuality are still needed. But we need to make sure that the people looking on—especially our gay and lesbian friends and neighbors—are more impressed with Jesus, not less. Being a Christian goes beyond just holding on to Christian views, but to expressing those views in a Christian manner. Only then will people be able to see Christ not just in the *content* but also in the *tone* of our doctrine.

INDEX

SCRIPTURE INDEX